"As a fellow dialectical behavior therapy (DBT) consumer, DBT therapist, and DBT author, I am always on the lookout for simple, practical, and effective ways of making DBT skills usable, accessible, and applicable to the average reader. In this book, you will find just that! Even after using, teaching, researching, and writing about DBT concepts for more than a decade, I now have a richer understanding of DBT that I am excited to try on myself…and share with others!"

—**Kirby Reutter, PhD**, bilingual clinical psychologist with the Department of Homeland Security, and author of *The Dialectical Behavior Therapy Skills Workbook for PTSD*

"For people who struggle with intense, painful emotions, this workbook is a great resource. It teaches the skills of DBT, including the newest skills, and provides examples and exercises to strengthen learning. Those who apply themselves to the program outlined in this book will acquire the skills necessary to experience strong emotions without resorting to behavior patterns that harm relationships and decrease quality of life. DBT skills, used daily as directed, change lives for the better!"

—**Cedar R. Koons, LCSW**, is an LBC-DBT-certified DBT therapist, a mindfulness retreat leader, an international DBT consultant, and author of *The Mindfulness Solution for Intense Emotions*

"The authors have produced yet another example of accessible and clear instructions for those coping with overwhelming emotions like guilt, anger, shame, and anxiety. The acronyms used are simple and easy to remember. The many examples and exercises in the book assist the reader to do the work that DBT demands. While staying true to the DBT model, the authors go beyond Linehan to synthesize adaptations of research and clinical instruments useful for both home and clinic. I was particularly impressed with their inclusion of exposure-based cognitive rehearsal, so the user deals with intense emotions in the moment."

—**Thomas Marra, PhD**, author of *Depressed and Anxious*, *Dialectical Behavior Therapy in Private Practice*, and the forthcoming *The Path of Wisdom on Emotion Regulation*

"Knowing how to effectively regulate emotions is not something we are born with. This updated manual provides a road map and step-by-step instructions for enhancing emotional well-being. It is easy to read and easy to use—with new techniques focusing on increasing compassion towards the self and others, and novel strategies for dealing with intense emotions. Highly recommended for anyone struggling with regulating emotions or interested in improving their emotional intelligence."

—**Thomas R. Lynch, PhD, FBPsS**, emeritus professor in the school of psychology at University of Southampton, United Kingdom; and author of *Radically Open Dialectical Behavior Therapy* and *The Skills Training Manual for Radically Open Dialectical Behavior Therapy*

"*The Dialectical Behavior Therapy Skills Workbook* update, by McKay, Wood, and Brantley, is remarkable in the attention it gives to explaining DBT skills, and in providing directions about how to practice and use the skills that are easy to follow. They have connected the skills in a way that makes sense, and that makes them understandable and eminently useful. This workbook, with its examples and exercises, provides many opportunities for anyone who has intense emotions to practice skills that will enhance their ability to manage their lives more effectively. I highly recommend it to anyone who has intense emotions, to clinicians, and to family members."

—**Pat Harvey, LCSW-C**, DBT parent coach, trainer, and consultant; and coauthor of *Parenting a Child Who Has Intense Emotions, Dialectical Behavior Therapy for At-Risk Adolescents*, and *Parenting a Teen Who Has Intense Emotions*

"Building on their original best seller, McKay, Wood, and Brantley have incorporated recent research and new developments in DBT into the second edition of *The Dialectical Behavior Therapy Skills Workbook*. The result is a comprehensive, user-friendly guide to DBT skills, chock-full of exercises that will help clients learn the skills that will help in their struggle with overwhelming emotions, and that will also make DBT more accessible to clinicians."

—**Sheri Van Dijk, MSW**, psychotherapist, international speaker, and author of several DBT books, including *Don't Let Your Emotions Run Your Life for Teens*

"This book has taken DBT skills, and provided a comprehensive framework to guide a client from first introduction to DBT through the development of a deeper proficiency in skill use. The additional focus on self-compassion and exposure-based cognitive rehearsal is vital to bridging the gap between learning new behaviors and using them when they truly matter—during times of emotional arousal and when it's a struggle to cope. I would highly recommend this book to clinicians and readers who want to build a rich array of strategies to survive painful emotions and live fully in everyday life."

—**Christy Matta, MA**, health manager at Stanford's Health Improvement Program, and author of *The Stress Response*

The Dialectical Behavior Therapy Skills Workbook

SECOND EDITION

Practical DBT Exercises for
Learning Mindfulness, Interpersonal
Effectiveness, Emotion Regulation

MATTHEW MᶜKAY, PhD
JEFFREY C. WOOD, PsyD
JEFFREY BRANTLEY, MD

New Harbinger Publications, Inc.

Publisher's Note

NEW HARBINGER PUBLICATIONS is a registered trademark of New Harbinger Publications, Inc.

Distributed in Canada by Raincoast Books

Copyright © 2019 by Matthew McKay, Jeffrey C. Wood, and Jeffrey Brantley
New Harbinger Publications, Inc.
5674 Shattuck Avenue
Oakland, CA 94609
www.newharbinger.com

Cover design by Amy Shoup

Acquired by Jess O'Brien

Edited by Jean Blomquist

All Rights Reserved

Library of Congress Cataloging-in-Publication Data

Names: McKay, Matthew, author. | Wood, Jeffrey C., author. | Brantley,
  Jeffrey, author.
Title: The dialectical behavior therapy skills workbook : practical DBT exercises for learning mindfulness,
  interpersonal effectiveness, emotion regulation, and distress tolerance / Matthew McKay, PhD, Jeffrey C.
  Wood, PsyD, and Jeffrey Brantley, MD.
Description: 2nd edition. | Oakland, CA : New Harbinger Publications, Inc., [2019] | Includes bibliographical
  references. |
Identifiers: LCCN 2019017394 (print) | LCCN 2019018365 (ebook) | ISBN 9781684034598 (PDF e-book) |
  ISBN 9781684034604 (ePub) | ISBN 9781684034581 (paperback)
Subjects: LCSH: Dialectical behavior therapy--Problems, exercises, etc. | BISAC: SELF-HELP / Mood Disorders.
  | PSYCHOLOGY / Psychopathology / General.
Classification: LCC RC489.B4 (ebook) | LCC RC489.B4 D52 2019 (print) | DDC 616.89/142076--dc23
LC record available at https://lccn.loc.gov/2019017394

Printed in the United States of America

23   22   21

15   14   13   12   11   10   9

In memory of my mother, Louise Long LaBrash, who was always there for me in the hard times.

—Matthew McKay

To my students and clients at Fresno City College and Reedley College, 2005–2006, whose strength, hope, and resilience inspired me while writing this book. And to all the readers of this book who have offered suggestions over the years about how to make this second edition a better healing tool for others.

—Jeffrey C. Wood

This work is dedicated to all who struggle with intense and unpredictable emotions in their inner and outer lives. May you find peace and happiness, and may all living beings benefit from your efforts.

—Jeffrey Brantley

Contents

Preface to the Second Edition

Dialectical behavior therapy (DBT) has been helping people reduce emotionally overwhelming feelings while stabilizing their lives and relationships for more than twenty-five years. A large number of published studies have proven the effectiveness of DBT, and hundreds of thousands of people—in DBT groups around the world—have experienced life-changing effects from the treatment.

In addition, DBT has evolved. The core skills are now used to treat many more problems than just the original target—borderline personality disorder. DBT has also been shown to be effective with anxiety and depression, shame, post-traumatic stress disorder, substance abuse relapse prevention, anger and aggression, interpersonal problems, and other difficulties. The treatment has even been adapted and extended for use with couples and adolescents.

The DBT treatment process has also evolved. Dozens of researchers and clinicians—including us—have augmented the original protocol with new and effective emotion regulation techniques. Some of these additions include values clarification, defusion, problem solving, exposure-based cognitive rehearsal, cue-controlled relaxation, compassion, meditations, new mindfulness processes, physiological coping skills (for extreme emotions), interpersonal negotiation skills, and others.

The original developer of DBT, Marsha Linehan, PhD, has acknowledged and documented the evolution of the treatment in the recent edition of her *DBT Skills Training Manual* (2015), where she has added new techniques that she and others have developed during the past twenty-five years. Some of the techniques that Dr. Linehan added appeared in the first edition of this book, while many other skills are the result of research by Dr. Linehan and independent behavioral scientists around the world.

The book you hold in your hand (or see on your screen), *The Dialectical Behavior Therapy Skills Workbook*, second edition, was necessitated by the evolution of DBT and the development of new and effective emotion regulation processes. This new edition contains techniques to build compassion for yourself and others, new skills for extreme emotions, skills to evaluate whether to cope or take action (FTB-Cope), a well-researched process to rehearse both values-based behavior and emotion-coping strategies, plus other updates.

The addition of a chapter on exposure-based cognitive rehearsal deserves special mention. This technique (Cautela, 1971; McKay & West, 2016) allows you to rehearse new coping skills in an emotionally activated state—the very condition in which you'll need to remember and use DBT skills. Up to now, one of the limitations of DBT was that the skills were learned in the relatively calm setting of a DBT group or at home reading a book. But when people are in an emotionally charged situation, they tend to forget the skills they learned while they were relaxed. Exposure-based cognitive rehearsal creates the emotional conditions that will help you remember and feel confident in using the skills when you need them. (For more information on why this works, see "The Problem of State-Dependent Learning" in chapter 11.)

We had one additional goal for this second edition: to present the skills and their component techniques accessibly, simply, and with a focus on usability. DBT is complex, and growing more so. To continue to be effective, it must be easy to understand and implement. That was the original impetus for this book, and we remain committed to clarity and usability in this new edition.

To our readers, we offer a warm welcome. Every page has been written with the intention to help you. DBT works. There is every reason to believe that you can feel better and live more fully if you learn the four core skills of dialectical behavior therapy. Remember, though—reading is one thing and doing is another. You'll need to practice the skills you learn every day. Use the DBT diary page in chapter 12 to help you. Or, if you'd like an additional tool to help you practice the skills in this workbook, consider using *The Dialectical Behavior Therapy Skills Card Deck: 52 Practices to Balance Your Emotions Every Day*, also available from New Harbinger Publications. Each of the fifty-two cards in the deck corresponds to a skill or exercise in this workbook that is marked by ⊠. These are the essential skills that you should be using on a regular basis; the card deck is an effective additional tool to help remind you to practice those skills. Either way you choose to practice, if you commit to using the DBT skills in this workbook, you can heal your life.

Matthew McKay, PhD

Jeffrey C. Wood, PsyD

Jeffrey Brantley, MD

INTRODUCTION

Dialectical Behavior Therapy: An Overview of the Treatment

Dialectical behavior therapy, developed by Marsha Linehan (1993a, 1993b), is extraordinarily effective at helping people manage their overwhelming emotions. Research shows that dialectical behavior therapy strengthens a person's ability to handle distress without losing control or acting destructively.

A lot of people struggle with overwhelming emotions. It's as if the knob is turned to maximum volume on much of what they feel. When they get angry or sad or scared, it shows up as a big, powerful wave that can sweep them off their feet.

If you've faced overwhelming emotions in your life, you know what we're talking about. There are days when your feelings hit you with the force of a tidal wave. And when that happens, it makes you—understandably—afraid to feel things because you don't want to get swept away by your emotions. The trouble is, the more you try to suppress or put a lid on your emotions, the more overwhelming they can get. We'll talk about that in chapters 7 and 8 on emotion regulation. What's important to know right now is that trying to stop your feelings doesn't work.

There's a fair amount of research to suggest that the likelihood of developing intense, overwhelming emotions may be hardwired from birth. But it can also be greatly affected by trauma or neglect during childhood. Trauma at critical points in our development can literally alter our brain structure in ways that make us more vulnerable to intense, negative emotions. However, even if your intense emotions are rooted in genetics or trauma, that doesn't mean the problem can't be overcome. Thousands of people have used the skills you'll learn in this book to achieve better emotional control. They have changed their lives—and you can too.

So what are these skills, and how will they help you? Dialectical behavior therapy teaches four critically important skills that can both reduce the size of emotional waves and help you keep your balance when those emotions overwhelm you.

1. *Distress tolerance* will help you cope better with painful events by building up your resiliency and giving you new ways to soften the effects of upsetting circumstances.

2. *Mindfulness* will help you experience more fully the present moment while focusing less on painful experiences from the past or frightening possibilities in the future. Mindfulness will also give you tools to overcome habitual, negative judgments about yourself and others.

3. *Emotion regulation* skills help you to recognize more clearly what you feel and then to observe each emotion without getting overwhelmed by it. The goal is to modulate your feelings without behaving in reactive, destructive ways.

4. *Interpersonal effectiveness* gives you new tools to express your beliefs and needs, set limits, and negotiate solutions to problems—all while protecting your relationships and treating others with respect.

This book is structured to make learning easier. Each of the key skills is covered in two chapters—basic and advanced—except distress tolerance and mindfulness, which both have a third, more advanced chapter. The basic skills chapters teach necessary concepts, identify the components of the new skill, and lead you through initial steps for acquiring the skill. The advanced skills chapters take you through the remaining components of the skill, building level by level. There will be examples to make each step clear as well as assessments, exercises, and worksheets to help you practice each thing you learn. (Many of these materials are available for download at the website for this book: http://www.newharbinger.com/44581. See the very back of this book for more details.) In this edition of the workbook, we have also included a new chapter on exposure-based cognitive rehearsal, to help you practice your skills under realistic, imaginary circumstances. Then in the final chapter, Putting It All Together, you'll learn how to integrate all those skills, in order to make them a regular part of your life.

The Dialectical Behavior Therapy Skills Workbook is written to make learning easy. The hard part will be making the commitment to *do* the exercises and put your new skills into practice. Nothing will change by just reading this workbook. The words on these pages will have no impact on your life unless you implement—behaviorally—the new techniques and strategies you will learn here. So now is a good time to think about why you are reading this book and what you want to change. Right here, on this page, write down three ways you currently react to your emotions that you want to change. In other words, identify three things that you do when you're upset or overwhelmed—things that are unhealthy or damaging—that you are committed to replacing with better ways to cope.

1. _____

2. _____

3. _____

WHO THIS BOOK IS FOR

There are two intended audiences for *The Dialectical Behavior Therapy Skills Workbook*. The first is people who are in dialectical behavior therapy (either group or individual) and need a workbook to help learn the four key skills. We also wrote this book so it could be used independently by *anyone* who struggles with overwhelming feelings. All the tools are here to achieve significant changes in your ability to control emotion. With that said, if you are reading this workbook on your own and are having a hard time implementing the new skills, we strongly recommend that you seek the services of a qualified dialectical behavior therapist.

THERE IS HOPE

Life is hard. You already know that. But you are not stuck or helpless in your struggle with your emotions. If you really do the work to implement the skills in this workbook, you can expect that your reactions to feelings will change. That's because—regardless of genetics or early pain—the key skills you'll learn here can affect the outcome of every conflict and every upset and can literally alter the course of your relationships. There is every reason to hope. All you have to do is turn the page and begin. Then keep working at it.

CHAPTER 1

Basic Distress Tolerance Skills

DISTRESS TOLERANCE SKILLS: WHAT ARE THEY?

At some point in our lives, we all have to cope with distress and pain. Either it can be physical, like a bee sting or a broken arm, or it can be emotional, like sadness or anger. In both cases, the pain is often unavoidable and unpredictable. You can't always anticipate when the bee will sting you or when something will make you sad. Often, the best you can do is to use the coping skills that you have and hope that they work.

But for some people, emotional and physical pain feels more intense and occurs more frequently than it does for other people. Their distress comes on more quickly and feels like an overwhelming tidal wave. Often, these situations feel like they'll never end, and the people experiencing them don't know how to cope with the severity of their pain. For the purposes of this book, we'll call this problem *overwhelming emotions*. (But remember, emotional and physical pain often occur together.)

People struggling with overwhelming emotions often deal with their pain in very unhealthy, very unsuccessful ways because they don't know what else to do. This is understandable. When a person is in emotional pain, it's hard to be rational and to think of a good solution. Nevertheless, many of the coping strategies used by people with overwhelming emotions only serve to make their problems worse.

Here's a list of some common coping strategies used by people dealing with this problem. Check (✔) the ones that you use to cope with your stressful situations:

☐ You spend a great deal of time thinking about past pains, mistakes, and problems.

☐ You get anxious worrying about possible future pains, mistakes, and problems.

☐ You isolate yourself from other people to avoid distressing situations.

☐ You make yourself feel numb with alcohol or drugs.

☐ You take your feelings out on other people by getting excessively angry at them or trying to control them.

☐ You engage in potentially dangerous behaviors, such as cutting, hitting, scratching, picking at, or burning yourself or pulling out your own hair.

☐ You engage in unsafe sexual activities, such as having sex with strangers or having frequent unprotected sex.

☐ You avoid dealing with the causes of your problems, such as an abusive or dysfunctional relationship.

☐ You use food to punish or control yourself by eating too much, not eating at all, or by throwing up what you do eat.

☐ You attempt suicide or engage in high-risk activities, like reckless driving or taking dangerous amounts of alcohol and drugs.

☐ You avoid pleasant activities, such as social events and exercise, maybe because you don't think that you deserve to feel better.

☐ You surrender to your pain and resign yourself to living a miserable and unfulfilling life.

All of these strategies are paths to even deeper emotional pain, because even the strategies that offer temporary relief will only cause you more suffering in the future. Use the Cost of Self-Destructive Coping Strategies worksheet to see how. Note the strategies that you use as well as their costs, and then include any additional costs that you can think of. At the end of the worksheet, feel free to add any of your own strategies that aren't included as well as their costs. (Visit http://www.newharbinger.com/44581 to download The Cost of Self-Destructive Coping Strategies worksheet.)

The Cost of Self-Destructive Coping Strategies

Self-Destructive Coping Strategy	Possible Costs
1. You spend a great deal of time thinking about past pain, mistakes, and problems.	Miss good things that might be happening now and then regret missing those things too; depression about the past Other:
2. You get anxious worrying about possible future pain, mistakes, and problems.	Miss good things that might be happening now; anxiety about the future Other:
3. You isolate yourself to avoid possible pain.	Spend more time alone and, as a result, feel even more depressed Other:
4. You use alcohol and drugs to numb yourself.	Addiction; loss of money; work problems; legal problems; relationship problems; health consequences Other:
5. You take your painful feelings out on others.	Loss of friendships, romantic relationships, and family members; other people avoid you; loneliness; feel bad about hurting other people; legal consequences of your actions Other:
6. You engage in dangerous behaviors, like cutting, burning, scratching, pulling out hair, and self-mutilation.	Possible death; infection; scarring; disfigurement; shame; physical pain Other:
7. You engage in unsafe sexual activity, like unprotected sex or frequent sex with strangers.	Sexually transmitted diseases, some life threatening; pregnancy; shame; embarrassment Other:

8. You avoid dealing with the causes of your problems.	Put up with destructive relationships; get burned out doing things for other people; don't get any of your own needs met; depression Other:
9. You eat too much, restrict what you eat, or throw up what you eat.	Weight gain; anorexia; bulimia; health consequences; medical treatment; embarrassment; shame; depression Other:
10. You have attempted suicide or engaged in other nearly fatal activities.	Possible death; hospitalization; embarrassment; shame; depression; long-term medical complications Other:
11. You avoid pleasant activities, like social events and exercise.	Lack of enjoyment; lack of exercise; depression; shame; isolation Other:
12. You surrender to your pain and live an unfulfilling life.	Lots of pain and distress; regrets about your life; depression Other:
13.	
14.	

The costs of these self-destructive coping strategies are clear. All of them lead to your pain being prolonged into long-term suffering. Remember, sometimes pain can't be avoided, but many times suffering can.

Take, for example, an argument between friends Maria and Sandra. For Maria, who doesn't have overwhelming emotions, the argument was initially painful. But after a few hours, she began to realize that she and Sandra were both to blame for the argument. So by the next day, Maria was no longer upset or mad at Sandra. But for Sandra, who struggles with overwhelming emotions, the argument was replayed in her memory over and over again for three days. Each word and gesture was remembered as an insult from Maria. So the next time Sandra saw Maria, three days later, Sandra was still angry and she restarted the argument just where it had ended. Both women experienced the initial pain of the argument, but only Sandra was suffering. Clearly, Sandra carried her emotional pain with her for days, and it made her life more of a struggle. While we can't always control the pain in our lives, we can control the amount of suffering we have in response to that pain.

To avoid this type of long-term suffering, chapters 1, 2, and 3 will teach you *distress tolerance skills.* These skills will help you endure and cope with your pain in a new, healthier way so that it doesn't lead to long-term suffering.

ABOUT THIS CHAPTER

The first group of distress tolerance skills you'll learn in this chapter will help you distract yourself from the situations that are causing you emotional pain. Distraction skills are important because (1) they can temporarily stop you from thinking about your pain and, as a result, (2) they give you time to find an appropriate coping response. Remember how Sandra carried her pain with her for three days? She couldn't stop thinking about her argument with Maria. Distraction can help you let go of the pain by helping you think about something else. Distraction also buys you time so that your emotions can settle down before you take action to deal with a distressing situation.

However, do not confuse distraction with avoidance. When you avoid a distressing situation, you choose not to deal with it. But when you distract yourself from a distressing situation, you still intend to deal with it in the future, when your emotions have calmed down to a tolerable level.

The second group of distress tolerance skills you'll learn in this chapter are self-soothing skills (Johnson, 1985; Linehan, 1993b). It's often necessary to soothe yourself before you face the cause of your distress, because your emotions might be too "hot." Many people with overwhelming emotions panic when faced with an argument, rejection, failure, or other painful events. Before you can address these problems with your new emotion regulation skills (chapters 7 and 8) or your new interpersonal effectiveness skills (chapters 9 and 10), it's often necessary to soothe yourself to regain your strength. In situations like these, distress tolerance skills are similar to refilling the gas tank in your car so that you can keep going. Self-soothing is meant to bring you some amount of peace and relief from your pain so that you can figure out what you're going to do next.

Self-soothing skills also serve another purpose. They'll help you learn to treat yourself compassionately. Many people with overwhelming emotions have been abused or neglected as children. As a result, they were taught more about how to hurt than to help themselves. The second purpose of the self-soothing skills, therefore, is to teach you how to treat yourself kindly and lovingly.

HOW TO USE THIS CHAPTER

As you read the following groups of skills, mark the ones that are helpful to you. This will make it easier to create a distraction plan for emergencies when you get to the end of this chapter. You'll also be shown how to create a list of relaxation skills to help soothe yourself, both at home and when you're away. Then, in the next two chapters, you'll learn more advanced distress tolerance skills.

TAKE A "REST" ⊠

Now that you've identified some of your own self-destructive and problematic behaviors—as well as their costs—the first distress tolerance strategy you need to learn is REST. REST is an acronym that reminds you to:

Relax

Evaluate

Set an intention

Take action

Changing any behavioral habit is difficult. It requires you to know what actions you want to change, when you want to change them, and what alternative actions you want to do instead. But equally important, it also requires that you *remember* that you want to do something differently in the first place. Often this is the hardest step—remembering that you want to change—especially when you're feeling overwhelmed by your emotions. When you get overwhelmed by painful emotions, often your first instinct is to act impulsively and to engage in some type of habitual self-destructive or problematic behavior (like the ones you previously identified). This happens because, unless you're prepared in those moments of heightened emotion, you might not even remember that you had planned to do something differently. So, how do you prepare to make healthier decisions when you're feeling overwhelmed? The first step to changing any problematic or self-destructive behavior—and to not act impulsively—is to use the REST strategy: Relax, Evaluate, Set an intention, and Take action.

- **Relax.** The first step of the process is to relax. Stop what you're doing. Freeze. Take a breath. Pause. Step away from the situation for a few seconds to get a different perspective. Just don't do what you normally do. Don't act impulsively. Do your best to remind yourself that you have an opportunity to behave differently. Create some "space" between your desire to act impulsively and your actual reaction. Maybe even say out loud, "Stop," "Relax," or "REST," just to remind yourself to not react so quickly and automatically. Then take a few slow breaths to help yourself calm down before choosing an alternative meaningful action.

- **Evaluate.** Next, ask yourself what's happening in this situation. What are the facts? Just do a quick evaluation. You *don't* have to figure it all out, and you *don't* have to do an in-depth analysis of why you're feeling the way you do. You *don't* even have to solve the problem if it's too compli-cated. Just do your best to get a general sense of what's occurring. For example, observe what is happening for you physically, emotionally, and mentally. Also observe what other people around you are doing. Maybe just ask yourself a few simple questions, like these: "How do I feel?" "What's happening?" "Is anyone in danger?"

- **Set an Intention.** The third step is to set an intention to do something. In this case, an intention is a target, goal, or plan about what you're going to do. Decide which action you're going to take. Pick one of the coping skills that you'll learn later in this book. Ask yourself, "What do I need right now?" Do you need to do something for yourself? Then maybe choose one of the coping skills or self-soothing skills that you'll soon learn. Or, do you need to solve a bigger problem? Then maybe choose one of the more advanced problem-solving or communication skills in the latter chapters of this book. Whatever you choose to do, it doesn't have to be the final or best solution to the problem right now, but hopefully it will be something healthy that will help you cope.

- **Take Action.** Finally, take action. Put your plan into motion. Proceed *mindfully*, which means move ahead slowly and with awareness of what you're doing. Whatever your intention was in the last step, do it now as calmly and effectively as you can. Again, this action may not be the ultimate solution to the problem at hand, but if you follow these steps, your mindful action is likely to be healthier and more effective than the self-destructive actions you would have taken if you had just reacted impulsively.

Although this might seem like a lot to do—especially when you're feeling overwhelmed by emotions—with practice, these steps can be accomplished in just a few seconds and become a new habit for you. Also, be aware that you might need to use REST more than once in the same situation. So if REST doesn't work the first time through, go back and use it again. Maybe you missed an important detail or maybe something has quickly changed. Keep "RESTing" until you feel like the situation is resolved, or until you can effectively get out of the situation.

So now that you know the REST strategy, the next step in changing your self-destructive and problematic behaviors is to identify and anticipate when you will likely have to use REST. Usually you'll know there's an opportunity to do something differently when you're feeling an intense negative emotion, especially an emotion that makes you want to avoid something or become aggressive with someone. When you do, it's usually an indicator that something is happening that's going to require you to make a choice: either you'll act impulsively and do what you normally do *or* you'll use one of the coping skills in this book and do something differently. Another good indicator that you need to use REST is if you're suddenly in pain emotionally, mentally, or physically; this is usually a good indicator that you need to make a choice to do something. And lastly, you might also need to use REST if you notice the desire to act impulsively, using one of your usual self-destructive behaviors, even if you don't know why. Each of these three conditions signals that you have a moment of choice: you can either do what you normally do—react impulsively and potentially cause pain for yourself or someone else—or you can relax, evaluate, set an intention, and take action using a healthier coping skill from this book. To understand how to use this, here are two examples. Let's see how Bryan and Sarah use the REST strategy.

Bryan had the problem of frequently starting arguments with his wife, Kelly. Usually, this would lead to him screaming at Kelly that she was "worthless" as a spouse and then further belittling her. Afterward, when he felt ashamed, Bryan would suddenly walk out and go to the local bar, where he'd drink too much alcohol and spend too much money. However, recently, Bryan had been using this book and learning new coping skills. He knew which skills worked for him, but he often had trouble remembering to use them when he was feeling overwhelmed by his anger and depression. He knew he needed to use the REST strategy, so he placed brightly colored sticky notes with the word "REST" on them in several places around their home. Luckily, the next time Bryan and Kelly began arguing, Bryan caught sight of one of the sticky notes he had put up and he was reminded to use the strategy. First, he simply stopped what he was doing and tried to relax. He stopped yelling at Kelly, took a deep breath, and released some of the muscle tension in his body. Next, he evaluated the situation. He quickly thought about what was happening. He was arguing with Kelly because she hadn't washed his uniform for work, but he wasn't going to work until the next morning and he had failed to tell her that he needed it washed in the first place. Plus, there was still plenty of time to do it. He also recognized that right now there was no emergency; he was just feeling extremely overwhelmed by his anger. He felt like leaving home to go to the bar to have a few drinks, but he didn't. Instead, he set an intention. He needed to stay home, calm down, and not do anything that would further destroy his relationship with Kelly. Bryan had been working on both his self-soothing skills and his communication skills, and he knew he needed to use them. So finally, he took action. He told Kelly that he recognized that he hadn't asked her to wash his uniform, that he was feeling angry, and that he needed to go into the bedroom to calm down. So he went to lie down on the bed, put on some soothing music, and practiced his diaphragmatic breathing (see chapter 2) until he felt calm enough to come out and apologize to Kelly.

Similarly, Sarah struggled with overwhelming emotions and would usually alienate people—even strangers—with her excessive anger. One day, she took a dress back to a clothing store to return it because after buying it she discovered that it was stained. Sarah was already bothered that she had to drive all the way back to the mall and then she made herself even angrier thinking about the "idiot" who made the stain and left it on the rack to be sold anyway. Then, to make matters worse, the cashier told Sarah that because she bought the dress on sale, she couldn't return it. Now Sarah was extremely angry. In the past, Sarah would have started screaming at the cashier in front of everyone, but she had been practicing her coping skills with her therapist, and she had been encouraged to use the REST strategy. So instead of screaming, Sarah paused, thought "Stop" in her mind, took a deep breath, and tried to relax. Then she evaluated the situation. She felt extremely angry and knew that if she attempted to talk to the cashier that it would collapse into an argument very quickly. This was not a "life or death" emergency, but Sarah had paid a lot of money and she wanted a refund. Next, she set an intention. She realized that she needed to calm down before she spoke with the cashier about this problem. She identified her coping skills as needing to briefly leave the store and use her coping thoughts to calm down. So finally, she took action. She told the cashier that she needed to step outside for a second, but she would be right back. Then Sarah sat down outside the store, took a few slow breaths, and repeated her coping thoughts: "I'm not in danger right now" and "These are just my feelings, but eventually they'll go away." When she felt sufficiently calm after a few minutes, she went back inside the store and again spoke with the cashier. Sarah explained that she didn't notice the stain until she got home and she wanted a refund. However, the cashier still insisted that she could not refund Sarah's money. Now Sarah was confused and angry. She had expected that using the REST strategy and calming down was going to solve her problem, but it didn't. So she decided to try it again. She again paused, took a slow breath, and relaxed as best she could. Then she quickly evaluated the situation. "What's happening here?" she thought to herself. She looked at the cashier's name tag and noticed that it said "Trainee." Sarah had been coming to this store for years and never had trouble returning items, so she wondered if this trainee was giving her accurate information. Sarah then set an intention of using some of her newly learned assertive communication skills and finally she took action by politely asking the cashier if she could speak with her manager. Naturally, the manager corrected the situation and allowed Sarah to return the dress. Sarah's problem hadn't been corrected automatically just because she used the REST strategy one time. But with her perseverance, the REST strategy helped during her second attempt to avoid alienating people with her anger.

Exercise: Take a REST

Now you try using the REST strategy. Remember a problematic situation you recently encountered that caused you to feel emotionally overwhelmed. Do your best to identify what you did impulsively, what self-destructive behavior you engaged in (if any), and how you might have coped with the situation better if you had used the REST strategy. Don't worry about not knowing the exact coping strategies you would use at this point—coping strategies you'll soon be learning—but rather, try to describe the general type of coping strategy that would have helped you. For example, "Learn how to calm myself down" or "Learn to communicate better with my wife." Then as you continue to read through this workbook, try to find the specific skill that would have helped. (A worksheet for this exercise is available at http://www.newharbinger.com/44581.)

What happened in this distressing situation? _____

_____

_____

How did you feel? _____

_____

_____

What did you do? _____

_____

_____

Did you engage in any self-destructive behaviors? If yes, what were they? _____

_____

_____

Now use the REST strategy and imagine what could have happened differently.

How could you have relaxed (**R**) in this situation? _____

_____

_____

If you had done an evaluation (**E**), what would you have discovered? _____

_____

_____

If you had set an intention (**S**), what would it have been? _____

_____

_____

If you would have taken action (**T**) in this situation, what might have happened? _____

_____

_____

What would the overall advantages have been if you had used the REST strategy? _____

_____

_____

Making any type of change in your behavior is hard. It's especially hard when you're also challenged by overwhelming emotions. That's why it's important to remind yourself to use REST throughout the remainder of this book. By itself, REST isn't much of a skill, it's more of a strategy that requires the use of all the other skills you'll learn in this book. So, as you continue to learn about each of the coping skills, ask yourself how you might incorporate that skill into the REST strategy. Then, each time you're presented with a challenging situation, feel overwhelmed by your emotions, or are required to make a choice about what to do, remember to REST and use your coping skills. Each time you remind yourself to REST, the more naturally you'll use it in the future. Like Bryan, you might even consider writing "REST" on colored sticky notes and posting them throughout your home and place of work, just to remind yourself.

RADICAL ACCEPTANCE

Increasing your ability to tolerate distress starts with a change in your attitude. You're going to need something called *radical acceptance* (Sherman, 1975; Linehan, 1993a). This is a new way of looking at your life. In the next chapter, you'll be given some key questions to help you examine your experiences using radical acceptance. But for now, it will be sufficient to cover this concept briefly.

Often, when a person is in pain, his or her first reaction is to get angry or upset or to blame someone for causing the pain in the first place. But, unfortunately, no matter whom you blame for your distress, your pain still exists and you continue to suffer. In fact, in some cases, the angrier you get, the worse your pain will feel (Greenwood, Thurston, Rumble, Waters, & Keefe, 2003; Kerns, Rosenberg, & Jacob, 1994).

Getting angry or upset over a situation also stops you from seeing what is really happening. Have you ever heard the expression "being blinded by rage"? This often happens to people with overwhelming emotions. Criticizing yourself or others all the time or being overly judgmental of a situation is like wearing dark sunglasses indoors. By doing this, you're missing the details and not seeing everything as it really is. By getting angry and thinking that a situation should never have happened, you're missing the point that it *did* happen and that you have to deal with it.

Being overly critical about a situation prevents you from taking steps to change that situation. You can't change the past. And if you spend your time fighting the past—wishfully thinking that your anger will change the outcome of an event that has already happened—you'll become paralyzed and helpless. Then, nothing will improve.

So, to review—being overly judgmental of a situation or overly critical of yourself or others often leads to more pain, missed details, and paralysis. Obviously, getting angry, upset, or critical doesn't improve a situation. So what else can you do?

The other option, which radical acceptance suggests, is to acknowledge your present situation, whatever it is, without judging the events or criticizing yourself. Instead, try to recognize that your present situation exists because of a long chain of events that began far in the past. For example, some time ago, you (or someone else) thought you needed help for the emotional pain you were experiencing. So, a few days later, you went to the bookstore (or went online) and bought this book. Then today, you thought about reading this chapter, and eventually you sat down, opened the book, and began reading. Now, you are up to the words you see here. Denying this chain of events does nothing to change what has already happened. Trying to fight this moment or say that it shouldn't be like this only leads to more suffering for you. Radical acceptance means looking at yourself and the situation and seeing it as it really is.

Keep in mind that radical acceptance does *not* mean that you condone or agree with bad behavior in others. But it does mean that you stop trying to change what's happened by getting angry and blaming the situation. For example, if you're in an abusive relationship and you need to get out, then get out. Don't waste your time and continue to suffer by blaming yourself or the other person. That won't help you. Refocus your attention on what you can do now. This will allow you to think more clearly and figure out a better way to cope with your suffering.

Radical Acceptance Coping Statements

To help you begin using radical acceptance, it's often helpful to use a coping statement to remind yourself. Below are a few examples and spaces to create your own. Check (✓) the statements that you would be willing to use to remind yourself that you should accept the present moment and the chain of events that created it. Then, in the next exercise, you'll begin using the statements that you chose.

☐ "This is the way it has to be."

☐ "All the events have led up to now."

☐ "I can't change what's already happened."

☐ "It's no use fighting the past."

☐ "Fighting the past only blinds me to my present."

☐ "The present is the only moment I have control over."

☐ "It's a waste of time to fight what's already occurred."

☐ "The present moment is perfect, even if I don't like what's happening."

☐ "This moment is exactly as it should be, given what's happened before it."

☐ "This moment is the result of a million other decisions."

☐ Other ideas: _____

_____

Exercise: Radical Acceptance

Now, using the coping statements that you checked, begin radically accepting different moments in your life without judging them. Naturally, it will be difficult to accept very painful situations, so start with smaller events. Here are some suggestions. Check (✓) the ones you're willing to do, and add any of your own ideas. Then use your coping statements to radically accept the situation without being judgmental or critical.

☐ Read a controversial story in the newspaper without being judgmental about what has occurred.

☐ The next time you get caught in heavy traffic, wait without being critical.

☐ Watch the world news on television without being critical of what's happening.

☐ Listen to a news story or a political commentary on the radio without being judgmental.

☐ Review an unpleasant event that happened in your life—one that is not too upsetting—and use radical acceptance to remember the event without judging it.

☐ Other ideas: _____

_____

DISTRACT YOURSELF FROM SELF-DESTRUCTIVE BEHAVIORS

One of the most important purposes of dialectical behavior therapy is to help you stop engaging in self-destructive behaviors, such as cutting, burning, scratching, and mutilating yourself (Linehan, 1993a). No one can deny the amount of pain you are in when you engage in one of these behaviors. Some people with over-whelming emotions say that self-injury even temporarily relieves them of some of the pain they're feeling. This might be true, but it's also true that these actions can cause serious permanent damage and even death if taken to an extreme.

Think about all the pain you've already been through in your life. Think about all the people who have hurt you physically, sexually, emotionally, and verbally. Clearly, it doesn't make sense to continue hurting yourself even more in the present, but obviously these self-destructive habits are very difficult to stop and change. You might even be addicted to the rush of natural painkillers called *endorphins* that are released when you hurt yourself. However, if you really want to recover from the pain you've already experienced, stopping these self-destructive behaviors should be one of the first steps you take. This can be very hard to do, but these types of self-destructive actions are highly dangerous and certainly deserve your best efforts to control them.

Instead of engaging in behaviors that can cause serious or even permanent damage, try using some of the alternative behaviors below. Some of them might sound strange, or even mildly painful themselves, but they're less destructive than cutting, burning, and mutilating yourself. The final goal is, of course, to stop engaging in all forms self-harming behaviors permanently. However, until you can do that, these behaviors offer less harmful alternatives. In psychology, this strategy of doing something less dangerous and destructive is called *harm reduction*, and it's frequently used with people struggling with addictions (Denning, 2000).

Exercise: Distract Yourself from Self-Destructive Behaviors

Here are some safer actions that you can use to distract yourself from your self-destructive emotions and thoughts. Check (✓) the ones you're willing to do, and then add any healthy, nonharming activities that you can think of:

☐ Instead of hurting yourself, hold an ice cube in one hand and squeeze it. The sensation from the cold ice is numbing and very distracting.

☐ Write on yourself with a red felt-tip marker instead of cutting. Draw exactly where you would cut. Use red paint or nail polish to make it look like you're bleeding. Then draw stitches with a black marker. If you need to make it even more distracting, squeeze an ice cube in the other hand at the same time.

☐ Gently snap a rubber band on your wrist each time you feel like hurting yourself. This might cause some minor temporary pain, but it causes less permanent damage than cutting, burning, or mutilating yourself.

☐ Gently dig your fingernails into your arm without breaking the skin.

☐ Draw faces of people you hate on balloons and then pop them.

☐ Write letters to people you hate or to people who have hurt you. Tell them what they did to you and tell them why you hate them. Then throw the letters away or save them to read later.

☐ Throw foam balls, rolled-up socks, or pillows against the wall as hard as you can.

☐ Scream as loud as you can into a pillow or scream someplace where you won't draw the attention of other people, like at a loud concert or in your car.

☐ Stick pins in a doll instead of hurting yourself. You can make a doll with some rolled-up socks or a foam ball and some markers. Or you can buy a doll in a store for the specific purpose of sticking pins in it. Buy one that's soft and easy to stick.

☐ Cry. Sometimes people do other things instead of crying because they're afraid that if they start to cry, they'll never stop. This never happens. In fact, the truth is that crying can make you feel better because it releases stress hormones.

☐ Go exercise. Go to the gym or yoga studio and take out your pain and frustration doing something healthy. Go for a long walk or a long run. Use all of that destructive energy you feel in a positive way.

☐ Other healthy, nonharming ideas: _____

☐ _____

☐ _____

Here's an example of using alternative actions to distract your self-destructive emotions. Lucy often cut herself when she felt upset or angry. She had dozens of scars on her wrists and forearms. She wore long-sleeved shirts even in the hot summer because she was embarrassed when other people saw what she had done to herself. But after getting some ideas from this workbook, she made a distraction plan. So the next time she got angry with herself and felt like cutting, she looked at her plan for alternative actions. She had written down the idea of drawing on herself with a red marker. She drew a line exactly where she would have cut herself. She even used red paint to make it look like she was bleeding. She carried the mark on her arm for the rest of the day to remind herself how sad and overwhelmed she felt. But then, before she went to sleep, she was able to erase the "scar" and "blood" from her arm, unlike the rest of the marks from her permanent injuries.

DISTRACT YOURSELF WITH PLEASURABLE ACTIVITIES ⊠

Sometimes doing something that makes you feel good is the best way to distract yourself from painful emotions. But remember, you don't have to wait until you feel overwhelmed by painful emotions in order to do one of these activities. It's also helpful to engage in these types of activities on a regular basis. In fact, you should try to do something pleasurable every day. Exercise is also especially important because not only is it good for your overall physical health, but it's also been shown to be an effective treatment for depression in some cases (Babyak et al., 2000). Plus, exercise makes you feel good almost immediately by releasing natural painkillers in your body called endorphins (the same painkillers that are released when you cut yourself).

Following is a list of over one hundred pleasurable activities you can use to distract yourself. (You can also download a copy of the list at http://www.newharbinger.com/44581.)

THE BIG LIST OF PLEASURABLE ACTIVITIES

Check (✓) the ones you're willing to do, and then add any activities that you can think of:

☐ Talk to a friend on the telephone.

☐ Go out and visit a friend.

☐ Invite a friend to come to your home.

☐ Text-message or email your friends.

☐ Organize a party.

☐ Exercise.

☐ Lift weights.

☐ Do yoga, tai chi, or Pilates, or take classes to learn.

☐ Stretch your muscles.

☐ Go for a long walk in a park or someplace else that's peaceful.

☐ Go outside and watch the clouds.

☐ Go jog.

☐ Ride your bike.

☐ Go for a swim.

☐ Go hiking.

☐ Do something exciting, like surfing, rock climbing, skiing, skydiving, motorcycle riding, or kayaking, or go learn how to do one of these things.

☐ Go to your local playground and join a game being played or watch a game.

☐ Go play something you can do by yourself if no one else is around, like basketball, bowling, handball, miniature golf, billiards, or hitting a tennis ball against the wall.

☐ Get a massage; this can also help soothe your emotions.

☐ Get out of your house, even if you just sit outside.

☐ Go for a drive in your car or go for a ride on public transportation.

☐ Plan a trip to a place you've never been before.

☐ Sleep or take a nap.

☐ Eat chocolate (it's good for you!) or eat something else you really like.

☐ Eat your favorite ice cream.

☐ Cook your favorite dish or meal.

☐ Cook a recipe that you've never tried before.

☐ Take a cooking class.

☐ Go out for something to eat.

☐ Go outside and play with your pet.

☐ Go borrow a friend's dog and take it to the park.

☐ Give your pet a bath.

☐ Go outside and watch the birds and other animals.

☐ Find something funny to do, like watching a funny video on YouTube.

☐ Watch a funny movie (start collecting funny movies to watch when you're feeling overwhelmed with pain).

- ☐ Go to the movie theater and watch whatever's playing.
- ☐ Watch television.
- ☐ Listen to the radio.
- ☐ Go to a sporting event, like a baseball or football game.
- ☐ Play a game with a friend.
- ☐ Play solitaire.
- ☐ Play video games.
- ☐ Go online to chat.
- ☐ Visit your favorite websites.
- ☐ Visit crazy websites and start keeping a list of them.
- ☐ Create your own website.
- ☐ Create your own online blog.
- ☐ Join an Internet dating service.
- ☐ Sell something you don't want on the Internet.
- ☐ Buy something on the Internet (within your budget).
- ☐ Do a puzzle with a lot of pieces.
- ☐ Call a crisis or suicide hotline and talk to someone.
- ☐ Go shopping.
- ☐ Go get a haircut.
- ☐ Go to a spa.
- ☐ Go to a library.
- ☐ Go to a bookstore and read.
- ☐ Go to your favorite café for coffee or tea.
- ☐ Visit a museum or local art gallery.
- ☐ Go to the mall or the park and watch other people; try to imagine what they're thinking.
- ☐ Pray or meditate.
- ☐ Go to your church, synagogue, temple, or other place of worship.
- ☐ Join a group at your place of worship.
- ☐ Write a letter to God.
- ☐ Call a family member you haven't spoken to in a long time.
- ☐ Learn a new language.
- ☐ Sing or learn how to sing.
- ☐ Play a musical instrument or learn how to play one.
- ☐ Write a song.
- ☐ Listen to some upbeat, happy music (start collecting happy songs for times when you're feeling overwhelmed).
- ☐ Turn on some loud music and dance in your room.
- ☐ Memorize lines from your favorite movie, play, or song.
- ☐ Make a movie or video with your smartphone.
- ☐ Take photographs.
- ☐ Join a public-speaking group and write a speech.
- ☐ Participate in a local theater group.
- ☐ Sing in a local choir.
- ☐ Join a club.
- ☐ Plant a garden.
- ☐ Work outside.
- ☐ Knit, crochet, or sew—or learn how to.

☐ Make a scrapbook with pictures.

☐ Paint your nails.

☐ Change your hair color.

☐ Take a bubble bath or shower.

☐ Work on your car, truck, motorcycle, or bicycle.

☐ Sign up for a class that excites you at a local college, adult school, or online.

☐ Read your favorite book, magazine, paper, or poem.

☐ Read a trashy celebrity magazine.

☐ Write a letter to a friend or family member.

☐ Write things you like about yourself on a picture of your body or draw them on a photograph of yourself.

☐ Write a poem, story, movie, or play about your life or someone else's life.

☐ Write in your journal or diary about what happened to you today.

☐ Write a loving letter to yourself when you're feeling good and keep it with you to read when you're feeling upset.

☐ Make a list of ten things you're good at or that you like about yourself when you're feeling good, and keep it with you to read when you're feeling upset.

☐ Draw a picture.

☐ Paint a picture with a brush or your fingers.

☐ Spend time with someone you care about, respect, or admire.

☐ Make a list of the people you admire and want to be like—it can be anyone real or fictional throughout history. Describe what you admire about these people.

☐ Write a story about the craziest, funniest, or most meaningful thing that has ever happened to you.

☐ Make a list of ten things you would like to do before you die.

☐ Make a list of ten celebrities you would like to be friends with and describe why.

☐ Make a list of ten celebrities you would like to date and describe why.

☐ Write a letter to someone who has made your life better and tell them why. (You don't have to send the letter if you don't want to.)

☐ Create your own list of pleasurable activities.

Other ideas: _____

_____

_____

Here's an example of using pleasurable activities to distract yourself. Karen was feeling lonely and had nothing to do. As she sat alone at home, she began to think about how lonely she'd been her whole life and how she was hurt by her father when she was growing up. Very quickly, Karen was overwhelmed with very painful emotions. In fact, the memories also triggered physical pain in her shoulder. Karen began to cry and didn't know what to do. Luckily, she remembered the distraction plan she had created. Exercise had always been a powerful tool for Karen, so she went for a long walk in the park while she listened to some of her favorite music. The activity didn't erase her memories or remove her pain completely, but the long walk did soothe her and prevent her from being overwhelmed with sadness.

DISTRACT YOURSELF BY PAYING ATTENTION TO SOMEONE ELSE

Another great way to distract yourself from pain is to put your attention on someone else. Here are some examples. Check (✓) the ones you're willing to do, and then add any activities that you can think of:

☐ *Do something for someone else.* Call your friends and ask if they need help doing something, such as a chore, grocery shopping, or housecleaning. Ask your parents, grandparents, or siblings if you can help them with something. Tell them you're feeling bored and you're looking for something to do. Call up someone you know and offer to take them out to lunch. Go outside and give money to the first needy person you see. If you can plan ahead for moments like these when you're overwhelmed with pain, call your local soup kitchen, homeless shelter, or volunteer organization. Plan to participate in activities that help other people. Join a local political activities group, environmental group, or other organization, and get involved helping other people.

☐ *Take your attention off yourself.* Go to a local store, shopping center, bookstore, or park. Just sit and watch other people or walk around among them. Watch what they do. Observe how they dress. Listen to their conversations. Count the number of buttons they're wearing on their shirts. Observe as many details about these other people as you can. Count the number of people with blue eyes versus the number of people with brown eyes. When your thinking returns to your own pain, refocus on the details of the people you're watching.

☐ *Think of someone you care about.* Keep a picture of this person in your wallet or in your purse. This could be your husband, wife, parent, boyfriend, girlfriend, children, or friend, or it could be someone else you admire, such as Mother Teresa, Gandhi, Jesus, the Dalai Lama, and so on. It could even be a movie star, an athlete, or someone you've never met. Then, when you're feeling distressed, take out the picture and imagine a healing, peaceful conversation you would have with that person if you could talk to them at that moment when you're feeling hurt. What would they say to you that would help make you feel better? Imagine them saying those words to you.

☐ Other ideas: _____

_____

Here's an example of distracting yourself by paying attention to someone else. Louis got upset by a fight he had with his boyfriend, Roger. Very quickly, Louis became overwhelmed by sadness as he started to remember all the other fights he and Roger had had in the past. Louis went to his desk, where he kept a picture of his mother. He sat down and started to talk to his mother as if she were there with him. He asked for strength and guidance to handle the situation with Roger. Then he imagined what she would say to him, and he started to feel better. Later, when he was able to think more clearly, he returned to what he needed to do that day.

DISTRACT YOUR THOUGHTS ⊠

The human brain is a wonderful thought-producing machine. It turns out millions of thoughts every day. Most of the time, this makes our lives much easier. But unfortunately, we can't fully control what our brain thinks about. Here's an example. Imagine a picture of your favorite cartoon character, such as Bugs Bunny, Snoopy, Superman, or whoever. Close your eyes and see the character in vivid detail in your mind's eye. Remember exactly what it looks like. Think about the character for about fifteen seconds. Got it? Now, for the next thirty seconds do your best not to think about the character. Try to block the character from your thoughts. But be honest with yourself and notice how often the character pops into your thoughts. It's impossible not to think about the character. In fact, the harder you try not to think about it, the more power you give to the image and the more your brain keeps bringing it into your thoughts. It's almost as if the harder you try to forget something, the harder your brain tries to remember it. This is why forcing yourself to forget about something that happened to you is impossible. It's also why you can't simply force yourself to get rid of emotions that you don't want.

So, instead of trying to force yourself to forget a memory or thought, try to distract your thoughts with other memories or creative images. Here are some examples. Check (✔) the ones you're willing to do, and then add any activities that you can think of:

☐ Remember events from your past that were pleasant, fun, or exciting. Try to remember as many details as possible about these happy memories. What did you do? Who were you with? What happened?

☐ Look outside at the natural world around you. Observe the flowers, trees, sky, and landscape as closely as you can. Observe any animals that are around. Listen to the sounds that they make. Or if you live in a city without much nature around you, either do your best to observe what you can or close your eyes and imagine a scene you've observed in the past.

☐ Imagine yourself as a hero or heroine correcting some past or future event in your life. How would you do it? What would people say to you?

☐ Imagine yourself getting praise from someone whose opinion matters to you. What did you do? What does this person say to you? Why does this person's opinion matter to you?

☐ Imagine your wildest fantasy coming true. What would it be? Who else would be involved? What would you do afterward?

☐ Keep a copy of your favorite prayer or favorite saying with you. Then, when you feel distressed, pull it out and read it to yourself. Imagine the words calming and soothing you. Use imagery (such as a white light coming down from heaven or the universe) that soothes you as you read the words.

☐ Other ideas: _____

_____

Here's an example of using distracting thoughts. Joel was in a bad relationship that often reminded him of the way he was treated by his mother. She was always criticizing him and telling him he was wrong. When these memories overwhelmed him, Joel never knew what to do. Sometimes he would just scream at his friends or whoever else was around. But after creating a distraction plan, Joel thought of other ideas. The next time he had memories of his mother berating him, he remembered to use his REST strategy. First, he did his best to relax by taking a few slow breaths. Then he evaluated the situation and realized he wasn't in any danger. Next, he set an intention to distract his thoughts, so he took action and went to his bedroom to lie down. Then he started to imagine himself as a child confronting his mother about her abusive language. He told her all the things he wished he could have said to her years ago. He told her she was wrong and that she should stop criticizing him. Joel controlled the details of the fantasy in the way he wished it could have happened years ago. Afterward, he slowly felt better. He had escaped the cycle of letting his painful emotions overwhelm him.

DISTRACT YOURSELF BY LEAVING

Sometimes the best thing that you can do is leave. If you're in a very painful situation with someone and you recognize that your emotions are going to overwhelm you and possibly make the situation worse than it is already, then often it's best to just leave. Remember, if you're already overwhelmed by your emotions, it will be harder for you to think of a healthy resolution to your problem. Maybe it's best to put some distance between you and the situation in order to give yourself time to calm your emotions and think of what to do next. Just walk away if that's the best you can do. It will be better than adding fuel to the emotional fire.

Here's an example of leaving to distract yourself. Anna was in a large department store shopping for a blouse. She wanted one of the clerks to help her find her size, but the store clerk was busy with other customers. Anna waited as long as she could and kept trying to get the clerk's attention, but nothing worked. Anna recognized that she was getting angry very quickly. She was ready to tear the blouse in half. She didn't know what else to do. In the past, she would have stayed in the store and gotten angrier, but this time she remembered to leave. She walked out of the store, did some shopping elsewhere, and returned to get the blouse later, when the store was less crowded and when she was feeling more in control of her behaviors.

DISTRACT YOURSELF WITH TASKS AND CHORES

Strangely, many people don't schedule enough time to take care of themselves or their living environments. As a result, tasks and chores go uncompleted. Here, then, is the perfect opportunity to do something to take care of yourself and your environment. The next time you're in a situation in which your emotions become too painful, temporarily distract yourself by engaging in one of the following activities. Check (✓) the ones you're willing to do, and then add any activities that you can think of:

☐ Wash the dishes.

☐ Make phone calls to people you haven't spoken to recently but not someone you're angry with.

☐ Clean your room or house, or go help a friend with their cleaning or gardening project.

- ☐ Clean out your closet and donate your old clothes.

- ☐ Redecorate a room or at least the walls.

- ☐ Organize your books, music playlists, computer desktop, and so forth.

- ☐ Make a plan for getting a job if you don't already have one, or make a plan for finding a better job.

- ☐ Go get a haircut.

- ☐ Go get a manicure or pedicure, or both.

- ☐ Go get a massage.

- ☐ Wash your or someone else's car.

- ☐ Mow the lawn.

- ☐ Clean your garage.

- ☐ Wash the laundry.

- ☐ Do your homework.

- ☐ Do work that you've brought home from your job.

- ☐ Polish your shoes.

- ☐ Polish your jewelry.

- ☐ Clean the bathtub and then take a bath.

- ☐ Water your plants or work in the garden.

- ☐ Cook dinner for yourself and some friends.

- ☐ Pay the bills.

- ☐ Go to a support meeting, like Narcotics Anonymous, Alcoholics Anonymous, or Overeaters Anonymous.

- ☐ Other ideas: _____

   _____

   _____

Here's an example of using tasks and chores to distract yourself. Mike called his girlfriend, Michelle, to go to a movie. Michelle had already made plans with her friends to do something else. Mike felt incredibly rejected and abandoned. He started yelling at Michelle, who hung up on him. This made Mike feel worse. He didn't know what to do. Quickly, he began to feel light-headed and confused, and his emotions became very angry. But this time, instead of calling Michelle back and arguing, he opened his wallet and pulled out the distraction plan he had made (which you'll also create at the end of this chapter). He had written down "Take a REST and distract with chores." So he took a few breaths to relax and then evaluated the situation. He recognized that he was angry—but not in danger. Next, he set an intention to go get a haircut, because it would take him at least two hours, by which time he'd probably calm down. And finally he took action by walking a half mile to his barber. Getting out of his house helped soothe his anger, and when he returned home, he had cooled down enough to call Michelle back to see if she was busy the next day.

DISTRACT YOURSELF BY COUNTING

Counting is a simple skill that can really keep your mind busy and help you focus on something other than your pain. Here are some examples. Check (✔) the ones you're willing to do, and then add any activities that you can think of:

- ☐ *Count your breaths.* Sit in a comfortable chair, put one hand on your belly, and take slow, long breaths. Imagine breathing into your stomach instead of your lungs. Feel your belly expand like a balloon with each inhalation. Start counting your breaths. When you inevitably start thinking about whatever it is that's causing you pain, return your focus to counting.

- ☐ *Count anything else.* If you're too distracted by your emotions, simply count the sounds that you're hearing. This will take your attention outside of yourself. Or try counting the number of cars that are passing by, the number of sensations that you're feeling, or anything else you can put a number on, such as the branches of a tree you're looking at.

- ☐ *Count or subtract by increments of seven.* For example, start with one hundred and subtract seven. Now take that answer and subtract seven more. Keep going. This activity will really distract you from your emotions because it requires extra attention and concentration.

- ☐ Other counting ideas: _____

_____

_____

Here's an example of using counting to distract yourself. Dawn became upset when her mother told her to help set the table for dinner. "She's always telling me what to do," Dawn thought. She could feel her anger getting worse, so she went to her room and remembered that the last time this happened, counting her breaths had helped soothe her emotions. She sat down and did it again. After ten minutes, she felt calmer, so she went back to the dining room.

CREATE YOUR DISTRACTION PLAN

Now identify those distraction skills that you're willing to use the next time you're in a situation that's causing you pain and discomfort. These chosen skills will make up your distraction plan. Remember, the first step in your distress tolerance plan should be to use the REST strategy, which will likely include distraction techniques. Write your chosen distraction techniques below. When you're done, write them down again on a sticky note to carry around with you in your wallet or purse, or use a note app to record them in your smartphone. Then the next time you're in a distressing situation, you can pull out the note or open the app to remind yourself of your distraction plan.

MY DISTRACTION PLAN

1. Use REST: relax (R), evaluate (E), set an intention (S), and take action (T).

2. _____

3. _____

4. _____

5. _____

6. _____

7. _____

8. _____

9. _____

10. _____

RELAX AND SOOTHE YOURSELF

Now that you've learned some healthy and effective ways to distract yourself when you become overwhelmed by painful emotions, you'll need to learn new ways to help soothe yourself (Johnson, 1985; Linehan, 1993b). The activities in this section will help you relax, which is the first step in the REST strategy—relax, evaluate, set an intention, and take action. Then, later in this book, you'll learn specific skills to cope with problematic situations. These will include emotion regulation skills, mindfulness skills, and interpersonal effectiveness skills.

Learning to relax and soothe yourself is very important for many reasons. When you're relaxed, your body feels better. It also functions in a healthier way. In a state of relaxation, your heart beats more slowly and your blood pressure is reduced. Your body is no longer in a state of constant emergency, preparing to either confront a stressful situation or run away from it. As a result, it's easier for your brain to think of healthier ways to cope with your problems.

Included here are some simple relaxation and soothing activities that utilize your five senses of smell, sight, hearing, taste, and touch. These activities are meant to bring you a small amount of peace in your life. So if one of these activities doesn't help you feel relaxed, or makes you feel worse, don't do it. Try something else. And remember, each one of us is different. For example, some people will become more relaxed by listening to music and others will find that taking a hot bubble bath works for them. As you explore this list, think about what works best for you and be willing to try something new if it sounds exciting.

Self-Soothing Using Your Sense of Smell ⌫

Smell is a very powerful sense that can often trigger memories and make you feel a certain way. Therefore, it's very important that you identify smells that make you feel good, not bad. Here are some ideas. Check (✓) the ones you're willing to do, and then add any activities that you can think of:

☐ Burn scented candles or incense in your room or house. Find a scent that's pleasing to you.

☐ Wear scented oils, perfume, or cologne that makes you feel happy, confident, or sexy.

☐ Cut out perfumed cards from magazines and carry them with you in your handbag or wallet.

☐ Go someplace where the scent is pleasing to you, like a bakery or restaurant.

☐ Bake your own food that has a pleasing smell, like chocolate chip cookies.

☐ Lie down in your local park and smell the grass and outdoor smells.

☐ Buy fresh-cut flowers or seek out flowers in your neighborhood.

☐ Hug someone you know whose smell makes you feel calm.

☐ Other ideas: _____

_____

_____

Self-Soothing Using Your Sense of Vision

Vision is very important to humans. In fact, a large portion of our brain is devoted solely to our sense of sight. The things you look at can often have very powerful effects on you, for better or for worse. That's why it's important to find images that have a very soothing effect on you. And again, for each person, it comes down to individual taste and preference. Here are some ideas. Check (✓) the ones you're willing to do, and then add any activities that you can think of:

☐ Go through magazines and books to cut out pictures that you like. Make a collage of them to hang on your wall or keep some of them with you in your handbag or wallet to look at when you're away from home.

☐ Find a place that's soothing for you to look at, like a park or a museum. Or find a picture of a place that's soothing for you to look at, like the ocean.

☐ Go to the bookstore and find a collection of photographs or paintings that you find relaxing, such as the nature photographs of Ansel Adams.

☐ Draw or paint your own picture that's pleasing to you.

☐ Carry a picture or photograph of someone you love, someone you find attractive, or someone you admire.

☐ Other ideas: _____

_____

_____

Self-Soothing Using Your Sense of Hearing ⊠

Certain sounds can soothe us. Listening to gentle music, for example, may be relaxing. In fact, this entire chapter was written while listening to classical music. However, each one of us has our own tastes. You have to find what works best for you. Use these examples to identify the sounds that help you relax. Check (✓) the ones you're willing to do, and then add any activities that you can think of:

☐ Listen to soothing music. This can be anything that works for you. It might be music with singing or without. Go online to sample some soothing music before you buy it, and listen to a wide variety of genres to determine which ones help you relax. Then download the music on your smartphone so you can listen to it anywhere you want.

☐ Listen to audio books. Many public libraries will let you borrow books on CDs or temporarily download audio books. Borrow a few to see if they help you relax. You don't even have to pay attention to the story line. Sometimes just listening to the sound of someone talking can be very relaxing. Again, keep some of these recordings with you in your car or loaded on your smartphone.

☐ Turn on the television and just listen. Find a show that's boring or sedate, not something agitating like the news. Sit in a comfortable chair or lie down, and then close your eyes and just listen. Make sure you turn the volume down to a level that's not too loud. Many years ago, there was a show on public television featuring a painter named Bob Ross. His voice was so soothing and relaxing that many people reported falling asleep while watching him. Find a show like this that will help you relax.

☐ Listen to a soothing podcast or video online, or find a soothing talk show on the radio. Remember—a *soothing* podcast or talk show, not something that's going to make you upset or angry. Again, stay away from political talk shows and the news. Find something neutral in discussion, like the *TED Talks* series online or *This American Life* on public radio. Again, some-times just listening to someone else talk can be relaxing. Bookmark the links or download your favorite podcasts on your smartphone so you can listen to them when you're feeling upset or angry.

☐ Open your window and listen to the peaceful sounds outside. Or, if you live in a place without relaxing sounds outside, go visit a place with relaxing sounds, such as a park.

☐ Listen to a recording of nature sounds, such as birds and other wildlife. You can often download these online and then take them with you to listen on your smartphone.

☐ Listen to a white-noise machine. *White noise* is a sound that blocks out other distracting sounds. You can buy a machine that makes white noise with circulating air, turn on a fan to block out distracting sounds, or download a white-noise app on your smartphone. Some white-noise machines and apps even have other recorded sounds on them, such as the sounds of birds, water-falls, and rain forests. Many people find these sounds very relaxing.

☐ Listen to the sound of a personal water fountain. These small electronic fountains can be bought online and many people find the sound of the trickling water in their homes to be very soothing.

☐ Listen to a recording of a meditation or relaxation exercise. Exercises such as these will help you imagine yourself relaxing in many different ways. Other recorded exercises can even teach you self-hypnosis techniques to help you relax. Recordings like these can be found online or on the websites of self-help publishers, such as New Harbinger Publications. Go to www.newharbinger .com and look under "Audiobooks." Then you can take the programs with you on your smart-phone to listen to whenever you're feeling overwhelmed. (Just don't listen to them while you're driving or operating equipment where it might be dangerous if you fell asleep.)

☐ Listen to the sound of rushing or trickling water. Maybe your local park has a waterfall, or the nearby mall has a fountain. Or maybe just sit in your bathroom with the water running for a few minutes.

☐ Other ideas: _____

_____

_____

Self-Soothing Using Your Sense of Taste

Taste is also a very powerful sense. Our sensations of flavor can trigger memories and feelings, so again, it's important that you find the tastes that are pleasing to you. However, if eating is a problem for you, such as eating too much, bingeing, purging, or restricting what you eat, talk to a professional counselor about getting help for yourself. If the process of eating can make you upset or nervous, use your other senses to calm yourself. But if food soothes you, use some of these suggestions. Check (✓) the ones you're willing to do, and then add any activities you can think of:

☐ Enjoy your favorite meal, whatever it is. Eat it slowly so you can enjoy the way it tastes.

☐ Carry lollipops, gum, or other candy with you to eat when you're feeling upset.

☐ Eat a soothing food, like ice cream, chocolate, pudding, or something else that makes you feel good.

☐ Drink something soothing, such as tea, coffee, or hot chocolate. Practice drinking it slowly so you can enjoy the way it tastes.

☐ Suck on an ice cube or an ice pop, especially if you're feeling warm, and enjoy the taste as it melts in your mouth.

☐ Buy a piece of juicy fresh fruit and then eat it slowly.

☐ Other ideas: _____

_____

_____

Self-Soothing Using Your Sense of Touch ⊠

We often forget about our sense of touch, and yet we're always touching something, such as the clothes we're wearing or the chair we're sitting in. Our skin is our largest organ, and it's completely covered with nerves that carry feelings to our brain. Certain tactile sensations can be pleasing, like petting a soft dog, while other sensations are shocking or painful in order to communicate danger, like touching a hot stove. Again, each of us prefers different sensations. You have to find the ones that are most pleasing for you. Here are some suggestions. Check (✓) the ones you're willing to do, and then add any activities that you can think of:

☐ Carry something soft or velvety in your pocket to touch when you need to, like a piece of cloth.

☐ Take a warm or cold shower and enjoy the feeling of the water falling on your skin.

☐ Take a warm bubble bath or a bath with scented oils and enjoy the soothing sensations on your skin.

☐ Get a massage. Many people who have survived physical and sexual abuse do not want to be touched by anyone. This is understandable. But not all types of massage require you to take off your clothes. Some techniques, such as traditional Japanese shiatsu massage, simply require you to wear loose-fitting clothes. A shoulder and neck massage, received while seated in a massage chair, can also be done without removing any clothes. If this is a concern for you, just ask the massage therapist what kind of massage would be best to have while wearing your clothes.

☐ Massage yourself. Sometimes just rubbing your own sore muscles is very pleasing.

☐ Play with your pet. Owning a pet can have many health benefits. Pet owners often have lower blood pressure, lower cholesterol levels, and reduced risk for heart disease (Anderson, Reid, & Jennings, 1992), and they also experience other general health improvements (Serpell, 1991). In addition, playing with your pet and stroking the animal's fur or skin can provide you with a soothing tactile experience. If you don't have a pet, consider getting one. Or if you can't afford one or if you can't have one where you live, visit a friend who has a pet or volunteer at your local animal shelter where you can play with the rescued animals.

☐ Wear your most comfortable clothes, like your favorite worn-in T-shirt, baggy sweat suit, or old jeans.

☐ Other ideas: _____

_____

_____

CREATE A RELAXATION PLAN

Now that you've read the suggestions to help you relax and soothe yourself using your five senses, construct a list of techniques you're willing to use. For ideas, review the activities that you checked. Be specific about what you're going to do. Make a list of ideas to try at home and a list of ideas you can take with you when you're away from home.

RELAXATION AND SOOTHING SKILLS TO USE AT HOME

1. _____

2. _____

3. _____

4. _____

5. _____

6. _____

7. _____

8. _____

9. _____

10. _____

Keep this list in a convenient place that's easy to remember, like in an app on your smartphone. You might even want to copy this list and put it in places where you see it all the time, such as on your refrigerator, above your desk, or next to your bed. This way you'll remind yourself to relax and soothe yourself as often as possible. It will also make it easier to soothe yourself when your painful emotions overwhelm you and prevent you from thinking clearly.

Now create a similar list to use when you're away from home. Again, review the soothing skills you checked in the last few pages to give yourself ideas. But make sure that it's possible to use these skills when you're away from home. For example, don't list "take a hot bath" because, most likely, there won't be a hot bath available to you when you're not at home.

RELAXATION AND SOOTHING SKILLS TO USE AWAY FROM HOME

1. _____

2. _____

3. _____

4. _____

5. _____

6. _____

7. _____

8. _____

9. _____

10. _____

Now copy these last ten ideas on a sticky note or put them in your smartphone to remind yourself what to do when you're away from home. Keep this list with you and make sure you have whatever else is needed, such as candy, your favorite music, pictures, and so forth. This way you can practice relaxing when you're not at home, especially when your painful emotions overwhelm you and prevent you from thinking clearly.

CONCLUSION

You've now learned some basic distraction and relaxation skills. You should begin using these skills immediately when you become overwhelmed with painful emotions. Also, don't forget to use your REST strategy too. The next chapter will build on these skills and teach you more advanced distraction and relaxation skills.

CHAPTER 2

Advanced Distress Tolerance Skills

In the last chapter, you learned many important skills that you can use in a crisis. These skills will distract you from painful situations and then help you soothe yourself and relax so that you can deal with the situation in a more effective way. Remember, your initial plan for handling a crisis should be to use the REST strategy in conjunction with these skills.

Now that you've been practicing the distress tolerance skills from the last chapter, you'll be ready for the advanced distress tolerance skills found in this chapter. These techniques will help you feel more empowered when you encounter painful situations in the future, and they'll help you build a more relaxing and fulfilling life for yourself.

After trying each technique, mark the ones that are helpful so you can identify them later.

SAFE-PLACE VISUALIZATION ☒

Safe-place visualization is a powerful stress-reduction technique. Using it, you can soothe yourself by imagining a peaceful, safe place where you can relax. The truth is, your brain and body often can't tell the difference between what's really happening to you and what you're just imagining. So if you can successfully create a peaceful, relaxing scene in your thoughts, your body will often respond to those soothing ideas.

Make sure you conduct this exercise in a quiet room where you'll be free from distractions. Turn off your phone, television, computer, and radio. Tell the people in your home, if there are any, that you can't be disturbed for the next twenty minutes. Allow yourself the time and the freedom to relax. You deserve it. Read the following directions before you begin. If you feel comfortable remembering them, close your eyes and begin the visualization exercise. Or, if you would prefer, record the instructions on your smartphone. Read them aloud using a slow, soothing voice. Then close your eyes and listen to the guided visualization you created.

Before you begin the exercise, think of a real or imaginary place that makes you feel safe and relaxed. It can be a real place that you've visited in the past, such as the beach, a park, a field, a church/temple/

synagogue, your room, and so on. Or it can be a place that you've completely made up, such as a white cloud floating in the sky, a medieval castle, or the surface of the moon. It can be anywhere. If you have trouble thinking of a place, think of a color that makes you feel relaxed, such as pink or baby blue. Just do your best. In the exercise, you'll be guided through exploring this place in more detail. But before you begin, make sure you already have a place in mind, and remember—thinking of it should make you feel safe and relaxed.

Complete the following sentences about your safe place before beginning the visualization:

- My safe place is _____

- My safe place makes me feel _____

Instructions

To begin, sit in a comfortable chair with your feet and hands resting comfortably. Close your eyes. Take a slow, long breath in through your nose. Feel your belly expand like a balloon as you breathe in. Hold it for five seconds: 1, 2, 3, 4, 5. Then release it slowly through your mouth. Feel your belly collapse like a balloon losing its air. Again, take a slow, long breath in through your nose and feel your stomach expand. Hold it for five seconds: 1, 2, 3, 4, 5. Then exhale slowly through your mouth. One more time: take a slow, long breath in through your nose and feel your stomach expand. Hold it for five seconds: 1, 2, 3, 4, 5. Then exhale slowly through your mouth. Now begin to take slow, long breaths without holding them, and continue to breathe smoothly for the rest of this exercise.

Now, with your eyes closed, imagine that you enter your safe place using all of your senses to ground yourself in the scene.

First, look around using your imaginary sense of sight. What does this place look like? Is it daytime or nighttime? Is it sunny or cloudy? Notice the details. Are you alone or are there other people or animals? What are they doing? If you're outside, look up and notice the sky. Look out at the horizon. If you're inside, notice what the walls and the furniture look like. Is the room light or dark? Choose something soothing to look at. Then continue looking for a few seconds using your imaginary sense of sight.

Next, use your imaginary sense of hearing. What do you hear? Do you hear other people or animals? Do you hear music? Do you hear the wind or the ocean? Choose something soothing to hear. Then listen for a few seconds using your imaginary sense of hearing.

Then use your imaginary sense of smell. If you're inside, what does it smell like? Does it smell fresh? Do you have a fire burning that you can smell? Or, if you're outside, can you smell the air, the grass, the ocean, or the flowers? Choose to smell something soothing in your scene. Then take a few seconds to use your imaginary sense of smell.

Next, notice if you can feel anything with your imaginary sense of touch. What are you sitting or standing on in your scene? Can you feel the wind? Can you feel something you're touching in the scene? Choose to touch something soothing in your scene. Then take a few seconds to use your imaginary sense of touch.

Last, use your imaginary sense of taste. Are you eating or drinking anything in this scene? Choose something soothing to taste. Then take a few seconds to use your imaginary sense of taste.

Now take a few more seconds to explore your safe place using all of your imaginary senses. Recognize how safe and relaxed you feel here. Remember that you can come back to this place in your imagination whenever you need to feel safe and relaxed. You can also come back whenever you're feeling sad, angry, restless, or in pain. Look around one last time to remember what it looks like.

Now keep your eyes closed and return your focus to your breathing. Again, take some slow, long breaths in through your nose and exhale through your mouth. Then, when you feel ready, open your eyes and return your focus to the room.

CUE-CONTROLLED RELAXATION

Cue-controlled relaxation is a quick and easy technique that will help you reduce your stress level and muscle tension. A *cue* is a trigger or command that helps you relax. In this case, your cue will be a word, like "relax" or "peace." The goal of this technique is to train your body to release muscle tension when you think about your cue word. Initially, you'll need the help of the guided instructions to help you release muscle tension in different sections of your body. But after you've been practicing this technique for a few weeks, you'll be able to relax your whole body at one time simply by taking a few slow breaths and thinking about your cue word. With practice, this can become a very quick and easy technique to help you relax. Before you begin, choose a cue word that will help you relax.

- My cue word is _____

To begin this exercise, you'll need to find a comfortable chair to sit in. Later, after you've practiced this exercise for a few weeks, you'll be able to do it wherever you are, even if you're standing. You'll also be able to do it more quickly. But to begin, choose a comfortable place to sit in a room where you won't be disturbed. Make sure you'll be free from distractions. Turn off your phone, television, computer, and radio. Tell the people in your home, if there are any, that you can't be disturbed for the next twenty minutes. Allow yourself the time and the freedom to relax. You deserve it. Read the following directions before you begin. If you feel comfortable remembering them, close your eyes and begin the relaxation exercise. Or, if you would prefer, record the instructions on your smartphone. Then close your eyes and listen to the guided relaxation technique that you created.

Instructions

To begin, sit in a comfortable chair with your feet flat on the floor and your hands resting comfortably, either on the arms of the chair or in your lap. Close your eyes. Take a slow, long breath in through your nose. Feel your belly expand like a balloon as you breathe in. Hold it for five seconds: 1, 2, 3, 4, 5. Then release it slowly through your mouth. Feel your belly collapse like a balloon losing its air. Again, take a slow, long breath in through your nose and feel your stomach expand. Hold it for five seconds: 1, 2, 3, 4, 5. Then exhale slowly through your mouth. One more time: take a slow, long breath in through your nose and feel your stomach expand. Hold it for five seconds: 1, 2, 3, 4, 5. Then exhale slowly through your mouth. Now begin to take slow, long breaths without holding them, and continue to breathe smoothly for the rest of this exercise.

Now, with your eyes still closed, imagine that a white beam of light shines down from the sky like a bright laser and lands on the very top of your head. Notice how warm and soothing the light makes you feel. This could be a light from God, the universe, or whatever power makes you feel comfortable. As you continue to breathe smoothly, taking slow, long breaths, notice how the light makes you feel more and more relaxed as it continues to shine on the top of your head. Now, slowly, the warm, white light begins to spread over the top of your head like soothing water. And as it does, the light begins to loosen any muscle tension that you're feeling on the top of your head. Slowly, the light begins to slide down your body, and as it moves across your forehead, all the muscle tension there is released. Then the white light continues down past your ears, the back of your head, your eyes, nose, mouth, and chin, and it continues to release any tension you're holding there. Notice how pleasantly warm your forehead feels. Now, slowly, imagine that the light begins to move down your neck and over your shoulders, releasing any muscle tension. Then the light slowly proceeds down both of your arms and the front and back of your torso. Feel the muscles in your upper and lower back release. Notice the soothing sensation of the white light as it moves across your chest and stomach. Feel the muscles in your arms release as the light moves down to your forearms and then across both sides of your hands to your fingertips. Now notice the light moving down through your pelvis and buttocks and feel the tension being released. Again, feel the light move like soothing water across your upper and lower legs until it spreads across both the upper and lower surfaces of your feet. Feel all of the tension leaving the muscles of your body as the white light makes your body feel warm and relaxed.

Continue to notice how peaceful and calm you feel as you continue to take slow, long, smooth breaths. Observe how your stomach continues to expand as you inhale, and feel it deflate as you exhale. Now, as you continue breathing, silently think to yourself "breathe in" as you inhale, and then silently think your cue word as you exhale. [If your cue word is something other than "relax," use that word in the following instructions.] Slowly inhale and think: "breathe in." Slowly exhale and think: "relax." As you do, notice your entire body feeling relaxed at the same time. Feel all the muscle tension in your body being released as you focus on your cue word. Again, inhale and think: "breathe in." Exhale and think: "relax." Notice your entire body releasing any muscle tension. Again, inhale… "breathe in." Exhale…"relax." Feel all the tension in your body releasing.

Continue breathing and thinking these words at your own pace for several minutes. With each breath, notice how relaxed your entire body feels. When your mind begins to wander, return your focus to the words "breathe in" and "relax."

Practice the cue-controlled relaxation technique twice a day, and record how long it takes you to feel relaxed. With daily practice, this technique should help you relax more quickly each time. Again, remember that the ultimate goal of this technique is to train your entire body to relax simply when you think of your cue word, such as "relax." This will only come with regular practice. Initially, you might also have to think of the white-light imagery and engage in slow, deep breathing to help yourself relax. But with practice, this technique can help you relax in many distressing situations. You can also combine this exercise with the previous safe-place visualization. Engaging in cue-controlled relaxation first will help you feel even more safe and calm in that visualization process.

REDISCOVER YOUR VALUES ⊠

The word "values" can be defined as your ethics, principles, ideals, standards, or morals. These are literally the ideas, concepts, and actions that fill your life with worth and importance. Remembering what you value in life can be a very powerful way to help you tolerate a stressful situation. It can also be particularly helpful when you find yourself upset over and over again in the same situation or with the same person. Sometimes we forget why we're doing something that's hard, and this makes it difficult for us to continue. Maybe you have a job that you don't like, and you wonder why you keep going to work. Perhaps you're going to school, and you don't remember what your goals are. Or maybe you're in a relationship that isn't fulfilling, and you wonder why you keep maintaining that relationship. In cases like these, remembering what you value can help you tolerate stressful situations and also help you create a more fulfilling life for yourself. Use the following exercises to explore what you value in life.

Exercise: Valued Living Questionnaire

This first exercise will ask you to identify how you value ten different components of your life using the Valued Living Questionnaire (Wilson, 2002; Wilson & Murrell, 2004). (Visit http://www.newharbinger .com/44581 to download the Valued Living Questionnaire.) For most people, these ten components represent the most important aspects of their lives. As you read each component, ask yourself how important each of these areas is to your life *ideally*—regardless of how much time or effort you now put into fulfilling the needs of that area. For example, maybe you highly value "self-care" regardless of the fact that you actually devote little time to it. Rate the ideal importance of each component on a scale of 0 to 10, with 0 being not important at all and 10 being extremely important. Do your best to rate them honestly, according to your own true feelings, not to what you think you *should* rate them. Put a circle around your answers. Do this now before reading the next paragraph.

Next, evaluate each component based on how much time and effort you *actually* put into the component. For example, you might highly value "self-care" at a 10, but maybe you only put a 5's worth of actual energy and effort into fulfilling that component. Again, do your best to rate yourself honestly and put a square around your answers for actual effort. Do this before reading the next paragraph.

Now, look at your two answers for each component. If your ideal answer is much higher than your answer for actual effort—for example, 10 ideal importance and 2 actual effort—that means you have room to grow. There is clearly more you can do to reach your ideal level of value. However, if your ideal is much lower than your answer for actual effort—for example, 2 ideal importance and 10 actual effort—that means you might be putting extra effort and energy into a component of your life that you don't highly value. Maybe this is a component that you can spend less time focusing on, in order to free up more time and effort to give to another component that you value more. For example, maybe you are giving much time and energy to "citizenship and community life" when you don't highly value it, and, as a result, you have little time to spend on "family," even though you do value that very highly. And finally, if your two answers for ideal importance and actual effort are the same, or very close, then you are putting in the right amount of effort just where it belongs.

Before moving on to the next exercise, look at the components with the largest spread between low actual effort and high ideal importance. Consider working on those components first in order to help shift your life toward doing more of what you value.

Valued Living Questionnaire
(Wilson, 2002)

Life Component	Less Important					Moderately Important					Extremely Important
Family (other than romantic relationships or parenting)	0	1	2	3	4	5	6	7	8	9	10
Romantic relationships (marriage, life partners, dating, and so on)	0	1	2	3	4	5	6	7	8	9	10
Parenting	0	1	2	3	4	5	6	7	8	9	10
Friends and social life	0	1	2	3	4	5	6	7	8	9	10
Work	0	1	2	3	4	5	6	7	8	9	10
Education and training	0	1	2	3	4	5	6	7	8	9	10
Recreation, interests, hobbies, music, and art	0	1	2	3	4	5	6	7	8	9	10
Spirituality and religion	0	1	2	3	4	5	6	7	8	9	10
Citizenship and community life	0	1	2	3	4	5	6	7	8	9	10
Self-care (exercise, diet, relaxation, and so on)	0	1	2	3	4	5	6	7	8	9	10

Exercise: Committed Action

This next exercise will help you create a more fulfilling life for yourself by formulating intentions and committed actions based on your values (Olerud & Wilson, 2002). Maybe you already dedicate a lot of time and effort to each of the components of your life that you value, or maybe you don't. Either way, this exercise will help you think about ways to make your life feel more fulfilling based on what you think is important.

First, using the Valued Living Questionnaire, identify the components of your life that you rated as having a high ideal importance and a lower actual effort. That is, identify the components where you think you have more work to do. Then, fill in the names of those components on the Committed Action Worksheet at the end of this section. (Make additional photocopies of it, or visit http://www.newharbinger.com/44581 to download the worksheet for future use.)

Next, identify one intention for each of those valued components that will help make your life feel more fulfilling. For example, if you rated "education" highly, maybe your intention would be "to go back to school." Or if you rated "romantic relationships" highly, maybe your intention would be "to spend more time with my spouse."

Then, finally, identify several *specific* actions you are willing to commit to doing that will move you toward your intention. Also, note when you're willing to begin that commitment. For example, if your intention is to go back to school, the actions you list might include "get a catalog of classes next week" and "sign up for a class within the next three weeks." If your intention is to spend more time with your spouse, your committed actions might include "do not work overtime for the next month" and "spend less time with friends for the next two weeks." Be as specific as you can about your intention and give yourself a time frame to complete that intention.

Again, the purpose of these exercises is to fill your life with activities that are important to you. Creating a life that you value can often help you deal with other situations that are distressing and less desirable. Having a fulfilling life can give you something to look forward to when you're doing something you don't like, and it can make you feel stronger during times of distress.

And remember, just because you might complete all of your committed actions for a particular life component, that doesn't mean that you're done or that the value is now "complete." Values are like compass directions—they point us toward where we want to go. But life is a journey, and we're never really "there" or "done" with any of the components. For example, as a parent, a mother or father can never say, "Okay, I've fed my children, I'm a good parent and now I can stop." Rather, the journey toward fulfilling each of these components is ongoing, and for the rest of your life, you'll need to continue reviewing these worksheets and identifying new committed actions—so make lots of copies of the worksheets.

Committed Action Worksheet

(Adapted from Olerud & Wilson, 2002)

1. A component of my life that I value is _____

   My intention for this component is _____

   The committed actions that I'm willing to take include the following (be sure to note when you'll begin these actions):

   _____

   _____

   _____

2. A component of my life that I value is _____

   My intention for this component is _____

   The committed actions that I'm willing to take include the following (be sure to note when you'll begin these actions):

   _____

   _____

   _____

3. A component of my life that I value is _____

   My intention for this component is _____

   The committed actions that I'm willing to take include the following (be sure to note when you'll begin these actions):

   _____

   _____

   _____

REHEARSING VALUES-BASED BEHAVIOR ⊠

Whenever you turn values into action, you're likely to face challenges and barriers. Sometimes values-based actions bring up negative thoughts like, "I can't do this," or "People will judge me." Often fear of being rejected or failing gets in the way. Feelings of shame or discouragement can also make it hard to act on values.

A good way to overcome these barriers is to mentally practice each step of a values-based action, including identifying likely obstacles and how you'll face them. This is called *cognitive rehearsal* (Cautela, 1971; McKay & West, 2016). Using this strategy, you'll even visualize yourself with a confident facial expression and posture, moving toward your goal despite painful thoughts and feelings. Here's a simplified version of how to do cognitive rehearsal:

How to Do Cognitive Rehearsal

- Identify the exact situation where you want to enact your values: where are you; who's there; what are other people saying and doing?

- What intentions do you want to act on in this situation? What would you say or do in order to turn this value into action?

- Break your values-based behavior into specific steps. As vividly as possible, imagine yourself in the situation acting on your value and intentions.

- Notice the barriers that come up—anxiety, discouragement, thoughts of failure, and so on. Stick with the visualization long enough to experience the more prominent obstacles.

- Now, from the beginning, do a full visualized rehearsal of the situation and each step of your values-based behavior—while noticing any distressing feelings and thoughts that arise. As barriers show up, try to accept whatever discomfort they bring while seeing yourself successfully completing your values-based goal.

- Imagine people responding well to what you do, and congratulate yourself for choosing values over old emotion-driven behavior.

- Repeat the full visualization (values-based behavior, barriers, and positive outcome) at least one more time.

(Visit http://www.newharbinger.com/44581 to download How to Do Cognitive Rehearsal.)

EXAMPLE: JARED'S COGNITIVE REHEARSAL

Jared, over the past year, had been fighting more with his wife. The most frequent triggers occurred when she said or asked for anything that implied he'd done something wrong. His immediate response was to get defensive and angry. As a result, their marriage was deteriorating.

Jared had identified that he highly valued his romantic relationship with his wife. His main intention for that component of his life was to further develop his understanding of her and caring for her. He wanted to know how she felt and how she saw things, and he wanted to care for her needs. Here's how he used cognitive rehearsal to better act on his values:

1. Jared identified a recent event where his wife appeared to complain that he'd been quiet and preoccupied lately. This conversation was typical of what led to their fights. He visualized where they were and how she looked.

2. Now Jared thought about a series of things he could say and do that would reflect his intentions of understanding and caring. This included touching her shoulder and inviting her to sit down, then asking how his quietness affected her. Then he planned to ask what would help. Jared was clear that his value and intentions did *not* include defending his behavior with countercriticism, so he made a commitment to avoid doing this.

3. While imagining his new, values-based behavior, Jared noticed some barriers: he had the thought that she was too demanding and another thought that maybe she didn't like him anymore. He was also aware of feelings of shame and anger, and a strong urge to accuse her of something—like being unfair and never satisfied.

4. Now Jared did a full, step-by-step rehearsal of his values-based behavior:

   - He imagined the scene and his wife's comment.

   - He tried to allow and accept the anger and shame while visualizing touching her shoulder and inviting her to sit.

   - He noticed critical thoughts about her, and doubts about her feelings for him.

   - He visualized asking about *her* feelings and needs, looking interested and caring rather than being defensive.

   - He imagined her appreciating his asking, and having a sense of accomplishment that he'd responded so much better than usual.

5. Finally, Jared repeated the cognitive rehearsal process, and committed himself to acting on his values and intention the next time his wife seemed critical.

IDENTIFY YOUR HIGHER POWER AND MAKE YOURSELF FEEL MORE POWERFUL

Whether you believe in one God, many gods, a divine universe, or the goodness that exists within each human being, having faith in something bigger and more powerful than yourself can often make *you* feel empowered, safe, and calm. This is what people mean when they talk about believing in a "higher power" or seeing "the big picture" in life. Believing in something divine, holy, or special can help you endure stressful situations as well as help you soothe yourself.

At some point in life, we all feel hopeless or powerless. We've all experienced unfortunate situations during which we felt alone and needed strength. Sometimes unexpected circumstances hurt us or the people we care about. These situations often include being the victim of a crime, getting into an accident, having someone close to us die, or being diagnosed with a serious illness. Having faith in something special during times like these can often help you feel connected to a bigger purpose in life. And remember, your faith doesn't have to involve God if that's not what you believe in. Some people only put their faith in the goodness of the people they love. Yet basic beliefs like these are often powerful enough to help people find the strength and comfort to lead happy, healthy lives.

While you're exploring your spirituality, remember that your spiritual beliefs can change over time. Sometimes a person is raised in a spiritual tradition that no longer makes sense or feels helpful. Yet, despite these feelings, a person will sometimes continue to attend the services of that tradition because he or she thinks "it's the right thing to do." The truth is, if your spiritual tradition is no longer giving you peace and strength, it's okay to reexamine that faith and to change traditions if necessary.

Also, for more help on developing your own sense of spiritual connection, spiritual values, and life purpose, read *The New Happiness* (McKay & Wood, 2019) by two of this book's authors. In many ways, *The New Happiness* is the second part of the self-growth work you've already started in this workbook. (The introduction to *The New Happiness* is included at the end of this book.)

Connect to Your Higher Power

Use the following questions to help you identify your beliefs and to identify some ways in which you can strengthen and use your beliefs on a regular basis.

- What are some of your beliefs about a higher power or a big picture that give you strength and comfort?

  _____

  _____

  _____

- Why are these beliefs important to you?

  _____

  _____

  _____

- How do these beliefs make you feel?

  _____

  _____

  _____

- How do these beliefs make you think about others?

  _____

  _____

  _____

- How do these beliefs make you think about life in general?

  _____

  _____

  _____

- How do you acknowledge your beliefs throughout your daily life? For example, do you go to church, synagogue, or temple? Do you pray? Do you talk to other people about your beliefs? Do you read books about your beliefs? Do you help other people?

  _____

  _____

- What else would you be willing to do in order to strengthen your beliefs?

  _____

  _____

  _____

- What can you do to remind yourself of your beliefs on a regular basis?

  _____

  _____

  _____

- What can you say or do to remind yourself of your beliefs the next time you're feeling distressed?

  _____

  _____

  _____

Exercise: Higher-Power Activities

Here are some additional activities to help you feel more connected to your higher power, the universe, and the big picture. Check (✓) the ones that you're willing to do:

☐ *If you do believe in the teachings of a particular religion or faith, find related activities that make you feel more empowered and calm.* Go to your church, synagogue, or temple for services. Talk to the person who runs your services. Talk to other members of your faith about how they've handled difficult experiences. Join discussion groups formed at your place of worship. Read the books that are important to your faith. Find passages that give you strength, and mark them or copy them to keep with you in your wallet or purse so you can read them no matter where you are.

☐ *Remember that your higher power can also be something other than God.* Your higher power can be a person who makes you feel stronger and more confident to deal with the challenges that you face. Think of someone you admire who can be your higher power. Describe that person. What makes that person special? Then, the next time you're in a difficult or distressing situation, act as if you are that person, and notice how you handle the situation differently.

☐ *Look up at the stars.* The light you're seeing is millions of years old, and it has traveled from stars that are billions of miles away. In fact, each time you look up at the stars, you're looking through a time machine and seeing the universe as it looked billions of years ago. Strangely, many of the stars you're looking at have already died, but their light is just reaching your eyes on the Earth. Look up at the stars and recognize that whatever created them also created you, whether it was God or a cosmic force. You are connected to the stars. Imagine yourself connecting with the universe. Sit in a comfortable chair, close your eyes, and imagine a white beam of light shining down from the universe. Like a laser beam, the white light shines on the top of your head and fills you with a feeling of peace. Now imagine the white light spreading all over your body, relaxing every muscle. Now imagine your legs stretching down through the floor like giant tree roots, going all the way down into the center of the Earth. Imagine these roots tapping into the energy that drives the planet. Feel your body fill with confidence as your legs absorb the golden energy flowing up from the Earth.

☐ *Think about our planet Earth.* Water is the most important substance for sustaining life on our planet. Yet if we were much closer to the sun, all the water on our planet would evaporate because the temperature would be too hot, and if we were much farther away, all the water would freeze because the temperature would be too cold. Somehow, we've been lucky enough to be in just the right place for life to form. Even if you don't believe in a religious purpose, ask yourself what it means that you live on a planet with just the right climate and elements for life to exist. How did this happen, and what does it mean about your life?

☐ *Go to the beach.* Try to count the grains in a handful of sand. Now try to imagine how many handfuls of sand there are in the world, on all the beaches and in all the deserts. Try to imagine how many billions of years must have passed to create so many grains of sand. And again, recognize that the chemical elements that make up the sand also exist in you. Stand with your feet in the sand and imagine feeling connected to the planet.

☐ *Go to a park or to a field and observe the trees, the grass, and the animals.* Again, recognize that whatever created all of that also created you. Remember that all living things are made of the same chemical elements. On a subatomic scale, there isn't much difference between you and many other life forms. Yet you are still different and special. What is it that makes you unique from other life?

☐ *Think about the human body, especially your own.* Each human being is more wonderful than a piece of artwork and more complex than any computer ever invented. Everything about you is largely determined by your *DNA* (deoxyribonucleic acid), the instructions that are found in every cell of your body. Yet amazingly, each set of instructions that creates every part of your body is composed of just four chemical elements that are repeated in different combinations. These different combinations are called *genes*, and these are the instructions you inherit from your parents that determine everything from your eye color to the structure of your heart. Incredibly, it only takes an estimated thirty to forty thousand genes to design a human being. Imagine trying to write so few instructions in order to create a body that thinks, breathes, eats, moves, and does everything else you do. Plus, remember that this same number of instructions is also responsible for creating approximately 100 billion neurons in your brain, 60,000 miles (!) of blood vessels throughout your body, 600 skeletal muscles, 206 bones, 32 teeth, and 11 pints of blood.

TAKE A TIME-OUT ⊠

Time-outs aren't just for kids. We all need to relax in order to refresh our bodies, minds, and spirits. Yet many people don't take time out for themselves because they feel like they'd be disappointing someone else, like their boss, spouse, family, or friends. Many people struggle with the constant need to please others, and, as a result, they neglect to take care of themselves. But people who don't take care of themselves lead very unbalanced lives. Many people ignore their own needs because they feel guilty or selfish about doing anything for themselves. But how long can you continue to take care of someone else without taking care of yourself? Imagine a woman who stands on a street corner on a hot, summer day holding a jug of cold water. She pours drinks for every pedestrian who walks by and, of course, everyone is grateful. But what happens when she's thirsty and goes to get a drink? After a long day of helping everyone else and neglecting herself, the jug is now empty. How often do you feel like this woman? How often do you run out of time for yourself because you've spent all of it taking care of other people? Helping others is a good thing to do as long as it doesn't come at the expense of sacrificing your own health. You need to take care of yourself, and that doesn't mean you're selfish.

Exercise: Time-Out

Here are some simple ideas you can use to take time out for yourself. Check (✓) the ones you're willing to do.

- ☐ Treat yourself as kindly as you treat other people. Do one nice thing for yourself that you've been putting off.

- ☐ Take time to devote to yourself, even if it's just a few hours during the week, by doing things like taking a walk or preparing your favorite meal.

- ☐ Or if you're feeling really brave, take a half day off from work. Go someplace beautiful, like a park, the ocean, a lake, the mountains, a museum, or even someplace like a shopping center.

- ☐ Take time to do things for your own life, like shopping, errands, doctor's appointments, and so on.

- ☐ Other ideas: _____

_____

_____

LIVE IN THE PRESENT MOMENT

Time travel is possible. We all do it occasionally, but some people do it more often than others. People who time travel spend a large portion of each day thinking about all the things they should've done yesterday, all the things that went wrong in the past, and all the things they're supposed to do tomorrow. As a result, that's where they live, in the past or in the future. They rarely pay attention to what's happening to them right now, so they miss living in the present moment—the only true moment in which anyone can really live. For example, notice what's happening to you right now as you read this. Are you thinking of something else? Are you thinking of something that happened in the past or something that's coming up in the future? What does your body feel like right now? Pay attention to it. Do you notice any spots of tension or physical pain? How are you breathing? Are you taking full, deep breaths, or are you breathing very shallowly?

Often, we don't pay attention to what's happening to us. We don't pay attention to what people are saying to us or to the things that we read. We don't even pay attention to who's around us while we're walking. And to make it even more problematic, we often try to do more than one thing at the same time, like driving, eating, texting, and talking on the phone simultaneously. As a result, we miss a lot of what life has to offer, and we often make easy situations more difficult.

But even worse, not living in the present moment can also make life more painful. For example, maybe you anticipate that the person with whom you're talking is going to say something insulting, which makes you feel angry—even though the person hasn't even said anything yet! Or maybe just thinking about past events makes you feel physically or emotionally upset, which then interferes with whatever you're trying to do at the moment. Obviously, both types of time traveling can make any event unnecessarily painful.

In chapters 4 through 6 on mindfulness skills, you'll learn advanced skills to help you stay in the moment. But for now, try the following exercises to help you live in the moment and tolerate distressing events more skillfully.

Exercise: "Where Are You Now?"

The next time you're in a distressing situation, ask yourself the following questions:

- Where am I right now?

- Am I time traveling in the future, worrying about something that might happen, or planning something that might happen?

- Am I time traveling in the past, reviewing mistakes, reliving bad experiences, or thinking about how my life could have been under different circumstances?

- Or am I in the present, really paying attention to what I'm doing, thinking, and feeling?

If you're not in the present moment, refocus your attention on what's happening to you now by using the following steps:

- Notice what you're thinking about and recognize if you're time traveling. Bring your focus back to the present moment.

- Notice how you're breathing. Take slow, long breaths to help you refocus on the present.

- Notice how your body feels and observe any tension or pain you might be feeling. Recognize how your thoughts might be contributing to how you're feeling. Use cue-controlled relaxation to release any tension.

- Notice any painful emotions you might be feeling as a result of time traveling, and use one of the distress tolerance skills to help you relieve any immediate pain.

Exercise: Listening to Now

Another exercise to help you refocus on the present moment is the Listening to Now exercise. Dedicate at least five minutes to help yourself refocus.

Instructions

Sit in a comfortable chair. Turn off any distractions, like your phone, radio, computer, and television. Take slow, long breaths, in through your nose and out through your mouth. Feel your stomach expand like a balloon each time you breathe in and feel it deflate each time you exhale. Now, as you continue to breathe, simply listen. Listen to any sounds you hear outside your home, inside your home, and inside your own body. Count each sound that you hear.

When you get distracted, return your focus to listening. Maybe you hear cars, people, or airplanes outside. Perhaps you hear a clock ticking or a fan blowing inside. Or maybe you hear the sound of your own heart beating inside your body. Actively and carefully listen to your environment and count as many sounds as you can. Try this exercise for five minutes and notice how you feel afterward.

A variation of this listening exercise will help you stay focused on the present moment while you're in a conversation with another person. If you notice that your attention is beginning to wander and you start thinking about your past or future, focus your attention on something that the person is wearing, like a button on their shirt, a hat they're wearing, or their collar. Note to yourself what color the item is and what it looks like. Sometimes this can snap you out of your time traveling. Now continue to listen, and if your mind begins to wander again, do the same thing and try to keep listening.

Exercise: Mindful Breathing

Another exercise that will help you stay focused in the present moment is breathing. It sounds simple, but we often don't breathe as well as we should. Think about it: who taught you how to breathe? If you're like the rest of us, probably no one. And yet, you do it about fifteen times a minute or almost 22,000 times a day! Everyone knows that we breathe air to take in oxygen. But how much of the air you breathe is actually oxygen— 100 percent, 75 percent? The correct answer is that the air you breathe is only about 21 percent oxygen, and when your body doesn't get enough oxygen it can knock your biological system off balance. For this reason alone, taking full, slow breaths is important. But another benefit of breathing correctly is that this simple technique can help you relax and focus. Many spiritual traditions combine slow breathing techniques with guided meditations to help people focus and relax.

Here's a breathing exercise that many people find helpful. This type of breathing is also called *diaphragmatic breathing* because it activates the diaphragm muscle at the bottom of your lung cavity. Engaging the diaphragm helps you take fuller, deeper breaths, which also helps you relax.

Read the instructions before beginning the exercise to familiarize yourself with the experience. If you feel more comfortable listening to the instructions, use your smartphone to record the directions in a slow, even voice so that you can listen to them while practicing this technique. Set a timer for three to five minutes and practice breathing until the alarm goes off. Then as you get more accustomed to using this technique to help you relax, you can set the alarm for longer periods of time, like ten or fifteen minutes. But don't expect to be able to sit still that long when you first start. In the beginning, three to five minutes is a long time to sit still and breathe.

When using this new form of breathing, many people often feel as if they become "one" with their breathing, meaning that they feel a deep connection to the experience. If that happens for you, great. If not, that's okay too. Just keep practicing. Also, some people feel light-headed when they first begin practicing this technique. This may be caused by breathing too fast, too deeply, or too slowly. Don't be alarmed. If you begin to feel light-headed, stop if you need to, or return your breathing to a normal rate and begin counting your breaths.

Instructions

To begin, find a comfortable place to sit in a room where you won't be disturbed for as long as you've set your timer. Turn off any distracting sounds. Take a few slow, long breaths and relax. Place one hand on your stomach and imagine your belly filling up with air as you breathe instead of your lungs. Now slowly breathe in through your nose and then slowly exhale through your mouth as if you're blowing out birthday candles. Feel your stomach rise and fall as you breathe. Imagine your belly filling up with air like a balloon as you breathe in, and then feel it effortlessly deflate as you breathe out. Feel the breath moving in across your nostrils, and then feel your breath blowing out across your lips. As you breathe, notice the sensations in your body. Feel your lungs fill up with air. Notice the weight of your body resting on whatever you're sitting on. With each breath, notice how your body feels more and more relaxed.

Now, as you continue to breathe, begin counting your breaths each time you exhale. You can count either silently to yourself or aloud. Count each exhalation until you reach 4 and then begin counting at 1 again. To begin, breathe in slowly through your nose and then exhale slowly through your mouth. Count 1. Again, breathe in slowly through your nose and slowly out through your mouth. Count 2. Repeat, breathing in slowly through your nose, and then slowly exhale. Count 3. Last time—breathe in through your nose and out through your mouth. Count 4. Now begin counting at 1 again.

When your mind begins to wander and you catch yourself thinking of something else, return your focus to counting your breaths. Try not to criticize yourself for getting distracted. Just keep taking slow breaths into your belly, in and out. Imagine filling up your belly with air like a balloon. Feel it rising with each inhalation and falling with each exhalation. Keep counting each breath, and with each exhale, feel your body relaxing, deeper and deeper.

Keep breathing until your alarm goes off, and then slowly return your focus to the room.

USE SELF-ENCOURAGING COPING THOUGHTS ⊗

There are many distressing times in life when we all need to hear some encouraging words to keep us motivated or to help us endure the pain that we're experiencing. But there are many distressing times like these when you are also alone, and you need to encourage yourself to stay strong. Often, this can be done with self-encouraging coping thoughts. Coping thoughts are reminders of how strong you've been in the past when you survived distressing situations, and they're also reminders of encouraging words that have given you strength. Coping thoughts are especially helpful when you first notice that you're feeling agitated, nervous, angry, or upset. If you can recognize your distress early on, you'll have a better chance of using one of these thoughts to help soothe yourself. Maybe there are even situations in your life that occur on a regular basis, when you can predict that one of these coping thoughts might be useful.

List of Coping Thoughts

Here is a list of some coping thoughts that many people have found to be helpful (McKay, Davis, & Fanning, 1997). Check (✓) the ones that are helpful to you and create your own.

☐ "This situation won't last forever."

☐ "I've already been through many other painful experiences, and I've survived."

☐ "This too shall pass."

☐ "My feelings make me uncomfortable right now, but I can accept them."

☐ "I can be anxious and still deal with the situation."

☐ "I'm strong enough to handle what's happening to me right now."

☐ "This is an opportunity for me to learn how to cope with my fears."

☐ "I can ride this out and not let it get to me."

☐ "I can take all the time I need right now to let go and relax."

☐ "I've survived other situations like this before, and I'll survive this one too."

☐ "My anxiety/fear/sadness won't kill me; it just doesn't feel good right now."

☐ "These are just my feelings, and eventually they'll go away."

☐ "It's okay to feel sad/anxious/afraid sometimes."

☐ "My thoughts don't control my life; I do."

☐ "I can think different thoughts if I want to."

☐ "I'm not in danger right now."

☐ "So what?"

☐ "This situation sucks, but it's only temporary."

☐ "I'm strong and I can deal with this."

☐ Other ideas: _____

_____

_____

Coping thoughts can help you tolerate distressing situations by giving you strength and motivation to endure those experiences. Now that you know about coping thoughts, you can begin using them immediately. Write your five favorite coping thoughts on a sticky note and put them in your wallet or hang them in a conspicuous place where you can see them every day, like on your refrigerator or bathroom mirror. Or, if you want to have them with you all the time, put them in a note app in your smartphone. The more you see your coping thoughts, the more quickly they will become part of your automatic thought process.

Use the following worksheet to record stressful situations in which you can use your coping thoughts to give you strength. Make photocopies of the Coping Thoughts Worksheet (or download it at http://www .newharbinger.com/44581), and keep one with you so that you can record the experience as soon as it happens. Recording the experience quickly might be awkward or inconvenient for you, but doing it this way will help you remember to use your self-encouraging coping thoughts more often. Read the example worksheet for ideas about when coping thoughts might be helpful to you.

Example: Coping Thoughts Worksheet

Distressing Situation	New Coping Thought
1. My boss yelled at me.	"This job stinks, but it's only temporary."
2. The weatherperson on television said that there is a really bad storm approaching that might cause some minor flooding.	"I can keep taking deep breaths and remind myself that this will pass soon. I can cope."
3. I couldn't get my gardening done before my friends came over, and I really wanted them to see how nice my backyard looks.	"It's disappointing, but I can cope. I'll talk about my plans for the backyard."
4. My sister called me "selfish" for not leaving work early to take her shopping.	"She lives in a world of pain herself; that's how she copes with disappointment."
5. I got sad while watching a movie.	"These are just my feelings, and eventually they'll go away. I can use my skills to cope."
6. I heard police sirens coming down the street, and it made me nervous.	"I'm not in danger right now. I'm safe and I'm comfortable behind the closed doors of my house."
7. The store clerk gave me the wrong change, and I have to go back and ask for more money.	"I can deal with this. I can say what I want, and deal with the disappointment if I don't get it."
8. My daughter is leaving for college, and I'm really going to miss her.	"My sadness won't kill me; it just doesn't feel good right now."
9. I get nervous when I don't have anything to keep me busy.	"I can take all the time I need right now to let go and relax."
10. I really hate to fly, but I need to go visit my grandmother in Tulsa.	"This is an opportunity for me to learn how to cope with my fears. I'll use my breathing and visualization skills."

Coping Thoughts Worksheet

Distressing Situation	New Coping Thought
1.	
2.	
3.	
4.	
5.	
6.	
7.	
8.	
9.	
10.	

RADICAL ACCEPTANCE ⊠

The word "dialectic" (in *dialectical behavior therapy*) means to balance and compare two things that appear very different or even contradictory. In dialectical behavior therapy, the balance is between change and acceptance (Linehan, 1993a). You need to change the behaviors in your life that are creating more suffering for yourself and others while simultaneously also accepting yourself the way you are. This might sound contradictory, but it's a key part of this treatment. Dialectical behavior therapy depends on acceptance *and* change, not acceptance *or* change. Most of this book will focus on skills you can develop to change your life. But this section will focus on how to accept your life. In fact, it will teach you how to *radically* accept your life.

Radical acceptance, which we first explored in chapter 1, is one of the hardest skills in this chapter to master because it will require you to look at yourself and the world in a different way. However, it's also one of the most important skills in dialectical behavior therapy (Linehan, 1993a). (You'll be exploring it further in chapters 4 through 6 on mindfulness skills.) *Radical acceptance* means that you accept something completely, without judging it. For example, radically accepting the present moment means that you don't fight it, get angry at it, or try to change it into something that it's not. To radically accept the present moment means that you must acknowledge that the present moment is what it is due to a long chain of events and decisions made by you and other people *in the past*. The present moment never spontaneously leaps into existence without being caused by events that have already taken place. Imagine that each moment of your life is connected like a line of dominoes that knock each other down.

But remember, radically accepting something doesn't mean that you give up and simply accept every bad situation that happens to you. Some situations in life are unjust, such as when someone abuses or assaults you. But for other situations in life, you share at least some responsibility. There's a balance between what you created and what others have created. However, many people struggling with overwhelming emotions often feel like life just "happens" to them, not recognizing their own role in creating a situation. As a result, their first reaction is to get angry. In fact, a woman told one of the authors of this workbook that anger was her "default emotion," meaning that when she was just being herself, she was angry. Her excessive hostility caused her to hurt herself—by drinking heavily, cutting herself, and constantly berating herself—and it also led to her hurting the people she cared about by constantly arguing with them.

In contrast, radically accepting the present moment opens up the opportunity for you to recognize the role that you have played in creating your current situation. And, as a result, it also creates an opportunity to respond to that situation in a new way that's less painful for yourself and others. In many ways, radical acceptance is like the Serenity Prayer, which says: "Grant me the serenity to accept the things I cannot change, the courage to change the things I can, and the wisdom to know the difference." In the exercise below, you will find some questions to ask yourself when you want to use radical acceptance. But first, let's look at an example of how radical acceptance can help a person in a distressing situation.

Example: Using Radical Acceptance

Christine and her boyfriend, John, had a difficult relationship. John spent a lot of his free time at the bar drinking with his friends, and, in response, Christine would get mad, threaten to leave him, and then do something destructive to "piss him off." This occurred regularly for five years. Then one night, Christine came home from work angry, and when John wasn't around to talk to, she suddenly felt hopeless about their relationship. So she called John at the bar to tell him that she was going to kill herself because she couldn't put up with his behavior any longer. John raced home to find Christine swallowing a handful of pills, and he made her spit them out. Then he made her promise that she wouldn't do it again. She promised, and then John left, taking the keys to Christine's car so that she couldn't go anywhere. Now Christine got even angrier and called the police to report that her keys had been stolen. Then she walked up to the bar, found John's car, and smashed his windshield with a brick. She would have broken the other windows too, but the police stopped her and arrested her. Needless to say, neither Christine nor John gave any consideration to using radical acceptance in this situation. Both of them were angry at each other, and by acting on their anger, they both ended up hurting themselves and the other person.

So how could this situation have occurred differently if radical acceptance had been used?

Let's consider the situation from Christine's point of view. Instead of threatening to kill herself, maybe she could have used the REST strategy and one of the distress tolerance skills you learned in the last chapter. Remember your strategy for dealing with distressing situations is to relax, evaluate, set an intention, and take action. Maybe Christine could have (1) stopped what she was doing and taken a few breaths to relax, (2) evaluated the situation and recognized that she was very upset, (3) set an intention to use a distress tolerance skill to help her relax, and then (4) taken action by screaming into a pillow and going outside for a long walk. Or maybe she could have called one of her friends to talk for a little while. Then after she'd cooled off a bit, she could have asked herself some questions and used radical acceptance to reexamine her situation. Let's look at this situation and see how it could have been handled a bit differently.

- *What events led up to Christine's situation?* She and John had been behaving and fighting like this for years. This night was nothing new. But she had come home angry about work, and she became even angrier with John because he wasn't around.

- *What role did Christine play in creating this situation?* Instead of trying to cope with her anger and frustration in a healthy way, she took her emotions out on herself and John. Also, Christine had had many reasons and opportunities in the past to end this relationship if she wanted to, but she had chosen to stay in this destructive relationship.

- *What role did John play in creating this situation?* John had an alcohol addiction that had been interfering with their relationship for five years. This night, he also didn't take the time to discuss Christine's suicidal behaviors with her. Instead, he chose to return to the bar, which made her even angrier.

- *What does Christine have control of in this situation?* She can end the relationship if she wants to, or she can choose a different way to cope with this distressing situation.

- *What doesn't Christine have control of in this situation?* Ultimately, it is John who has to seek help to stop his alcohol addiction. Christine can't make him stop drinking. She also doesn't have control of how John chooses to behave toward her in this situation.

- *What was Christine's response to this situation?* She tried to kill herself, and then she smashed John's windshield.

- *How did her response affect her own thoughts and feelings?* Her actions made her feel worse about herself and her relationship, and she kept thinking about why she was still in this destructive relationship.

- *How did her response affect the thoughts and feelings of other people?* Christine was arrested, which made both of them feel worse than they already did about themselves and their relationship.

- *How could Christine have changed her response to this situation so that it led to less suffering for her and John?* She could have used the REST strategy and other distress tolerance skills to cope with her pain and anger. She could also have used radical acceptance to reevaluate the situation so that she could choose to react in a different way. And perhaps she could even have chosen to leave John that evening, even temporarily, which might have been less painful for both of them.

- *How could the situation have occurred differently if Christine had decided to radically accept the situation?* If she had used some type of distress tolerance skills that evening, maybe she could have waited until the next morning to talk to John about how angry she felt at work and how upset his drinking made her feel. Or maybe if she had ended the relationship, she could have made space in her life for a healthier relationship or simply spared herself the reoccurring pain of a destructive relationship.

Exercise: Radical Acceptance

Now answer the same questions for yourself. (A worksheet for the Radical Acceptance exercise is available to download at http://www.newharbinger.com/44581.) Think of a distressing situation that you experienced recently. Then answer these questions that will help you radically accept the situation in a new way:

- What happened in this distressing situation?

  _____

  _____

- What past events happened that led up to this situation?

  _____

  _____

- What role did you play in creating this situation?

  _____

  _____

- What roles did other people play in creating this situation?

  _____

  _____

- What *do* you have control of in this situation?

  _____

  _____

- What *don't* you have control of in this situation?

  _____

  _____

- What was your response to this situation?

  _____

  _____

- How did your response affect your own thoughts and feelings?

  _____

  _____

- How did your response affect the thoughts and feelings of other people?

  _____

  _____

- How could you have changed your response to this situation so that it led to less suffering for yourself and others?

  _____

  _____

- How could the situation have occurred differently if you had decided to radically accept the situation?

  _____

  _____

It's very important to remember that radical acceptance also applies to accepting yourself. In this case, radical acceptance means embracing who you are without judging or criticizing yourself. Or, to put it another way, radically accepting yourself means loving yourself just the way you are, with all of your goodness and all of your faults. Finding the goodness inside of yourself might be a difficult challenge, especially if you're strug- gling with overwhelming emotions. Many people with this problem often think of themselves as being defective, bad, or unlovable. As a result, they overlook their good qualities and add more pain to their lives. However, this is why radically accepting yourself is so extremely important.

SELF-AFFIRMING STATEMENTS

To begin building a healthier self-image, many people find it helpful to use self-affirming statements. The purpose of these statements is to remind yourself of the good qualities you possess in order to give you strength and resilience when confronted with distressing situations. This type of statement will remind you that hidden underneath your overwhelming emotions is a caring, loving person who is capable of handling a distressing situation in a healthier way.

Example: Self-Affirming Statements

Here are some examples of self-affirming statements. Check (✓) the ones you're willing to use, and then create your own:

☐ "I might have some faults, but I'm still a good person."

☐ "I care about myself and other people."

☐ "I accept who I am."

☐ "I love myself."

☐ "I'm a good person, not a mistake."

☐ "I'm good and nobody's perfect."

☐ "I embrace both my good and bad qualities."

☐ "Today I take responsibility for everything I do and say."

☐ "I'm becoming a better person every day."

☐ "I'm a sensitive person who experiences the world differently."

☐ "I'm a sensitive person with rich emotional experiences."

☐ "Each day I do the best I can."

☐ "Even though I forget sometimes, I'm still a good person."

☐ "Even though bad things happened to me in the past, I'm still a good person."

☐ "Even though I've made mistakes in the past, I'm still a good person."

☐ "I'm here for a reason."

☐ "There's a purpose to my life, even though I might not always see it."

☐ "I radically accept myself."

☐ Other ideas: _____

_____

Some people find it helpful to write their self-affirming statements on sticky notes and then post them throughout their home. One woman wrote her statement on her bathroom mirror with an erasable marker so it was the first thing she saw in the morning. One man wrote his on a sticky note and kept it posted on his computer as he worked. You can choose to remind yourself of your self-affirming statement in any way that works. But choose a technique that will remind you many times throughout the day. If you choose to write your statement in a note app in your smartphone, make sure to check it every day. The more often you can see the statement, the more it will help change the way you think about yourself.

FEELINGS-THREAT BALANCE (FTB-COPE) ⊠

As you know, strong emotions usually carry an impulsive urge to do something. Anger and anxiety, in particular, make you want to do something to overcome a threat. Sometimes the threat actually requires action if there's a serious danger or if someone is trying to hurt you, but often your emotion is probably far bigger than the actual threat you face. FTB-Cope is a skill that can help you recognize the feeling-threat balance (FTB) and then cope with the stressor appropriately. For example, on a scale of 1 to 10, is your fear and urge to avoid at a 10 but the actual danger is only a 2? Or, is your anger and urge to attack a 9, while the provocation and threat only a 3?

The FTB-Cope process will help you assess the actual level of threat versus the strength of your feelings. The bigger the gap between them, the more reason there is to cope rather than act on your emotions. The gap between a high intensity of emotion and a low level of actual threat is usually fueled by something called *emotional reasoning*—the human tendency to believe that strong emotions confirm some truth about a situation. For example, maybe you believe:

• . Intense anger means something really bad was done to you.

• Intense anxiety means that you are facing something really dangerous.

• Intense shame means you have done something reprehensible.

The problem with emotional reasoning is that emotions don't prove anything—they're just feelings. Sometimes there's very little relationship between the strength of a negative emotion and any real-life problem, threat, or failure. As you'll learn in chapter 7, Basic Emotion Regulation Skills, emotions are merely messages. Sometimes they are accurate, but sometimes they aren't. So how can you assess the actual level of threat versus what your emotions are telling you?

Assessing the Feeling-Threat Balance

(The worksheet for assessing your feeling-threat balance is available to download at http://www.newharbinger .com/44581.)

First, rate the intensity of your emotion on a 0 to 10 scale of distress (where 10 represents the most intense level you've ever felt for this emotion).

0	1	2	3	4	5	6	7	8	9	10

Low
Distress

Moderate
Distress

High
Distress

Now rate the threat.

For anger:

How much actual damage has the offending person or situation done to your well-being?

0	1	2	3	4	5	6	7	8	9	10

Little
Damage

Moderate
Damage

Excessive
Damange

How much sustained damage has the offending person or situation done to your self-worth?

0	1	2	3	4	5	6	7	8	9	10

Little
Damage

Moderate
Damage

Excessive
Damange

For anxiety/fear:

How potentially harmful is this situation?

0	1	2	3	4	5	6	7	8	9	10

Little
Harm

Moderate
Harm

Excessive
Harm

How likely is that harm to occur?

0	1	2	3	4	5	6	7	8	9	10

Not   Moderately   Very
Likely   Likely   Likely

For guilt/shame:

How much harm have I caused?

0	1	2	3	4	5	6	7	8	9	10

None   Some   A Lot

How much did my behavior deviate from my values or beliefs about what's right?

0	1	2	3	4	5	6	7	8	9	10

None   Some   A Lot

For sadness:

How serious is the loss I've suffered?

0	1	2	3	4	5	6	7	8	9	10

Little   Moderate   Excessive
Loss   Loss   Loss

How serious or long-lasting is the effect of my failure or mistake?

0	1	2	3	4	5	6	7	8	9	10

Little   Moderate   Serious
Effect   Effect   Effect

Now put the feeling intensity and the greatest threat intensity (the item with the highest number) together. If the numbers are close, your emotions are in balance with the actual threat level, and because your feelings reflect a realistic threat, it might be time to take action. For example, use "Rediscover Your Values" and the Committed Action Worksheet in this chapter to guide your behavioral choices; you can also use "Wise Mind" decisions in chapter 5 or "Problem Solving" in chapter 8.

However, if there is a significant imbalance between your feelings and threat levels—meaning your emotion is high and the threat is actually low—then do your best to *not respond with emotion-driven behavior*. Don't act on your impulses or urges. This is the time to *cope*. Instead of reacting, use skills from the distress tolerance chapters to help turn the knob down on your emotions:

- REST strategy
- Distraction
- Self-soothing
- Safe-place visualization
- Cue-controlled relaxation
- Time-out
- Mindfulness
- Coping thoughts
- Radical acceptance
- Self-affirming statements

Summary of FTB-Cope

So remember to use FTB-Cope whenever you're feeling an intense emotion and have a strong urge to do something. Rather than acting on that impulse, do the following:

1. Calculate the intensity of your feeling (0–10).

2. Calculate the actual threat level (0–10).

3. If the feeling and threat level are in balance (the numbers are close), you may wish to take action based on values, wise mind (chapter 5), or problem solving (chapter 8).

4. However, if the intensity of the feeling is significantly higher than the threat, then don't act on your emotion. Choose a coping skill that you've learned to soothe your emotions.

CREATE NEW COPING STRATEGIES

Now that you're familiar with all the distress tolerance skills, you can create new coping strategies for your future. The easiest way to do this is to examine some of the distressing situations you've experienced in the past and to identify how you've coped with them. Often, people with overwhelming emotions go through similar distressing situations over and over again. So, in some ways, these situations are predictable. In this exercise, you'll identify what those past situations were, how you coped with them, and what the unhealthy consequences were. Then you'll identify what new coping strategies you can use in the future if you experience similar situations and what the healthier consequences might be as a result of using those new strategies.

But as you'll notice below, you've been given two different New Coping Strategies worksheets. This is because you'll need different coping strategies to use in situations when you're alone or when you're with someone else. For example, when you're alone and feel overwhelmed, it might be most effective to use cue-controlled relaxation or mindful breathing techniques to soothe yourself. But these techniques might be awkward or impossible to use when you're with someone else. So, you'll need to be prepared with other skills for those situations.

Here's an example of preparing for both kinds of situations. Carl identified a distressing situation that occurred when he was with someone else. He wrote: "When I'm with my brother, he always corrects everything I do." This is a good situation for Carl to examine because it's predictable that the next time he's with his brother, Carl will experience a similar distressing situation. Next, Carl identified how he usually coped with that situation with his brother, using his old coping strategies. He wrote: "We fight. I eat too much. I scratch myself. I think about all the times he's insulted me in the past." Then Carl recorded the unhealthy consequences of his actions: "We both get angry. I gain weight. I get cuts all over my face and arms. I feel horrible for days thinking about the past." Obviously, none of Carl's strategies has had any long-term benefits. Next, Carl identified new distress tolerance skills he could use the next time this situation arose with his brother. Under "New Coping Strategies," Carl wrote the most appropriate distress tolerance skills for this type of situation. He chose them from the skills he found helpful in this chapter and chapter 1. He wrote: "Take a time-out. Use my new coping thought: 'I'm strong and I can deal with him.' Radically accept myself and the situation in a new way." Then he predicted what the healthier possible consequences of these new strategies would be: "We won't fight as much. I won't eat as much. I'll feel stronger. Maybe I can deal with the situation better in the future." Obviously, the consequences of using his new distress tolerance skills will be much healthier for Carl.

But these coping strategies are probably different from the strategies he might choose when he's in a distressing situation by himself. So Carl also filled out the worksheet for coping with distressing situations when he's alone. The situation he selected was this: "Sometimes I feel scared when I'm alone." Again, this is a good situation for Carl to examine because it's predictable that he will experience this same overwhelming feeling the next time he's alone. The old coping strategies that Carl used to deal with this situation were these: "I smoke pot. I go to the bar and drink. I cut myself. I spend money on my credit card." And the unhealthy consequences of these actions were these: "I feel sick after smoking or drinking too much. I get into fights at the bar. I bleed. I spend too much money for things I don't need." Next, in order to prepare for the future, Carl chose new coping strategies to deal with this situation: "Use mindful breathing. Remember my connection to the universe. Use safe-place visualization. Remember what I value." And finally, he predicted the healthier possible consequences: "I won't feel as anxious. I won't hurt myself. I'll have more money. I'll feel more relaxed." Again, it's easy to see that Carl's new distress tolerance skills are much healthier for him than his old coping strategies. The same results can also benefit you if you take the time to prepare for predictable situations in your own future.

Create New Coping Strategies for Distressing Situations When You're with Someone Else

Distressing Situation	Old Coping Strategies	Unhealthy Consequences	New Coping Strategies	Healthier Possible Consequences
Example: When I'm with my brother, he always corrects everything I do.	We fight. I eat too much. I scratch myself. I think about all the times he's insulted me in the past.	We both get angry. I gain weight. I get cuts all over my face and arms. I feel horrible for days thinking about the past.	Take a time-out. Use my new coping thought: "I'm strong and I can deal with him." Radically accept myself and situation in a new way.	We won't fight as much. I won't eat as much. I'll feel stronger. Maybe I can deal with the situation better in the future.
1.				
2.				
3.				
4.				

Create New Coping Strategies for Distressing Situations When You're Alone

Distressing Situation	Old Coping Strategies	Unhealthy Consequences	New Coping Strategies	Healthier Possible Consequences
Example: Sometimes I feel scared when I'm alone.	I smoke pot. I go to the bar and drink. I cut myself. I spend money on my credit cards.	I feel sick after smoking or drinking too much. I get into fights at the bar. I bleed. I spend too much money for things I don't need.	Use mindful breathing. Remember my connection to the universe. Use safe-place visualization. Remember what I value.	I won't feel as anxious. I won't hurt myself. I'll have more money. I'll feel more relaxed.
1.				
2.				
3.				
4.				

On each worksheet, pick four distressing situations from the past and examine how you coped with them. Identify the unhealthy coping strategies you used and what the consequences were for you and anyone else who was involved. Then record which new distress tolerance skills could have been used to cope with those situations in a healthier way. Review this chapter and chapter 1 and pick the distress tolerance skills that you found to be helpful. Consider these to be options for the "New Coping Strategies" column as you're completing the two worksheets. Most importantly, be specific. If you write, "Use a new coping thought," write what that thought is. Or if you write, "Take a time-out," include what you're going to do. Be specific so you don't forget in the future. Finally, record what the healthier consequences will be if you use your new distress tolerance skills.

Use the examples provided to guide you. If you need additional space, make photocopies of the worksheets or download extras from http://www.newharbinger.com/44581.

CREATE AN EMERGENCY COPING PLAN

Hopefully, you've been practicing the new distress tolerance skills from this chapter and chapter 1—including the REST strategy—and you now have a good idea about which ones work best for you. Or maybe using the New Coping Strategies worksheets in the last section helped you predict which ones are going to work best for you. Now you'll be ready for the next step, which will help you create a personally tailored plan for dealing with some common distressing situations, both when you're with other people and when you're alone.

For situations when you're with other people, list four coping strategies that you think will be the most effective for you. Again, be specific and include as many details about that strategy as you can. Begin with your most effective strategy, then the second most effective strategy, and so on. The plan is that you'll try the first strategy to see if it helps you cope with the distressing situation; then if it doesn't, you'll move on to the next strategy, and so on. Again, refer to any distress tolerance skills you found helpful in this chapter and chapter 1, your REST strategy, your New Coping Strategies worksheets in the last section, and any experience you have using the distress tolerance skills so far. (Visit http://www.newharbinger.com/44581 to download the Emergency Coping Plan forms.) In the next chapter, you'll also learn some physiological coping skills that you might want to add to your emergency coping plans after trying each of them.

My Emergency Coping Plan for Dealing with Situations

When I'm Upset and Dealing with Other People

First, I'll _____

_____

Next, I'll _____

_____

Then, I'll _____

_____

Finally, I'll _____

_____

- -

My Emergency Coping Plan for Dealing with Situations

When I'm Upset and Alone

First, I'll _____

_____

Next, I'll _____

_____

Then, I'll _____

_____

Finally, I'll _____

_____

Then, when you've finished making both plans, copy each of them onto a single note card to keep with you in your wallet or purse, or put the two plans in your smartphone app. This strategy will provide you with constant reminders about your new distress tolerance skills, and you'll no longer have to rely on your old, ineffective strategies. Plus, you won't have to try to remember what to do the next time you're feeling angry, hurt, or upset. You can simply pull out your card or smartphone and follow your own emergency coping plan.

CONCLUSION

Remember to practice your new distress tolerance skills as often as possible, and don't get frustrated if you don't get them right on the first try. Learning new skills is hard, and it often feels awkward. But anyone can learn these distress tolerance skills, and they have already helped thousands of people just like you. Good luck.

CHAPTER 3

More Distress Tolerance Skills

PHYSIOLOGICAL COPING SKILLS FOR DISTRESS TOLERANCE

In addition to all of the cognitive and behavioral distress tolerance skills that you've learned in the last two chapters, a few physiological coping skills are also helpful. Some of these skills have already been suggested, but they are worth repeating.

These skills can quickly reduce the intensity of your overwhelming emotions, especially when you're too sad, irritated, or angry to use one of the other distress tolerance skills. In many ways, the physiological distress coping skills bypass your need to "think clearly," because they are largely based on biological principles and physiological reflexes that are effective whether or not you remember *how* they work; you just have to *do* them.

Later, in chapter 7, you'll learn a little more about the "fight, flight, or freeze" response in the nervous system, which helps you to survive dangerous situations. But for now, it's sufficient to know that two of the many purposes of your nervous system are survival and relaxation. In survival mode, the nervous system turns on the "fight, flight, or freeze" responses in your body that are necessary for survival, like a faster heart rate and increased muscle tension. In contrast, the relaxation response causes an opposite set of reactions to occur—such as decreased heart rate and reduced muscle tension—which helps you to rest and feel at ease. The physiological coping skills that you're about to learn turn on the relaxation response by triggering biological responses in the human body.

Some of these coping skills will work better for you than others. Keep track of which ones work best for you, and make them a part of your emergency coping plan, which you completed at the end of chapter 2. Also, keep in mind that if you struggle with any medical issues that affect your balance, blood pressure, or heart rate—especially heart conditions, breathing problems, high blood pressure, or pregnancy—you should always check with a medical professional before trying any of these skills, because some of these skills might quickly decrease your heart rate and blood pressure. This is also important if you take any medications to regulate these types of issues.

SIDE-TO-SIDE EYE MOVEMENTS

Moving your eyes back and forth rather quickly, from side to side, while keeping your head still, has been shown in research to have a relaxing effect for people experiencing stress (Barrowcliff, Gray, MacCulloch, Freeman, & MacCulloch, 2003). This type of eye movement has also been shown to reduce the emotional distress related to painful memories and to making those memories less vivid (Barrowcliff, Gray, Freeman, & MacCulloch, 2004). One psychological treatment that incorporates this type of eye movement to ease chronically painful emotions related to trauma is called eye-movement desensitization and reprocessing, also known as EMDR (Shapiro, 2001). However, even in its simplest form, moving your eyes back and forth for about thirty seconds at a comfortably quick pace has a relaxing effect for many people. Researchers are still debating *why* this technique works (Lee & Cuijpers, 2013), but, regardless, the technique is quick to use, easy to do, and worth trying.

Instructions

Ideally, you should first practice this technique while you are relaxed and undisturbed by emotions. Find a comfortable place to sit, and while keeping your eyes open, simply move your eyes back and forth from side to side. Move your eyes at a comfortable rate of approximately one back-and-forth movement per second, as if you were watching a fast game of ping-pong. Do your best *not* to move your head, just allow your eyes to move from side to side, looking from one corner of the room to the other. Do this for about thirty seconds. Get used to the movement. Stop if you feel any excessive eye strain or pain, or slow the movement to a more comfortable pace.

Next, practice using this technique with a *mildly* disturbing memory. Recall the memory and the emotional response that it caused. Do your best to rate the emotional distress on a scale of 0 to 10, with 10 being the worst distress you can imagine. Also, note any stress or strain that the memory causes in your body. Now use the side-to-side eye movement for about thirty seconds. As you move your eyes, don't try to hold on to the disturbing memory; rather, let whatever memory or feeling comes up next to just appear naturally. After about thirty seconds, note any changes in how you feel emotionally or physically. Then try the technique again, starting again from the original disturbing memory and letting whatever comes up during those thirty seconds to appear naturally. Then again, note any changes in how you feel emotionally or physically. Try this for about four or five attempts and note any improvements in how you feel emotionally or physically.

If you did notice any improvements while practicing this technique, try it the next time you experience a painful or heightened emotional response to something. Identify what the most bothersome part of the event was, what emotion was most painful, or what triggered the painful emotion. Start from there. If you are somewhere private and can move your eyes from side to side without calling unwanted attention to yourself, sit down and try using the technique wherever you are. Otherwise, if you cannot openly move your eyes from side to side, try *closing your eyes* and using the same technique. Quickly move your eyes back and forth for about thirty seconds with your eyelids closed, note any changes in how you feel emotionally or physically, and then repeat the technique three or four times if necessary. Again, for each thirty-second interval, allow whatever memories or thoughts that come up to do so naturally. Then when you restart, go back to the original painful memory or emotion.

One of the authors of this workbook often recommends this technique to help with occasional insomnia and anxious thoughts at bedtime. Try it the next time you're having trouble sleeping. With your eyelids closed and while lying down, move your eyes back and forth in the same way you practiced above for about thirty seconds. Imagine "erasing" whatever thoughts or memories are bothering you as your eyes move from side to side. Again, continue using the technique for four or five attempts, then try sleeping again.

USE COLD TEMPERATURES TO RELAX

There are two helpful ways that you can use cold temperatures to help you relax. First, apply a cold, wet compress to your face, and second, hold something cold in your hands.

Exercise: Diving Response

It might seem counterintuitive, but research has shown that immersing your face in very cold water while holding your breath causes your body to turn on the nervous system's relaxation response and slow your heart rate (Kinoshita, Nagata, Baba, Kohmoto, & Iwagaki, 2006). This phenomenon is known as the *diving response* (Gooden, 1994), and it's a natural reflex in most mammals. It is believed that the response occurs in order to conserve oxygen in the brain and heart while underwater. Again, if you are pregnant or coping with medical problems related to your heart or blood pressure, check with your medical professional before trying this technique.

Instructions

In order to trigger the diving response to help you relax, it is recommended that you place a very cold, wet towel on your forehead or cheeks, or to use a semimelted ice pack wrapped in a towel. (Never place a fully frozen ice pack directly on your skin; always keep the ice pack wrapped to avoid injury.) Try one of these techniques rather than submerging your full face in a tub of very cold water. Placing the very cold compress on your forehead or your cheeks affects the trigeminal nerve in your face in a way that is similar to immersing your face in very cold water. (If you experience any pain while doing this, stop immediately.) If you're using a cold wet towel, make sure it is colder than 70 degrees Fahrenheit (below 21 degrees Celsius) in order to trigger the diving response. Next, in order to further simulate submerging your face in water, hold your breath for several seconds (or for as long as is comfortable) while maintaining the cold compress on your forehead or cheeks. However, never do anything else to purposely block your ability to breathe; doing so can lead to feeling faint, passing out, or even death.

Exercise: Cold Pressor Technique

Another way to use cold temperatures to help you experience emotional relief is to hold a very cold ice pack in your hand or to run your hands under very cold water for two to four minutes. In research studies examining people who commit purposeful self-injuring behaviors (such as cutting and scratching), the results indicate that engaging in such painful behavior does actually lead to a sense of emotional relief for some people. Obviously, however, engaging in such behavior also leads to injury and medical emergencies, and cannot be recommended. In fact, one of the goals of dialectical behavior therapy is to stop such self-harming behaviors. Instead, in some research studies that try to replicate similar painful behaviors the *cold pressor test* is often used. During the cold pressor test, the subject immerses their hand into a bucket of ice water, from 32 to 50 degrees Fahrenheit (0 to 10 degrees Celsius), up to their wrist, for two to four minutes before removing their hand from the bucket. In one study that used the cold pressor test, some of the participants with borderline personality disorder experienced a noticeable reduction in anger, confusion, depression, and anxiety (Russ et al., 1992), with similar results in a later study that also used the cold pressor test (Franklin et al., 2010). The exact reason as to why the removal of painful stimuli leads to such a great sense of emotional relief is still being debated (Klonsky, 2007), but the results of such experiments are promising for people who experience overwhelming painful emotions.

Instructions

It is recommended that instead of holding your hand in a bucket of ice water for two to four minutes, you instead run your hands under very cold water or hold onto a covered ice pack for the same amount of time. (Finding a bucket of ice water when you are very distressed is unlikely, especially if you are not at home, and it is more likely that you will have access to an ice pack or very cold water. Or, if neither of those is available, hold a very cold can of soda or a very cold bottle of water.) Make the temperature of the cold water or ice pack as cold as you can tolerate, between 32 and 50 degrees Fahrenheit (0 and 10 degrees Celsius). It is expected that you will experience a mild to moderate amount of discomfort, but it should never cause you a high level of pain. If at any point you do experience a great amount of pain or discomfort, stop immediately. Set a timer on your smartphone for no more than four minutes and do your best to tolerate the discomfort. If you need something else to focus on during the exercise, practice your mindful breathing technique.

HIGH-INTENSITY INTERVAL TRAINING (HIIT) EXERCISE

It probably comes as no surprise that physical exercise has been shown to have numerous health benefits (Warburton, Nicol, & Bredin, 2006), as well as being an effective treatment for mild to moderate depression, anxiety, phobias, panic attacks, and possibly even post-traumatic stress disorder (see Ströhle, 2009 for a review). Engaging in aerobic exercise even increases brain chemicals similar to the results of taking antidepressant and antianxiety medications (Dishman, 1997). For these reasons alone, exercise can be a very effective coping strategy for dealing with distressing feelings and overwhelming emotions. Yet, many people still avoid engaging in regular exercise because they find it unenjoyable, too difficult, or too time-consuming (Trost, Owen, Bauman, Sallis, & Brown, 2002). Luckily, over the last several years, there is good research to support a new type of exercise that is more enjoyable, is less time-consuming, and provides even more health benefits.

Previously, official recommendations from institutions such as the US Department of Health and Human Services recommended moderate-intensity exercise, five days a week for thirty minutes at a time (Physical Activity Guidelines Advisory Committee, 2008). However, new research in physical fitness has shown that shorter bursts of high-intensity exercise, followed by short periods of recovery, has equal health benefits to exercising for longer extended periods of time (Gibala & McGee, 2008). This type of exercise is commonly referred to as *high-intensity interval training* (HIIT). One version of HIIT exercise, used in a successful research study, showed beneficial results from performing just one minute of intense exercise followed by one minute of lower-intensity recovery periods, for a total of approximately ten "intense-moderate" paired intervals (Little, Safdar, Wilkin, Tarnopolsky, & Gibala, 2010). This means that the participants were only exercising intensively for about ten minutes. Perhaps due to these shorter periods of exertion, HIIT training has been shown to be more enjoyable and preferable to other more time-consuming forms of aerobic exercise (Jung, Bourne, & Little, 2014).

HIIT has gained much positive research to support its use for people of all ages (Robinson et al., 2017), as well as for people with illnesses such as type 2 diabetes (Little et al., 2011). In one study, HIIT even reversed some signs of aging within human cells (Robinson et al., 2017). In that study, participants performed four minutes of intensive pedaling on a bicycle, followed by three minutes of less intense pedaling, and repeated this "intense-moderate" routine four times. They exercised this way three days a week and then walked at a brisk pace two days a week, for a total of twelve weeks.

In some of the HIIT exercise studies, participants' exertion levels were measured by monitoring their heart rates. During the intensive periods of exercise, participants attempted to maintain an exertion level that forced their hearts to beat at approximately 90 percent of their maximum heart rates (Gibala, Little, MacDonald, & Hawley, 2012). Then during the less-intensive moderate level of activity, they decreased their exertion level and allowed their heart rates to slow down and recover. Although "*90 percent of your maximum heart rate*" might sound intimidating to maintain during exercise, and even to calculate, it doesn't have to be. For example, if you decide to try a HIIT exercise regimen and 90 percent sounds too intimidating, make an initial goal of maintaining only 75 or 80 percent of your maximum heart rate, until you gain strength, confidence, and endurance. Then increase your target heart rate to 90 percent.

One easy way to calculate your maximum workout heart rate is to multiply your age by 0.64 and then subtract the result from 211 (Nes, Janszky, Wisløff, Stølen, & Karlsen, 2013). For example, if you are forty-one years old: $41 \times 0.64 = 26.24$, and $211 - 26.24 = 184.76$. Then to calculate an exercise target of 90 percent of your maximum heart rate, you would multiply that number by 0.9, for example $184.76 \times 0.9 = 166.28$. Therefore, for a person who is forty-one years old, a target heart rate of 90 percent would be approximately 166 beats per minute. (However, remember that medications, medical conditions, and your general fitness level can all affect your target heart rate as well. And if you're just starting an exercise regimen, you might start with a lower target, such as 80 percent of your maximum heart rate, or even 75 percent. In which case, you would multiply your maximum heart rate by 0.8 for 80 percent or 0.75 for 75 percent.)

Monitoring your heart rate during exercise is easy using an exercise heart-rate monitor that can be purchased online and in most sporting goods stores. However, another general way to monitor your exertion level during exercise is to use the "talk test" (Downing, 2016). It's been suggested that if you can talk and sing while exercising—without running out of breath—then you're exerting yourself at a low-intensity level. At a moderate-intensity level, you can talk, but can only sing a few words before running out of breath, while at an exercise level of high intensity, you can't sing at all and will find it difficult to speak more than just a few words at a time. If you're using the talk test while performing HIIT, do your best to maintain this high intensity level during the exertion periods and keep checking yourself by attempting to talk. If you find it too easy to talk, you're likely not exerting yourself enough. At a higher intensity of exercising, it should be difficult to speak because you will be breathing more heavily as you exert more effort; it will also feel strenuous, like you cannot maintain that pace for longer than just a few minutes. Then, during the in-between recovery periods, slow down your exercise intensity level to where you can comfortably speak and easily breathe again.

So, in summary, physical exercise has been shown to have numerous health and psychological benefits, but HIIT exercise has also been shown to be more enjoyable and preferential to other forms of aerobic exercise. In addition, HIIT doesn't require a great amount of time to complete, it doesn't require an expensive gym membership (see below for some alternative ideas), it doesn't require expensive equipment to monitor your exertion level, it can reverse some effects of aging, it's safe for all ages of participants, and it can be an effective coping skill for dealing with unpleasant emotions. Hopefully, you will commit to using HIIT on a regular basis by engaging in HIIT exercise two or three times a week. But, at the very least, it will also benefit you to use HIIT when you're feeling distressed, angry, anxious, sad, or overwhelmed.

Use the general instructions below to begin a HIIT exercise program. But, of course, before you begin any exercise routine, check with your medical provider about your state of health, especially if you have a history of heart problems, stroke, diabetes, trouble breathing, chronic pain, or joint problems. Then, once you begin, remember to start exercising slowly and build up your intensity and endurance over time.

Instructions

To perform HIIT exercises, consider using a treadmill, stationary bike, elliptical trainer, stair-climber, rowing machine, or other piece of equipment that allows you to exert yourself at an intensive exertion level for several minutes. (If you need help using a piece of equipment that you're not familiar with, first consult a physical fitness expert.) However, if you don't have access to equipment like this, consider other forms of high-intensity exercise, such as running sprints outside, running in place, skipping rope, performing "burpees," or even doing exercises like jumping jacks.

Before beginning each set of HIIT exercise, consider warming up with stretching or performing a set of slow movements to loosen and warm your muscles. As with starting any new exercise regimen, "start low and go slow," which means start with a lower amount of total exercise time and don't immediately aim to maintain 90 percent of your maximum heart rate while exercising if that sounds too hard or too intimidating. Instead, maybe start with thirty seconds of high-intensity exercise, aiming to maintain only 75 percent of your maximum heart rate while exercising (or moderate intensity using the "talk test"), followed by two minutes of moving at a slower pace, allowing your heart rate to slow down and your breathing to become easier. Later, with improved strength and endurance, you can increase your time, intensity level, and targeted heart rate.

Also, consider adjusting the number of paired intervals that you will be performing. Maybe when you're just beginning HIIT, you can only perform three or four "intense-moderate" paired intervals of one minute (for six to eight minutes of total exercise time). Then as you gain stamina and experience, maybe you can build up to one minute of five or six paired intervals (for ten to twelve minutes of total exercise time). Remember, the level at which you begin exercising and the amount you progress is largely going to be determined by your age, activity level, medical conditions, and consistency of exercise. Keep your goals and expectations reasonable, and don't expect to do too much, too quickly.

Finally, consider these suggestions too. One fitness writer who interviewed expert HIIT trainers recommends that you avoid seven common mistakes that people sometimes make when starting a HIIT exercise regimen (Migala, 2017): (1) Don't skip performing a warm-up before exercising. (2) Don't exercise for longer than twenty or thirty minutes each time. (3) Make sure you exert yourself to a high-intensity level during the periods of exertion in order to gain the benefits of HIIT. (4) *Between each period of high-intensity exertion make sure you slow down and take enough time to recover so that you can then push yourself again during the next period of exertion. (5) Whichever exercise you are using to perform HIIT, make sure that the movements are simple, because you will tire quickly and lose the ability to do any movements that are too complex. (6) Don't extend the length of your overall workouts too quickly, such as going from five minutes to twenty minutes in the first week; rather, allow your body the time it needs to gain strength before you push it harder. And lastly, (7) don't perform HIIT exercise routines more than two or three times each week, because your body needs time to recover in between workouts.*

Use the HIIT Exercise Log below to monitor your exercise intensity, your overall progress, and the effect HIIT has on your mood. Make extra copies of the log as needed. (Visit http://www.newharbinger.com/44581 to download the log.)

HIIT Exercise Log

Date	Exercise Performed	Length of High-Intensity Intervals and # of Intervals	Maximum Intensity Level (Heart Rate or Talk Test)	Length of Moderate-Intensity Interval	Mood Before HIIT Exercise, Rate intensity 0 – 10 (max.)	Mood After HIIT Exercise, Rate intensity 0 – 10 (max.)
Example: Mon., June 12	Stationary bike @ the gym	1 min. intervals x 5 total intervals	High intensity, hard to talk while exercising; 80% max. HR on monitor	2 min. intervals, able to speak and breathe more easily	Felt very angry about work, 8/10	Felt better, not as angry, 4/10

Date	Exercise Performed	Length of High-Intensity Intervals and # of Intervals	Maximum Intensity Level (Heart Rate or Talk Test)	Length of Moderate-Intensity Interval	Mood Before HIIT Exercise, Rate intensity 0 – 10 (max.)	Mood After HIIT Exercise, Rate intensity 0 – 10 (max.)

SLOW BREATHING

You've already learned how to use mindful breathing as a skill to help you stay focused in the present moment. But regulating the overall rate at which you breathe can also help you relax when you're experiencing distress and anxiety (McCaul, Solomon, & Holmes, 1979). Here's why: the way you breathe has a direct influence on your heart rate and nervous system. Each time you inhale your heart rate speeds up a little bit, and each time you exhale your heart rate slows down a little bit (Hirsch & Bishop, 1981). As you exhale, it also triggers the relaxation response in your nervous system. In addition, slowing your overall breathing rate and exhaling more slowly than you inhale have both been shown to have relaxing effects (see the review in Lehrer & Gevirtz, 2014).

In one study, people who slowed their rate of breathing experienced a noticeable reduction in anxiety and tension (Clark & Hirschman, 1990). In that study, the participants slowed their breathing rate to six breaths per minute, meaning one cycle of inhaling and exhaling every ten seconds. This is much slower than the average person breathes, which is usually from nine to twenty-four breaths per minute (Lehrer & Gevirtz, 2014). Therefore, slowing your breath to six breaths per minute will likely take some time and practice to achieve.

Similarly, exhaling more slowly than you inhale has also been shown to have positive effects on your ability to relax. In another study, participants were able to reduce their agitation during a stressful situation by breathing in quickly over a period of two seconds and then breathing out slowly over eight second (Cappo & Holmes, 1984). And again, in that same study, the participants also slowed their breathing rate to six breaths per minute. (Six breaths per minute appears to be the "magic" number at which many people feel very relaxed.)

So, to briefly review: (1) slowing down your overall breathing rate and (2) slowing down the length of your exhalation can help you both to relax and to cope during stressful situations.

The slow-breathing technique that you'll learn below is a distress tolerance technique that you should practice for three to five minutes each day. But don't worry, you're *not* expected to breathe this slowly throughout an entire day. Rather, think of this as another distress tolerance skill that you should practice in a calm atmosphere before you really need it in a time of heightened emotion. With enough practice, you will then be able to use this coping technique when presented with a very stressful situation.

However, before you begin practicing the slow-breathing technique, first determine how quickly you breathe in general. Using a clock or a stopwatch, sit down and count how many breaths you take in one minute while you are feeling generally relaxed. Count each pair of inhalation and exhalation as a single count. For example, inhale-exhale, count 1. Next inhale-exhale, count 2, and so on. After one full minute, record the number of breaths you've taken and use the chart below to identify the closest approximation of how quickly you are breathing. For example, if you counted twenty-three breaths per minute, look at 24 on the chart or if you counted fourteen look at 15 on the chart.

Breaths per Minute	Length of Each Paired Inhale and Exhale
24	2.5 seconds
20	3 seconds
15	4 seconds
10	6 seconds
8	8 seconds (approximately)
6	10 seconds

You might find it difficult to immediately reduce your rate of breathing to six breaths per minute (one breath in and out every ten seconds), especially if you're currently breathing at a faster rate, such as twenty breaths per minute (one breath in and out every two and a half seconds). Instead, we recommend reducing your rate of breathing incrementally, over a period of several days or weeks, using the chart above as a guide. Reduce your breathing by one row every several days or weeks—as it becomes easier—until you reach six breaths per minute. For example, if you're currently breathing at fourteen breaths per minute, try reducing your rate of breathing in the first week to ten breaths per minute. Then when that feels comfortable, reduce it to eight breaths per minute. And finally, in several more days or weeks, reduce your rate to six breaths per minute.

In addition to reducing your overall rate of breathing, do your best to focus on extending your exhalation for a second or two longer than your inhalation. For example, once you are able to slow your breathing to ten breaths per minute (one inhale-exhale every six seconds), you can then focus on breathing in for two seconds and out for four seconds. Then, once you can slow your breathing to six breaths per minute (one inhale-exhale every ten seconds), you can inhale for four seconds and exhale for six seconds, or inhale for two seconds and exhale for eight seconds. But again, don't expect to be able to do this right away, especially if you typically breathe at a much faster pace.

If at any point during this exercise you feel dizzy, light-headed, faint, or notice tingling in your lips or fingertips, stop the exercise and return your breathing rate to normal. Feelings like this typically indicate that you're hyperventilating, meaning you're breathing too quickly. Try the technique again later, breathing more slowly, once you feel stable.

Finally, it is *very* helpful to conduct this exercise using a breathing app that you can download on your smartphone. Many breathing apps that you can find online are free and provide visual guidance to show you when to inhale and when to exhale. Plus, on some of the apps, you can even set the length of each inhale-exhale breath (for example, ten seconds), as well as the length of each individual inhale and exhale (for example, two-second inhale and eight-second exhale). Then you can watch the visual guide on the app and breathe accordingly. Otherwise, use a timer on your smartphone to count the seconds. Then, do your best to inhale and exhale by counting as you breathe, for example: "In, 2, 3. Out, 2, 3, 4, 5."

Read the instructions below before beginning the exercise to familiarize yourself with the experience. If you feel more comfortable listening to the instructions, use your smartphone to record the directions in a slow, even voice so that you can listen to them while practicing this technique.

If you're using a breathing app on your smartphone, set the overall length of your breath, as well as the length of each inhale and exhale, and then follow the visual guide until your time has expired. Otherwise, set a timer on your smartphone for three to five minutes and watch the seconds while you count your breaths. The example below is using ten breaths per minute (six seconds for each inhale-exhale), with two-second inhales and four-second exhales. However, you should change the numbers according to whatever length of inhales and exhales you are practicing.

Instructions

To begin, find a comfortable place to sit in a room where you won't be disturbed for as long as you've set your timer. Turn off any distracting sounds. Take a few slow, long breaths and relax. Place one hand on your stomach. Now slowly breathe in through your nose and then slowly exhale through your mouth. Feel your stomach rise and fall as you breathe. Imagine your belly filling up with air like a balloon as you breathe in, and then feel it effortlessly deflate as you breathe out. Feel the breath moving in across your nostrils, and then feel your breath blowing out across your lips, as if you're blowing out birthday candles.

Now, as you continue to breathe, begin counting the length of both your inhalations and exhalations. Count silently to yourself as you watch your timer. As you slowly breathe in, think: "In, 2." Then as you start to breathe out, think: "Out, 2, 3, 4." Then start the pattern again: "In, 2. Out, 2, 3, 4. In, 2. Out, 2, 3, 4." Continue to silently pace your breaths with your timer, doing your best to take slow, steady breaths. Slow, steady breaths. Do your best not to breathe too quickly. Remember, you do not have to fill up your entire lung capacity. Rather, think of slow breaths moving in and out of your belly, gently filling it up with air like a balloon. "In, 2. Out, 2, 3, 4. In, 2. Out, 2, 3, 4. In, 2. Out, 2, 3, 4." When your mind gets distracted, or when you lose count of your breaths, just gently return your focus to your breath moving in and out of your belly, or refocus on your timer. "In, 2. Out, 2, 3, 4. In, 2. Out, 2, 3, 4. In, 2. Out, 2, 3, 4."

Keep breathing until your timer goes off, and then slowly return your focus to the room.

PROGRESSIVE MUSCLE RELAXATION

Progressive muscle relaxation is a technique of systematically tightening and relaxing specific muscle groups in order to soothe anxiety and help you relax. This technique was created by physician Edmund Jacobson in the early twentieth century, and the results of his research were eventually published in his book *Progressive Relaxation* in 1929. Dr. Jacobson was one of the pioneers in early *psychosomatic medicine*, meaning he investigated the relationship between mental-emotional states and their influence on the body. What he discovered was that humans react to stress and anxiety by tightening their muscles; put another way, he found that emotional stress causes muscle tension. To correct this and relieve anxiety, Dr. Jacobson promoted progressive relaxation, a system of tensing and releasing muscles, which simultaneously soothed mental and emotional distress. With regular practice, Dr. Jacobson discovered that this muscle relaxation technique not only relieves immediate distress, but it can also prevent future distress because the muscles of the body cannot be both relaxed and tense at the same time.

Nearly thirty years later, psychiatrist Joseph Wolpe adapted progressive relaxation into his own treatment for anxiety, and used a shorter version of the technique that included verbal suggestions to relax (1958). By repeatedly attaching a verbal *cue* (like the word "peace") with the muscular relaxation process, you can train your muscles to release tension simply by using the cue word in the future, that is, by simply saying "peace." Dr. Wolpe discovered that clients who used this version of progressive relaxation were able to better confront situations that caused them anxiety and fear.

Since Dr. Wolpe's adaptation of Dr. Jacobson's technique, numerous other mental health professionals have further adapted the technique for their own needs. The progressive muscle relaxation format described below is adapted from *The Relaxation & Stress Reduction Workbook*, by Davis, Eshelman, and McKay (1980).

Instructions

Unfortunately, most people are not aware of the muscle tension that they hold in their bodies. The next time you're in a group of people, notice how many people struggle with muscle tension in their bodies. Look for the hunched shoulders, the poor posture, the tight jaws, the clenched fists, and the grimaces on so many faces. Unfortunately, many of us have become so used to carrying tension in our bodies that we just accept it as being "normal." But whether it's normal or not, it can still be corrected in most cases.

Progressive muscle relaxation focuses on helping you recognize the difference between a tight, tense feeling in your muscles versus a loose, relaxed feeling. In order to help you recognize the sensations more easily, progressive muscle relaxation focuses on tensing and releasing small groups of muscles, one at a time. By slowly tensing and relaxing that group of muscles, you learn to recognize the difference, and in the future, when you do hold tension in those muscles, you'll be able to more easily spot the tension and release it. Using the technique below, you'll move through your entire body, tensing and releasing small groups of muscles, learning to recognize and release tension, as well as to create muscular relaxation.

As you move through each muscle group, you'll tighten the muscles for approximately five seconds, and then quickly release the muscle tension. It's important that you release the tension as quickly as you can so that you're better able to distinguish the relaxed feeling. Then take approximately fifteen to thirty seconds to notice the feeling of your muscles releasing and relaxing. Then tighten and release the same group of muscles again, and continue to notice the difference between the tight feeling and the relaxed feeling. In general, tighten and release each group of muscles at least twice, but if you need additional focus on a particular group of muscles to help them release, you can tighten and release them up to five times. You can practice progressive muscle relaxation while you are either seated or lying down, and with practice, you can even tense and release some muscles on the go while you are walking and standing.

Before beginning, there are three parts of general instructions to consider. First, you need to determine the type of tensing you're going to do. There are three kinds: active tensing, threshold tensing, and passive tensing. They are all explained below. Second, pick a verbal cue to use while you are relaxing. Some suggestions are provided. By repeatedly pairing a verbal cue with the act of relaxing your muscles, you can eventually train your muscles to relax simply by using your verbal cue. And third, decide whether you are using the basic procedure for progressive muscle relaxation or the shorthand procedure. When you are first learning how to tense and release your muscle groups, it is recommended that you use the basic procedure for several weeks until you are able to both easily notice muscle tension and effectively release it. Then you can begin using the shorthand procedure, which conglomerates muscles into several larger groups to relax at the same time. Consider recording either of the scripts on your smartphone so that you can close your eyes and relax while performing progressive muscle relaxation.

Before beginning progressive muscle relaxation, consider your physical limitations—if any—and proceed with extra caution if you currently have any back, neck, joint, or shoulder pain. If you have any doubts about your ability to tense and release muscles in your body, talk with a medical care provider before you begin. Also, if you are pregnant or prone to fainting, speak with a medical professional before trying this technique. And, even if your health is not a concern, proceed with caution as you tense muscles in your back, neck, and even your feet. Never tighten these areas so much that they cause you pain.

Three Levels of Tensing

When using progressive muscle relaxation, there are three different types of tensing that you can try. Typically, a person starts with active, then tries threshold, and finally, with experience, uses passive. But if, for whatever reason, you feel comfortable using one and not the others, do whatever works best for you.

1. *Active tensing* requires you to physically tighten a group of muscles until you notice the tension, holding the tension for five seconds, and then quickly releasing the tension. Some practitioners recommend squeezing the muscle groups as hard as you can, but this is often too much tension for most people, or sometimes people cause themselves pain by squeezing the muscles too hard. Instead, squeeze the muscle group tight enough to notice the tension, but not so much that it causes pain. While you are tensing one group of muscles, do your best to leave the rest of your body relaxed. Also, continue to breathe while you are actively tensing your muscles. Some people prefer to breathe normally or use diaphragmatic breathing throughout the exercise; others prefer to inhale, hold the tension, and then exhale while releasing the tension. Whichever way works best for you is okay. For people who are generally pain free, active tensing is often the preferred method, because the experience of holding tension and releasing it is often pleasurable, almost like giving yourself a minimassage.

2. *Threshold tensing* is subtler than active tension. Threshold tensing also requires you to actively tense your muscles but only to the point where the tension is barely noticeable. Again, hold the tension in a minimal way for five seconds. Then release the subtle tension and notice the more relaxed feeling for fifteen to thirty seconds. Continue to breathe throughout the process. Many people prefer threshold tensing after they've already become very familiar with the process of noticing and releasing tension using active tensing. However, other people use threshold tensing if they have a bad back or an injury that they're trying to protect.

3. *Passive tensing* requires you to simply notice the tension in a particular group of muscles, rather than tensing that group of muscles at all. Again, notice the tension in the muscles for five seconds, and then focus on releasing the tension using your creative thoughts. For example, imagine the muscles getting longer and looser, like wax melting in the sun. Or, take a breath in, hold it, and then when you exhale imagine the tension from those muscles releasing. Then focus on the relaxed physical sensation for fifteen to thirty seconds. Passive tensing is often easier to perform after you've already

practiced physically tensing muscles and noticing the tension. But again, some people prefer passive tensing due to injuries and health conditions that prevent them from physically tensing any muscles. If you are using passive tensing, when following the basic procedure below substitute the phrase "notice the tension" when the script instructs you to physically tense a muscle.

Relaxation Cues

Pick a verbal cue to use while you are releasing tension in your muscles. Not only will your verbal cue give you a reminder to relax, but by repeatedly pairing the cue with the act of relaxing you can eventually train your muscles to release simply by saying your cue word(s). Here are some suggestions to help you relax, or you can create one of your own:

- Release and let go

- Relax

- Calm and rested

- Peace

- Letting go more and more

- Loosening and relaxing

- Smooth, relaxed muscles

- Calm

- _____

Basic Procedure

To begin, find a comfortable place to sit or lie down in a room where you won't be disturbed. Turn off any distracting sounds. Loosen any articles of clothing that are too tight or might be distracting. Take a few slow, long breaths and relax.

Now as you let the rest of your body relax, start by clenching your fists and bend them back at the wrist. Tighten them until you notice the tension in your fists, wrists, and forearms. Hold for five seconds. [If recording, count 1, 2, 3, 4, 5 here and do the same below for the other muscle groups.] _Then release the tension and relax. If you're using a cue word to help you relax, say it as you release the tension: "Peace."_ [If you are using a cue word, insert your own phrase here and below each time you release tension.] _Notice the difference between the tight feeling and the relaxed feeling as your muscles lengthen, loosen, and relax. Now take several seconds to become more fully aware of the sensation of your muscles relaxing._ [If recording, pause here for fifteen seconds and do the same for the other muscle groups below.] _Now repeat tightening and releasing this same group of muscles._ [If recording, repeat the same instructions here and for each muscle group below.]

Now bend your arms at the elbows and tense your biceps. Tighten them until you notice the tension in your arms. Hold for five seconds. Then drop your hands, release the tension, and relax. [Insert your cue word if you are using one.] *Feel the difference and take several seconds to become more fully aware of the relaxed feeling.* [Repeat.]

Now turn your attention to your head and wrinkle your forehead as you raise your eyebrows. Tighten the muscles there until you notice the tension in your forehead and scalp. Hold for five seconds. Then release the tension and imagine your forehead and scalp becoming smooth again. [Insert your cue word if you are using one.] *Feel the difference, then take several seconds to become more fully aware of the relaxed feeling.* [Repeat.]

Now frown and notice the tension around your forehead and brow as they stretch. Tighten the muscles there until you notice the tension in your forehead. Hold for five seconds. Then release and imagine your forehead and brow becoming smooth and relaxed again. [Insert your cue word if you are using one.] *Feel the difference and take several seconds to become more fully aware of the relaxed feeling.* [Repeat.]

Now squeeze your eyes closed tightly and notice the tension around your eyes, nose, and cheeks. Hold for five seconds. Then release the tension while still keeping your eyes closed and imagine the muscles around your eyes becoming smooth and relaxed again. [Insert your cue word if you are using one.] *Feel the difference and take several seconds to become more fully aware of the relaxed feeling.* [Repeat.]

Now open your mouth wide and feel the tension in your jaw. Hold for five seconds. Then release the tension by closing your mouth. [Insert your cue word if you are using one.] *Feel the difference and take several seconds to become more fully aware of the relaxed feeling.* [Repeat.]

Now press your tongue against the roof of your mouth. Press your tongue tighter until you feel the tension in your tongue and in the back of your mouth. Hold for five seconds. Then release the tension and let your tongue relax. [Insert your cue word if you are using one.] *Feel the difference and take several seconds to become more fully aware of the relaxed feeling.* [Repeat.]

Now pucker your lips into an "O" and feel the tension around your mouth and jaw. Hold for five seconds. Then release your lips and let your mouth relax. [Insert your cue word if you are using one.] *Feel the difference and take several seconds to become more fully aware of the relaxed feeling.* [Repeat.]

Now notice the overall sense of relaxation in your forehead, scalp, eyes, jaw, tongue, and lips. Mentally scan those areas, and if you still notice any tension, go back to that muscle group and repeat tensing and releasing that area. Allow the overall sensation of relaxation to spread throughout your body. [Insert your cue word if you are using one.]

Now roll your head slowly. Beginning with one ear nearly touching your shoulder, slowly roll your chin down to your chest and over to the other shoulder. Feel the points of tension shift as your head moves from side to side. Then slowly roll your chin down again and back to the other shoulder. Now relax and allow your head to return to a comfortable upright position. [Insert your cue word if you are using one and/or repeat the process.]

Now shrug your shoulders, bringing them up toward your ears. Continue pulling them up until you notice the tension in your neck, shoulders, and upper back. Hold for five seconds. Then release your shoulders quickly, allowing them to drop. Feel the relaxation spread through your neck, shoulders, and upper back. [Insert your cue word if you are using one.] *Feel the difference and take several seconds to become more fully aware of the relaxed feeling.* [Repeat.]

Now inhale and fill your lungs completely. Feel the tension in your chest. Hold your breath and the tension for five seconds. Then release the tension in your chest and breathe normally. [Insert your cue word if you are using one.] *Feel the difference and take several seconds to become more fully aware of the relaxed feeling.* [Repeat.]

Now tighten the muscles in your lower abdominal area. Hold the tension for five seconds, then release the tension. [Insert your cue word if you are using one.] *Notice the relaxed feeling in your abdomen. Now place your hand on your belly in your lower abdominal area. Breathe slowly and fully, allowing your belly to gently expand like a balloon as you breathe in. Then hold your breath, noticing the tension in your abdominal area. Finally, release and allow your abdomen to effortlessly relax as you breathe out. Feel the tension disappear as you exhale.* [Insert your cue word if you are using one.] *Feel the difference and take several seconds to become more fully aware of the relaxed feeling.* [Repeat.]

Now gently arch your back without straining. Just go far enough to notice the tension building in your lower back muscles. Keep the rest of your body as relaxed as possible. Hold the gentle tension in your lower back for five seconds. Then release the tension by returning your posture to a straight position. [Insert your cue word if you are using one.] *Feel the difference and take several seconds to become more fully aware of the relaxed feeling.* [Repeat.]

Now tighten your upper legs and buttocks area. Squeeze the quadriceps and hamstring muscles in your legs, as well as your gluteus muscles. Hold the tension for five seconds. Then release the tension and relax. [Insert your cue word if you are using one.] *Feel the difference and take several seconds to become more fully aware of the relaxed feeling.* [Repeat.]

Now straighten and tense your legs by pointing your toes downward. Feel the tension throughout the entire length of your legs. Hold the tension for five seconds. Then release the tension and relax. [Insert your cue word if you are using one.] *Feel the difference and take several seconds to become more fully aware of the relaxed feeling.* [Repeat.]

Now straighten and tense your legs by curling your toes upward toward the sky. Feel the tension throughout the entire length of your legs, especially in your calf muscles. Hold the tension for five seconds. Then release the tension and relax. [Insert your cue word if you are using one.] *Feel the difference and take several seconds to become more fully aware of the relaxed feeling.* [Repeat.]

Finally, notice your entire body relaxing and releasing. Allow the comfortable warmth of this relaxation to continue to spread throughout your body, growing and expanding. [Insert your cue word if you are using one.] *Mentally scan your body from your toes to your head, noting any muscles that need to relax more fully, and allow those muscles to lengthen, loosen, and relax. Starting with your legs, relax your feet…your ankles…your calves…your shins…your knees…your thighs…and your buttocks. Then let the relaxation expand to your abdominal area and lower back. Then let the sensation of relaxation spread to your chest and upper back. Allow all of those muscles to lengthen, loosen, and relax. Now allow the relaxation to grow and expand in your shoulders…arms…hands…and fingers. Then allow the relaxation to continue to grow and expand in your neck…jaw…mouth…cheeks…around your eyes…forehead…scalp…and the back of your head. Continue to breathe slowly and notice the sensation of relaxation growing and expanding with each breath.* [Insert your cue word if you are using one.]

When you are ready, slowly open your eyes and return your focus to the room, feeling relaxed, alert, and aware of your surroundings.

Shorthand Procedure

After you've experienced success relaxing individual muscles using the basic procedure above, try the shorthand procedure. The shorthand procedure groups muscles into five basic poses that will help you relax more quickly. In each pose, whole muscle groups are tensed and relaxed together, shortening the length of time it takes to relax your entire body. The process for using the shorthand procedure is the same as the basic procedure: during each pose hold the tension for five seconds, then release the tension and notice the relaxed feeling for fifteen to thirty seconds. Then repeat the tension at least one more time. Also, if you want to continue to use your cue word, say it when you release the tension each time.

1. Clench your hands into fists, flex your biceps and forearms, and raise your arms like a bodybuilder posing in front of a mirror. Feel the tension in your hands, arms, shoulders, and upper back. Then release and relax the muscles. [Repeat.]

2. Attempt to place your left ear on your left shoulder and then slowly roll your chin down to your chest; continue to slowly roll your head until your right ear nearly touches your right shoulder. Then reverse the roll and return your head to your left shoulder by moving your chin down past your chest again. Feel the tension in your neck, upper back, and jaw as your head slowly rolls. Release and relax the muscles. [Repeat.]

3. Contract all the muscles in your face and shoulders, squeezing your face and pulling up your shoulders as if you just ate something very sour. (Or imagine wrinkling your face like a walnut as you hunch your shoulders.) Contract the muscles around your eyes, mouth, forehead, and shoulders. Then release and relax the muscles. [Repeat.]

4. Gently arch your shoulders back and stretch your chest. Then take a full breath, expanding your chest and abdomen. Hold the breath for five seconds while noticing the tension in your chest, shoulders, back, and abdomen. Then exhale and release the muscle tension. [Repeat.]

5. Straighten your legs and point your toes back toward your face. Feel the tension in your upper and lower leg. Then release and relax. Now straighten your legs and point your toes away from your face. Again, feel the tension in your upper and lower leg, then release and relax. [Repeat.]

Finally, as you begin to use progressive muscle relaxation, here are some tips to make the practice more effective:

1. Progressive muscle relaxation requires regular use in order to be effective. Try using it once a day for the first two weeks. Or at the very least, use it three times a week. Remember to start with the basic procedure and then transition to the shorthand procedure after you can recognize the difference between the tense and relaxed feelings in your muscles. The more you practice progressive muscle relaxation, the more effective the technique will be as a distress tolerance skill when you get overwhelmed by emotions.

2. Be very cautious when tensing the muscles in your neck and back, especially if you suspect or have been diagnosed with injuries or degenerative conditions in your neck and back. Avoid any tension that causes pain. Also avoid excessively tightening your toes or feet, as this, too, can cause cramping.

3. When releasing tension from your muscles, do so quickly. For example, if you are pulling up your shoulders, when you release the tension let your shoulders drop quickly rather than slowly lowering them. Releasing the muscles quickly will accentuate the relaxed feeling.

4. As you practice progressive muscle relaxation, you will become more aware of the places where you hold tension. As you gain awareness, check those muscles periodically throughout the day, even if you are at work or someplace else where you can't do a full relaxation routine. Most likely, you can tense and release those muscles on the go, no matter where you are.

5. If you are recording the instructions for yourself on your smartphone or other device, make sure you take long enough pauses to allow yourself to experience both the tension and the longer periods of relaxation.

USING PHYSIOLOGICAL COPING SKILLS

Of course, each of these physiological coping skills requires practice. You can't expect to simply try the technique for the first time when you are overwhelmed with emotions and expect it to work. Plus, some skills will be more effective for you than other skills, and some skills might not be appropriate in every situation even if they do work. For example, it might not be practical—or safe—to use the diving technique while you are driving a car. So be sure to try each technique and regularly practice the ones that you find to be effective. Also, be sure to include the physiological coping skills that work for you in your emergency coping plan, which you completed at the end of chapter 2.

In addition, you might want to take some time to imagine yourself using the physiological coping skills in stressful situations. This will make it more likely that you will use the skills in future stressful situations. For example, remember a past stressful experience that led to overwhelming emotions. What was the situation? How did you feel? How did you react? What was the end result of the experience? Now imagine that you had used one of the physiological coping skills when you first started to feel overwhelmed. Which one could you have used? How would the technique have made you feel? How might you have reacted differently? How might the situation have ended differently? Use the space below to record your answers.

What was the situation in the past that led to overwhelming emotions?

_____

_____

_____

How did I feel in that situation?

_____

_____

_____

How did I react?

_____

_____

_____

What was the end result of that situation?

_____

_____

_____

Which of the physiological coping skills could I have used in that situation?

_____

_____

_____

How would the technique have made me feel?

_____

_____

_____

How would I have reacted differently?

_____

_____

_____

How might the situation have ended differently?

_____

_____

_____

Now imagine a future stressful event, maybe even one that you know will occur, like having a difficult conversation with your spouse or partner. What do you think will happen? How do you imagine that you will react emotionally? What physiological coping skill might be the most effective in that situation? Now, imagine yourself performing the skill, even if you have to step away from the situation for a little while, such as going to the restroom to practice slow breathing. How do you imagine the technique will help you cope? How might the situation proceed differently if you do use the technique? How can you remind yourself to use the technique when the situation occurs? Use the space below to record your answers.

What is the likely situation that will occur?

_____

_____

_____

What do you think will happen?

_____

_____

_____

How might you react emotionally?

_____

_____

_____

What physiological coping skill might be the most effective in that situation?

_____

_____

_____

.How do you imagine the technique will help you cope?

_____

_____

_____

How might the situation proceed differently if you do use the technique?

_____

_____

_____

How can you remind yourself to use the technique when the situation occurs?

_____

_____

_____

CHAPTER 4

Basic Mindfulness Skills

An operational working definition of mindfulness is: the awareness that emerges through paying attention on purpose, in the present moment, and nonjudgmentally to the unfolding of experience moment by moment.

—Jon Kabat-Zinn (2003)

MINDFULNESS SKILLS: WHAT ARE THEY?

Mindfulness, also known as meditation, is a valuable skill that has been taught for thousands of years in many of the world's religions, including Christianity (Merton, 1960), Judaism (Pinson, 2004), Buddhism (Rahula, 1974), and Islam (Inayat Khan, 2000). Beginning in the 1980s, Jon Kabat-Zinn began using nonreligious mindfulness skills to help hospital patients cope with chronic pain problems (Kabat-Zinn, 1982; Kabat-Zinn, Lipworth, & Burney, 1985; Kabat-Zinn, Lipworth, Burney, & Sellers, 1987). More recently, similar mindfulness techniques were also integrated into other forms of psychotherapy (Segal, Williams, & Teasdale, 2002), including dialectical behavior therapy (Linehan, 1993a). Studies have shown mindfulness skills to be effective at reducing the odds of having another major depressive episode (Teasdale et al., 2000); reducing symptoms of anxiety (Kabat-Zinn et al., 1992); reducing chronic pain (Kabat-Zinn et al., 1985; Kabat-Zinn et al., 1987); decreasing binge eating (Kristeller & Hallett, 1999); increasing tolerance of distressing situations; increasing relaxation; and increasing skills to cope with difficult situations (Baer, 2003). As a result of findings like these, mindfulness is considered one of the most important *core skills* in dialectical behavior therapy (Linehan, 1993a).

So what exactly is mindfulness? One definition is offered above by mindfulness researcher Jon Kabat-Zinn. But for the purposes of this book, mindfulness is *the ability to be aware of your thoughts, emotions, physical sensations, and actions—in the present moment—without judging or criticizing yourself, others, or your experience.*

Have you ever heard the expressions "be in the moment" or "be here now"? These are both different ways of saying "be mindful of what's happening to you and around you." But this isn't always an easy task. At any moment in time, you might be thinking, feeling, sensing, and doing many different things. For example, consider what's happening to you right now. You're probably sitting somewhere, reading these words. But at the same time, you're also breathing, listening to the sounds around you, noticing what the book feels like, noticing the weight of your body resting in the chair, and maybe you're even thinking about something else. It's also possible that you're aware of your emotional and physical states of being happy, sad, tired, or excited. Maybe you're even aware of bodily sensations, such as your heart beating or the rising and falling of your chest as you breathe. You might even be doing something that you're completely unaware of, like shaking your leg, humming, or resting your head in your hand. That's a lot to be aware of, and right now, you're just reading a book. Imagine what's happening to you when you're doing other things in your life, like talking with someone or dealing with people at work. The truth is, no one is 100 percent mindful all the time. But the more mindful you learn to be, the more control you will gain over your life.

But remember, time never stands still and each second of your life is different. Because of this, it's important that you learn to be aware "in each present moment." For example, by the time you finish reading this sentence, the moment that you started reading it is gone and your present moment is now different. In fact, you are now different. The cells in your body are constantly dying and being replaced, so physically you're different. Equally important, your thoughts, feelings, sensations, and actions are never exactly the same in every situation, so they're different too. For these reasons, it's important that you learn to be mindful of how your experience changes in each individual moment of your life.

And lastly, in order to be fully aware of your experiences in the present moment, it's necessary that you do so without criticizing yourself, your situation, or other people. In dialectical behavior therapy, this is called radical acceptance (Linehan, 1993a). As described in chapter 2, radical acceptance means tolerating something without judging it or trying to change it. This is important because if you're judging yourself, your experience, or someone else in the present moment, then you're not really paying attention to what's happening in that moment. For example, many people spend a lot of time worrying about mistakes they've made in the past or worrying about mistakes that they might make in the future. But while they're doing this, their focus is no longer on what's happening to them *now*; their thoughts are somewhere else. As a result, they live in a painful past or future, and life feels very difficult.

So to review, mindfulness is the ability to be aware of your thoughts, emotions, physical sensations, and actions—in the present moment—without judging or criticizing yourself, others, or your experience.

A "MINDLESS" EXERCISE

Obviously, mindfulness is a skill that requires practice. Most people get distracted, "zone out," or spend most of their daily lives being unmindful or running on autopilot. As a result, they then get lost, anxious, and frustrated when a situation doesn't happen as they expect it to. Here are some common ways in which all of us have experienced being unmindful. Check (✓) the ones that you've done:

☐ While driving or traveling, you don't remember the experience or which roads you took.

☐ While having a conversation, you suddenly realize that you don't know what the other person is talking about.

☐ While having a conversation, you're already thinking about what you're going to say next before the other person has even stopped speaking.

☐ While reading, you suddenly realize that you've been thinking about something else and have no idea what you just read.

☐ While walking into a room, you suddenly forget what you came to get.

☐ After putting something down, you can't remember where you just put it.

☐ While taking a shower, you're already planning what you have to do later and then you forget whether you've already washed your hair or some other body part.

☐ While having sex, you're thinking about other things or other people.

All of these examples are fairly harmless. But for people with overwhelming emotions, being unmindful can often have a devastating effect on their lives. Consider the example of Lee. Lee thought that everyone at work hated him. One day, a new employee whom Lee found attractive approached him in the cafeteria and asked to sit down. The woman tried to be friendly and make conversation, but Lee was more engaged in the conversation in his own head than he was in the one with the woman.

"She's probably just stuck up like the rest of them," he thought. "Why would someone like her be interested in me anyway? Why would she want to sit with me? It's probably just a joke someone else put her up to." From the moment the woman sat down and tried to talk with him, Lee just became angrier and more suspicious.

The woman did her best to make small talk. She asked Lee how he liked working at the company, how long he'd been there, and she even asked him about the weather, but Lee never noticed. He was so wrapped up in his own conversation, and in paying attention to his own self-critical thoughts, that he never even recognized that the woman was trying to be friendly.

After five minutes of unsuccessfully trying, the woman finally stopped talking to Lee. Then a few minutes later, she moved to a different table, and when she did, Lee congratulated himself. "I knew it," he thought, "I knew she wasn't really interested in me." But at the expense of being right, Lee's unmindfulness and self-criticism had cost him another opportunity to meet a potential friend.

WHY ARE MINDFULNESS SKILLS IMPORTANT?

Now that you have a better idea of what mindfulness is—and isn't—it's probably easy to see why this skill is so important. But for the purposes of this workbook, let's be very clear about why you need to learn mindfulness skills. There are three reasons:

1. Mindfulness skills will help you focus on one thing at a time in the present moment, and by doing this, you can better control and soothe your overwhelming emotions.

2. Mindfulness will help you learn to identify and separate judgmental thoughts from your experiences. These judgmental thoughts often fuel your overwhelming emotions.

3. Mindfulness will help you develop a skill that's very important in dialectical behavior therapy called "wise mind" (Linehan, 1993a).

Wise mind is the ability to make healthy decisions about your life based on both your rational thoughts and your emotions. For example, you've probably noticed that it's often difficult—or impossible—to make good decisions when your *emotions* are intense, out of control, or contradict what's rational. Similarly, it's often difficult to make informed decisions when your *thoughts* are intense, irrational, or contradict how you feel. Wise mind is a decision-making process that balances the reasoning of your thoughts with the needs of your emotions, and it is a skill that will be discussed further in chapter 5.

ABOUT THIS CHAPTER

Throughout this chapter and the next, you'll be presented with exercises to help you become more mindful of your moment-to-moment experiences. This chapter will introduce you to beginning mindfulness exercises to help you observe and describe your thoughts and emotions more carefully. In dialectical behavior therapy, these are called "what" skills (Linehan, 1993b), meaning they'll help you become mindful of *what* you're focusing on. Then in the next chapter, you'll be taught more advanced mindfulness skills. In dialectical behavior therapy, these are called "how" skills (Linehan, 1993b), meaning they'll help you learn *how* to be both mindful and nonjudgmental in your daily experiences.

The exercises in this chapter will teach you four "what" skills:

1. To focus more fully on the present moment

2. To recognize and focus on your thoughts, emotions, and physical sensations

3. To focus on your moment-to-moment stream of awareness

4. To separate your thoughts from your emotions and physical sensations

As you read the following exercises, it's important that you practice them in the order in which they're presented. The exercises in this chapter are grouped according to the four "what" skills, and each exercise builds on the previous exercise.

Exercise: Focus on a Single Minute ⊠

This is the first exercise that will help you focus more fully on the present moment. It's simple to do, but it often has an amazing effect. Its purpose is to help you become more mindful of your own sense of time. For this exercise, you'll need a watch with a second hand or a stopwatch app on your smartphone.

Many people feel that time goes by very quickly. As a result, they're always in a rush to do things and they're always thinking about the next thing they have to do or the next thing that could go wrong. Unfortunately, this just makes them more unmindful of what they're doing in the present moment. Other people feel that time goes by very slowly. As a result, they feel like they have more time than they actually do and they frequently find themselves running late. This simple exercise will help you become more mindful of how quickly or slowly time actually does go by.

Instructions

To begin this exercise, find a comfortable place to sit in a room where you won't be disturbed for a few minutes and turn off any distracting sounds. Begin timing yourself with your watch or smartphone. Then, without counting the seconds or looking at the watch, simply sit wherever you are. When you think that one minute has passed, check the watch again, or stop the timer. Note how much time really has passed.

Did you allow less than a full minute to pass? If so, how long was it—a few seconds, twenty seconds, forty seconds? If it wasn't a full minute, consider how this affects you. Are you always in a rush to do things because you don't think you have enough time? If so, what does the result of this exercise mean for you?

Or did you allow more than a minute to pass? If so, how long was it—one and a half minutes, two minutes? If so, consider how this affects you. Are you frequently late for appointments because you think that you have more time than you really do? If so, what does the result of this exercise mean for you?

Whatever your results were, one of the purposes of learning mindfulness skills is to help you develop a more accurate awareness of all your moment-to-moment experiences, including your perception of time. If you'd like, return to this exercise in a few weeks after you've been practicing your mindfulness skills and see whether your perception of time has changed.

Exercise: Focus on a Single Object ⊠

Focusing on a single object is the second mindfulness skill that will help you concentrate more fully on the present moment. Remember, one of the biggest traps of being unmindful is that your attention wanders from one thing to the next or from one thought to the next. And as a result, you often get lost, distracted, and frustrated. This exercise will help you focus your attention on a single object. The purpose of this exercise is to help you train your "mental muscle." This means you will learn to maintain your focus on whatever it is you're observing. And with practice, you'll get better at focusing your attention, just like an athlete who exercises certain muscles to become stronger.

During this exercise, you will eventually become distracted by your thoughts, memories, or other sensations. That's okay; this happens to everyone who does this exercise. Do your best not to criticize yourself or stop the exercise. Just notice when your mind wanders and return your focus to whatever object you're observing.

Pick a small object to focus on. Choose something that can rest on a table, is safe to touch, and is emotionally neutral. It can be anything, such as a pen, a flower, a watch, a ring, a cup, or something similar. Don't choose to focus on something that could hurt you or on a picture of someone you don't like. These will stir up too many emotions for you right now.

Find a comfortable place to sit in a room where you won't be disturbed for a few minutes, and put the object on a table in front of you. Turn off any distracting sounds. Set the timer in your smartphone for five minutes. Do this exercise once or twice a day for two weeks, choosing a different object to focus on each time.

You can use a voice-recording app on your smartphone to record the instructions in a slow, even voice and play them while you're exploring the object.

Instructions

·To begin, sit comfortably and take a few slow, deep breaths. Then, without touching the object, begin looking at it and exploring its different surfaces with your eyes. Take your time exploring what it looks like. Then try to imagine the different qualities that the object possesses.

- What does the surface of the object look like?

- Is it shiny or dull?

- Does it look smooth or rough?

- Does it look soft or hard?

- Does it have multiple colors or just one color?

- What else is unique about the way the object looks?

Take your time observing the object. Now hold the object in your hand or reach out and touch the object. Begin noticing the different ways it feels.

- Is it smooth or is it rough?

- Does it have ridges or is it flat?

- Is it soft or is it hard?

- Is it bendable or is it rigid?

- Does the object have areas that feel different from each other?

- What does the temperature of the object feel like?

- If you can hold it in your hand, notice how much it weighs.

- What else do you notice about the way it feels?

Continue exploring the object with both your sight and your sense of touch. Continue to breathe comfortably. When your attention begins to wander, return your focus to the object. Keep on exploring the object until your alarm goes off or until you have fully explored all the qualities of the object.

Exercise: Band of Light ⊠

This is the third exercise that will help you focus more fully on the present moment. It will help you become more mindful of the physical sensations in your body. Read the instructions before beginning the exercise to familiarize yourself with the process. Then you can keep these instructions near you if you need to refer to them while you're doing the exercise, or you can record them in a slow, even voice on your smartphone and play them while you're observing the sensations in your body.

As with the other exercises in this chapter, most likely your focus will begin to wander while you're doing this exercise. That's okay. When you recognize that your focus is drifting, gently return your attention to the exercise and do your best not to criticize or judge yourself.

Instructions

To begin, find a comfortable place to sit in a room where you won't be disturbed for ten minutes. Turn off any distracting sounds. Take a few slow, long breaths and then close your eyes. Using your imagination, envision a narrow band of white light circling the top of your head like a halo. As this exercise progresses, the band of light will slowly move down your body, and as it does, you will become aware of the different physical sensations you're feeling beneath the band of light.

As you continue to breathe with your eyes closed, continue to see the band of white light encircling the top of your head and notice any physical sensations you feel on that part of your body. Perhaps you will notice your scalp tingling or itching. Whatever sensations you notice are okay.

- *Slowly the band of light begins to descend around your head, passing over the tops of your ears, your eyes, and the top of your nose. As it does, become aware of any sensations you feel there, even small sensations.*

- *Notice any muscle tension you may be feeling on the top of your head.*

- *As the band of light slowly descends over your nose, mouth, and chin, continue to focus on any physical sensations you might be feeling there.*

- *Pay attention to the back of your head where you may be having sensations.*

- *Notice any sensations you may be feeling in your mouth, on your tongue, or on your teeth.*

- *Continue to watch the band of light in your imagination descend around your neck, and notice any feelings in your throat or any muscle tension on the back of your neck.*

- *Now the band widens and begins to move down your torso, across the width of your shoulders.*

- *Notice any sensations, muscle tension, or tingling you might be feeling in your shoulders, upper back, upper arms, and upper chest area.*

- *As the band of light continues to descend down around your arms, notice any feelings you're aware of in your upper arms, elbows, forearms, wrists, hands, and fingers. Become aware of any tingling, itching, or tension you might be holding in those places.*

- *Now become aware of your chest, the middle of your back, the side of your torso, your lower back, and stomach. Again, notice any tension or sensations, no matter how small they might be.*

- *As the band continues to move down your lower body, become aware of any sensations in your pelvic region, buttocks, and upper legs.*

- *Be sure to pay attention to the backs of your legs and notice any feelings there.*

- *Continue to watch the band of light descend around your lower legs, around your calves, shins, feet, and toes. Notice any feelings or tension you're experiencing.*

Then as the band of light disappears after completing its descent, take a few more slow, long breaths, and when you feel comfortable, slowly open your eyes and return your focus to the room.

Exercise: Inner-Outer Experience ⊠

Now that you've practiced being mindful of both an object outside of yourself and your internal physical sensations, the next step is to combine the two experiences. This is the first exercise that will teach you how to recognize and focus on your thoughts, emotions, and physical sensations. This will be done by teaching you to shift your attention back and forth in a mindful, focused way between what you are experiencing internally, such as your physical sensations and thoughts, and what you are experiencing externally, such as what you notice using your eyes, ears, nose, and sense of touch.

Read the instructions before beginning the exercise to familiarize yourself with the experience. Then you can either keep these instructions near you if you need to refer to them while you're doing the exercise, or you can record them in a slow, even voice on your smartphone so that you can listen to them while you practice shifting your focus between your internal and external awareness.

Instructions

To begin, find a comfortable place to sit in a room where you won't be disturbed for ten minutes. Turn off any distracting sounds. Take a few slow, long breaths and relax.

Now, keeping your eyes open, focus your attention on an object in the room. Notice what the object looks like. Notice its shape and color. Imagine what that object would feel like if you could hold it. Imagine what the object must weigh. Describe the object silently to yourself, being as descriptive as possible. Take a minute to do this. Keep breathing. If your focus begins to drift, simply return your attention to the exercise without criticizing yourself. [Pause here for one minute if you are recording the instructions.]

When you have finished describing the object, return your focus to your body. Notice any physical sensations that you might be experiencing. Scan your body from your head to your feet. Notice any muscle tension you might be holding, any tingling you might be experiencing, or any other sensations of which you are aware. Take a minute to do this, and keep breathing slow, deep breaths. [Pause here for one minute if you are recording the instructions.]

Now redirect your attention to your sense of hearing. Notice any sounds that you can hear. Notice sounds you hear coming from outside your room and note to yourself what they are. Now become aware of any sounds you hear coming from inside the room and note to yourself what they are. Try to notice even small sounds, such as the ticking of a clock, the sound of the wind, or the beating of your heart. If you become distracted by any thoughts, return your focus to your sense of hearing. Take a minute to do this, and keep breathing. [Pause here for one minute if you are recording the instructions.]

When you have finished listening to the sounds that you can notice, return your focus to your body. Again, notice any physical sensations. Become aware of the weight of your body resting in the chair. Notice the weight of your feet resting on the floor. Notice the weight of your head resting on top of your neck. Notice in general how your body feels. If you become distracted by your thoughts, just notice what they are and refocus your attention as best you can on your physical sensations. Take a minute to do this, and keep breathing slow, deep breaths. [Pause here for one minute if you are recording the instructions.]

Once again, redirect your attention. This time, put your focus on your sense of smell. Notice any smells that are in the room, pleasant or otherwise. If you don't notice any smells, just become aware of the flow of air moving into your nostrils as you breathe in through your nose. Try your best to maintain your focus on your sense of smell. If you become distracted by any thoughts, return your focus to your nose. Take a minute to do this, and keep breathing. [Pause here for one minute if you are recording the instructions.]

When you have finished using your sense of smell, once again return your focus to your physical sensations. Notice any sensations that you might be feeling. Once again, scan your body from your head to your feet and become aware of any muscle tension, tingling, or other physical feelings. If your thoughts distract you, do your best to return your focus to your physical sensations. Take a minute to do this, and keep breathing slow, deep breaths. [Pause here for one minute if you are recording the instructions.]

Now, finally, redirect your attention to your sense of touch. Reach out with one of your hands to touch an object that is within reach. Or, if there is no object within reach, touch the chair you're sitting on or touch your leg. Notice what the object feels like. Notice if it's smooth or rough. Notice if it's pliable or rigid. Notice if it's soft or solid. Notice what the sensations feel like on the skin of your fingertips. If your thoughts begin to distract you, simply return your focus to the object that you're touching. Take a minute to do this, and keep breathing slow, deep breaths. [Pause here for one minute if you are recording the instructions.]

When you've finished, take three to five slow, long breaths and return your focus to the room.

Exercise: Record Three Minutes of Thoughts

This is the second exercise that will help you recognize and focus on your thoughts, emotions, and physical sensations. In this exercise, you will identify the number of thoughts you have in a three-minute period. This will allow you to become more mindful of just how quickly your mind really works. This exercise will also help you prepare for the next exercise, Thought Defusion.

The instructions for this exercise are simple: set a timer for three minutes and begin writing down every thought you have on a piece of paper. But don't try to record the thought word for word. Just write down a word or two that represents the thought. For example, if you are thinking about a project you have to complete at work by next week, simply write "project" or "work project." Then record your next thought.

See how many of your thoughts you can catch in three minutes, no matter how small the thoughts are. Even if you start thinking about this exercise, write "exercise." Or if you start thinking about the paper you're writing on, write "paper." No one else ever has to see this record, so be honest with yourself.

When you've finished, count the number of thoughts you had in three minutes and multiply that number by twenty to get an idea of how many thoughts you might have in an hour.

Exercise: Thought Defusion ⊗

This is the third exercise that will help you recognize and focus on your thoughts, emotions, and physical sensations. *Thought defusion* is a technique borrowed from acceptance and commitment therapy (Hayes, Strosahl, & Wilson, 1999), which has proven to be a very successful treatment for emotional distress.

When distressing thoughts keep repeating, it's often easy to get "hooked" on them, like a fish biting on a bait hook (Chodron, 2003). In contrast, thought defusion will help you mindfully observe your thoughts without getting stuck on them. With practice, this skill will give you more freedom to choose which thoughts you want to focus on and which thoughts you want to let go of instead of getting stuck on all of them.

Thought defusion requires the use of your imagination. The object of this skill is to visualize your thoughts, either as pictures or words, harmlessly floating away from you without obsessing about them or analyzing them. Whichever way you choose to do this is okay. Here are some suggestions that other people have found helpful:

- Imagine sitting in a field watching your thoughts float away on clouds.

- Picture yourself sitting near a stream watching your thoughts float past on leaves.

- See your thoughts written in the sand and then watch the waves wash them away.

- Envision yourself driving a car and see your thoughts pass by on billboards.

- See your thoughts leave your head and watch them sizzle in the flame of a candle.

- Imagine sitting beside a tree and watch your thoughts float down on leaves.

- Picture yourself standing in a room with two doors, then watch your thoughts enter through one door and leave through the other.

If one of these ideas works for you, that's great. If not, feel free to create your own. Just make sure that your idea captures the purpose of this exercise, which is to visually watch your thoughts come and go without holding on to them and without analyzing them. Remember to use the concept of radical acceptance while doing this exercise. Let your thoughts be whatever they are and don't get distracted fighting them or criticizing yourself for having them. Just let the thoughts come and go.

Read the instructions before beginning the exercise to familiarize yourself with the experience. If you feel more comfortable listening to the instructions, record the instructions on your smartphone in a slow, even voice so you can listen to them while practicing this technique. When you are first using thought defusion, set a timer for three to five minutes and practice letting go of your thoughts until the alarm goes off. Then as you get more accustomed to using this technique, you can set the alarm for longer periods of time, like eight or ten minutes. But don't expect to be able to sit still that long when you first start. In the beginning, three to five minutes is a long time to use thought defusion. (For a copy of the instructions below, visit http://www .newharbinger.com/44581 and download How to Do Thought Defusion.)

Instructions

To begin, find a comfortable place to sit in a room where you won't be disturbed for as long as you've set your timer. Turn off any distracting sounds. Take a few slow, long breaths, relax, and close your eyes.

Now, in your imagination, picture yourself in the scenario that you chose, watching your thoughts come and go, whether it's on the beach, near a stream, in a field, in a room, or wherever. Do your best to imagine yourself in that scene. After you do, start to become aware of the thoughts that you're having. Start to observe the thoughts that are coming up, whatever they are. Don't try to stop your thoughts, and do your best not to criticize yourself for any of the thoughts. Just watch the thoughts arise, and then, using whatever technique you've chosen, watch the thoughts disappear. Whatever the thought is, big or small, important or unimportant, watch the thought arise in your mind and then let it float away or disappear by whichever means you've chosen.

Just continue to watch the thoughts arise and disappear. Use pictures to represent the thoughts or words, whatever works best for you. Do your best to watch the thoughts arise and disappear without getting hooked into them and without criticizing yourself.

If more than one thought comes up at the same time, see them both arise and disappear. If the thoughts come very quickly, do your best to watch them all disappear without getting hooked on any of them. Continue to breathe and watch the thoughts come and go until your timer goes off.

When you've finished, take a few more slow, long breaths and then slowly open your eyes and return your focus to the room.

Exercise: Describe Your Emotion

This is the fourth exercise that will help you recognize and focus on your thoughts, emotions, and physical sensations. So far, the exercises in this chapter have helped you learn to be more mindful of your physical sensations and thoughts. This next exercise will help you become more mindful of your emotions. As with some of the other exercises, the instructions for this exercise might sound simple, but the results can be powerful. This exercise will ask you to choose an emotion and then describe that emotion by drawing it and exploring it.

So, to begin, pick an emotion. It can be either a pleasant or an unpleasant emotion. Ideally, you should choose an emotion that you're feeling right now, *unless that emotion is overwhelmingly sad or self-destructive.* If it is, you should wait until you feel more in control of your emotions before beginning this exercise. On the other hand, if you can't identify what you're feeling now, choose an emotion that you were feeling recently, something that you can easily remember. But, whichever you choose, try to be specific about what the emotion is. For example, if you got into a fight with your spouse or partner recently because he or she did something to you, that's the situation, not the emotion. Maybe this situation made you feel angry, hurt, sad, stupid, or something else. Be specific about how you feel. Here's another example. Maybe someone recently gave you a gift. That's the situation. Your emotion would depend on how you felt about the gift. If it was something you've always wanted, you might feel elated. If the gift came from someone you don't know very well, you might feel anxious about its purpose. Be specific about how you feel.

To help you choose an emotion, use this list of some commonly felt emotions. (Visit http://www.newhar binger.com/44581 to download the List of Commonly Felt Emotions.)

List of Commonly Felt Emotions

Adored	Disgusted	Horrified	Sad
Afraid	Disturbed	Hurt	Satisfied
Angry	Embarrassed	Hysterical	Scared
Annoyed	Empty	Indifferent	Scattered
Anxious	Energetic	Infatuated	Secure
Apologetic	Enlightened	Interested	Shy
Ashamed	Enlivened	Irritated	Smart
Blessed	Enraged	Jealous	Sorry
Blissful	Enthusiastic	Joyful	Strong
Bored	Envious	Lively	Surprised
Bothered	Excited	Lonely	Suspicious
Broken	Exhausted	Loved	Terrified
Bubbly	Flirtatious	Loving	Thrilled
Cautious	Foolish	Mad	Tired
Cheerful	Fragile	Nervous	Unsure
Confident	Frightened	Obsessed	Upset
Content	Frustrated	Pleased	Vivacious
Curious	Glad	Proud	Vulnerable
Delighted	Guilty	Regretful	Worried
Depressed	Happy	Relieved	Worthless
Determined	Hopeful	Respected	Worthy
Disappointed	Hopeless	Restless	

When you finish identifying the emotion you want to explore, write it down at the top of the Describe Your Emotion form (on the next page) or use a blank piece of paper.

Then, using your imagination, draw a picture of what your emotion might look like. This might sound hard to do, but just do the best you can. For example, if you are feeling happy, maybe a picture of the sun expresses how you feel or maybe a picture of an ice-cream cone would do better. The picture doesn't have to make sense to anyone else but you. Just give it a try.

Next, try to think of a sound that would further describe the emotion. For example, if you are feeling sad, maybe the sound of a groan would describe how you feel, such as "ugh." Or maybe a certain song expresses your emotion better. Describe the sound as best you can, and write it near your drawing.

Then describe an action that "fits" your emotion. For example, if you are feeling bored, maybe the action would be to take a nap. Or if you are feeling shy, maybe the action would be to run away and hide. Do your best to describe the action, and write it near your drawing.

The next step of this exercise is to describe the intensity of the emotion on which you're focusing. This will require some thought. Do your best to describe the strength of this emotion. Feel free to be creative and use metaphors if you need to. For example, if you are feeling very nervous, you might write that the feeling is so strong that your "heart feels like a drum at a rock concert." Or if you are only feeling a little angry, you might write that the intensity is like a "mosquito bite."

After describing the intensity of the emotion, briefly describe the overall quality of what the emotion feels like. Again, feel free to be as creative as you need to be in your description. If you are nervous, maybe it makes you feel like your "knees are made of jelly." Or if you are getting angry, it might make you feel like "water that's about to boil." Be as accurate as you can in your description and be as creative as you need to be in order to convey your feelings.

Finally, add any thoughts that arise due to your emotion. But be clear that what you describe is a thought and not another emotion. For example, don't choose any of the words in the list above to describe your thoughts. Those are emotions, not thoughts. Your thoughts should be able to finish the following sentences: "My emotion makes me think that…" or "My emotion makes me think about…" It's important that you begin separating your thoughts and your emotions because this will give you better control over both of them in the future. Here are some examples of thoughts that can arise from emotions. If you are feeling confident, a related thought might be that you think you can ask your boss for a raise, or it makes you remember other times in your life when you felt confident and were successful. Or if you are feeling fragile, a related thought could be that you think you can't handle any more stress in your life, or it makes you think about how you're going to struggle with future problems if you don't get stronger. (Visit http://www.newharbinger.com/44581 to download the Describe Your Emotion form.)

Describe Your Emotion

Name the emotion: _____

Draw a picture of your emotion

Describe a related action: _____

_____

Describe a related sound: _____

_____

Describe the intensity of the emotion: _____

_____

Describe the quality of the emotion: _____

_____

Describe thoughts related to the emotion: _____

_____

Exercise: Focus Shifting

This next exercise will teach you the third "what" skill, which is learning to identify what you are focusing on in your moment-to-moment stream of awareness. Now that you've practiced being mindful of both your emotions and your sense experiences (seeing, hearing, touching), it's time to put the two experiences together. This exercise is similar to the Inner-Outer Experience exercise because it will also help you shift your attention back and forth in a mindful, focused way. However, this focus-shifting exercise will address the shift between your emotions and your senses and help you differentiate between the two.

At some point in our lives, we all get caught in our emotions. For example, when someone says something insulting to you, maybe you feel upset all day, think poorly of yourself, get angry at someone else, or look at the world in a much gloomier way. This "emotional trap" is a common experience for everyone. But for someone struggling with overwhelming emotions, these experiences happen more frequently and intensely. Mindfulness skills will help you separate your present-moment experience from what's happening inside you emotionally, thereby giving you a choice as to which one you'll focus on.

Before starting this exercise, you'll also need to identify how you are currently feeling. If you need to refer to the list of emotions in the previous exercise, go ahead. Do your best to be as accurate as possible about how you feel. Even if you think that you're not feeling anything, you probably are. A person is never completely without emotion. Maybe you're just feeling bored or content. Do your best to identify what it is.

Read the instructions before beginning this exercise to familiarize yourself with the experience. Then you can either keep these instructions near you if you need to refer to them while you're doing the exercise, or you can record them in a slow, even voice on your smartphone so that you can listen to them while you practice shifting your focus between your emotions and your senses.

If you need to, set a timer for five to ten minutes for this exercise.

Instructions

To begin, find a comfortable place to sit in a room where you won't be disturbed for ten minutes. Turn off any distracting sounds. Take a few slow, long breaths, and relax.

Now close your eyes and focus your attention on how you are feeling. Name the emotion silently to yourself. Use your imagination to envision what your emotion might look like if it had a shape. The image doesn't have to make sense to anyone but you. Just allow your imagination to give your emotion a form or shape. Take a minute to do this, and keep breathing slow breaths. [Pause here for one minute if you are recording the instructions.]

Now open your eyes and put your focus on an object in the room where you're sitting. Notice what the object looks like. Notice its shape and color. Imagine what that object might feel like if you could hold it. Imagine what the object must weigh. Describe the object silently to yourself, being as descriptive as possible. Take a minute to do this. Keep breathing. If your focus begins to drift, simply return your attention to the exercise without criticizing yourself. [Pause here for one minute if you are recording the instructions.]

When you've finished describing the object, close your eyes and return your focus to your emotion. Think of a sound that might be related to your emotion. The sound can be anything that you think describes your emotion. It can be a noise, a song, or whatever. When you're done describing the sound to yourself, think of an action related to your emotion. Again, it can be anything that further enhances your understanding of your emotion. Take a minute to do this, and keep breathing slow, deep breaths. [Pause here for one minute if you are recording the instructions.]

Now, keeping your eyes closed, redirect your attention to your sense of hearing. Notice any sounds that you can hear. Notice sounds you hear coming from outside your room and note to yourself what they are. Now become aware of any sounds you hear coming from inside the room and note to yourself what they are. Try to notice even small sounds, such as the ticking of a clock, the sound of the wind, or the beating of your heart. If you become distracted by any thoughts, return your focus to your sense of hearing. Take a minute to do this, and keep breathing. [Pause here for one minute if you are recording the instructions.]

When you have finished listening to the sounds that you can notice, return your focus to your emotion. Keeping your eyes closed, silently describe the intensity and quality of your emotion to yourself. Again, feel free to be creative and use comparisons if you need to. Take a minute to do this, and keep breathing slow, deep breaths. [Pause here for one minute if you are recording the instructions.]

Once again, redirect your attention. This time, put your focus on your sense of smell. Notice any smells that are in the room, pleasant or otherwise. If you don't notice any smells, just become aware of the flow of air moving into your nostrils as you breathe in through your nose. Try your best to maintain your focus on your sense of smell. If you become distracted by any thoughts, return your focus to your nose. Take a minute to do this, and keep breathing. [Pause here for one minute if you are recording the instructions.]

When you have finished using your sense of smell, once again return your focus to your emotion. Notice any thoughts you might be having that are related to your emotion. Be as specific about the thought as you can, and make sure your thought isn't really another emotion. Take a minute to do this, and keep breathing slow, deep breaths. [Pause here for one minute if you are recording the instructions.]

Now, finally, redirect your attention to your sense of touch. Reach out with one of your hands to touch an object that is within reach. Or if there is no object within reach, touch the chair you're sitting in or touch your leg. Notice what the object feels like. Notice if it's smooth or rough. Notice if it's pliable or rigid. Notice if it's soft or solid. Notice what the sensations feel like on the skin of your fingertips. If your thoughts begin to distract you, simply return your focus to the object that you're touching. Take a minute to do this, and keep breathing slow, deep breaths. [Pause here for one minute if you are recording the instructions.]

When you've finished, take three to five slow, long breaths and return your focus to the room.

Exercise: Mindful Breathing ⊠

This Mindful Breathing exercise will help you learn the fourth "what" skill, which is learning to separate your thoughts from your emotions and physical sensations. (You already learned the basics of mindful breathing in chapter 2, Advanced Distress Tolerance Skills, but this exercise will give you an additional understanding of the skill.) Very often, when you're distracted by your thoughts and other stimuli, one of the easiest and most effective things you can do is to focus your attention on the rising and falling of your breath. This type of breathing also causes you to take slower, longer breaths, which can help you relax.

In order to breathe mindfully, you need to focus on three parts of the experience. First, you must count your breaths. This will help you focus your attention, and it will also help you calm your mind when you're distracted by thoughts. Second, you need to focus on the physical experience of breathing. This is accomplished by observing the rising and falling of your chest and stomach as you inhale and exhale. And third, you need to be aware of any distracting thoughts that arise while you're breathing. Then you need to let the thoughts go without getting stuck on them, as in the previous Thought Defusion exercise. Letting go of the distracting thoughts will allow you to refocus your attention on your breathing and help you further calm yourself.

Read the instructions before beginning the exercise to familiarize yourself with the experience. If you feel more comfortable listening to the instructions, use your smartphone to record the directions in a slow, even voice so that you can listen to them while practicing this technique. When you first start this technique, set a timer for three to five minutes, and practice breathing until the alarm goes off. Then as you get more accustomed to using this technique to help you relax, you can set the alarm for longer periods of time, like ten or fifteen minutes. But don't expect to be able to sit still that long when you first start. In the beginning, three to five minutes is a long time to focus and breathe. Later, when you become more accustomed to using this style of breathing, you can also begin using it while you're doing other daily activities, like walking, doing the dishes, watching television, or having a conversation.

When using mindful breathing, many people feel as if they become "one" with their breathing, meaning that they feel a deep connection to the experience. If that happens for you, that's great. If not, that's okay too. Just keep practicing. Also, some people feel light-headed when they first begin practicing this technique. This may be caused by breathing too fast, too deeply, or too slowly. Don't be alarmed. If you begin to feel light-headed, stop if you need to, or return your breathing to a normal rate and begin counting your breaths. (For a copy of the instructions below, visit http://www.newharbinger.com/44581 and download How to Do Mindful Breathing.)

This is such a simple and powerful skill that, ideally, you should practice it every day.

Instructions

First, find a comfortable place to sit in a room where you won't be disturbed for as long as you've set your timer. Turn off any distracting sounds. If you feel comfortable closing your eyes, do so to help you relax.

To begin, take a few slow, long breaths, and relax. Place one hand on your stomach. Now slowly breathe in through your nose and then slowly exhale through your mouth. Feel your stomach rise and fall as you breathe. Imagine your belly filling up with air like a balloon as you breathe in, and then feel it effortlessly deflate as you breathe out. Feel the breath moving in across your nostrils, and then feel your breath blowing out across your lips, as if you're blowing out candles. As you breathe, notice the sensations in your body. Feel your belly move as you activate the diaphragm muscle and allow your lungs to fill up with air. Notice the weight of your body resting on whatever you're sitting on. With each breath, notice how your body feels more and more relaxed.

Now, as you continue to breathe, begin counting your breaths each time you exhale. You can count either silently to yourself or aloud. Count each exhalation until you reach 4 and then begin counting at 1 again. To begin, breathe in slowly through your nose, and then exhale slowly through your mouth. Count 1. Again, breathe in slowly through your nose and slowly out through your mouth. Count 2. Repeat, breathing in slowly through your nose, and then slowly exhale. Count 3. Last time—breathe in through your nose and out through your mouth. Count 4. Now begin counting at 1 again.

This time, though, as you continue to count, occasionally shift your focus to how you're breathing. Notice the rising and falling of your chest and abdomen as you inhale and exhale. Again, feel the breath moving in through your nose and slowly out through your mouth. If you want to, place one hand on your abdomen and feel your breath rise and fall. Continue counting as you take slow, long breaths. Feel your belly expand like a balloon as you breathe in, and then feel it deflate as you breathe out. Continue to shift your focus back and forth between counting and the physical experience of breathing.

Now, lastly, begin to notice any thoughts or other distractions that remove your focus from your breathing. These distractions might be memories, sounds, physical sensations, or emotions. When your mind begins to wander and you catch yourself thinking of something else, return your focus to counting your breath. Or return your focus to the physical sensation of breathing. Try not to criticize yourself for getting distracted. Just keep taking slow, long breaths into your belly, in and out. Imagine filling up your belly with air like a balloon. Feel it rising with each inhalation and falling with each exhalation. Keep counting each breath, and with each exhalation, feel your body relaxing, more and more deeply.

Keep breathing until your alarm goes off. Continue counting your breaths, noticing the physical sensation of your breathing and letting go of any distracting thoughts or other stimuli. Then, when your alarm goes off, slowly open your eyes and return your focus to the room.

Exercise: Mindful Awareness of Emotions

This is the second exercise that will help you learn to separate your thoughts, emotions, and physical sensations. Mindful awareness of your emotions starts with focusing on your breathing—just noticing the air moving in through your nose and out through your mouth, filling and emptying your lungs. Then, after four or five slow, long breaths, shift your attention to how you feel emotionally in the present moment. Start by simply noticing if you feel good or bad. Is your basic internal sense that you are happy or not happy?

Then see if you can observe your emotion more closely. What word best describes the feeling? Consult the list of emotions from the Describe Your Emotion exercise if you're having trouble finding the most accurate description. Keep watching the feeling, and while you do, continue describing to yourself what you observe. Notice the nuances of the feeling or perhaps the threads of other emotions woven into it. For example, sometimes sadness has veins of anxiety or even anger. Sometimes shame is intertwined with loss or resentment. Also notice the strength of your emotion and check to see how it changes while you watch it.

Emotions invariably come as a wave. They escalate, then they reach a crest, and finally they diminish. You can observe this, describing to yourself each point in the wave as the feeling grows and passes.

If you have difficulty finding an emotion that you're feeling in the present moment, you can still do this exercise by locating a feeling that you had in the recent past. Think back to a situation during the last several weeks when you had a strong emotion. Visualize the event—where you were, what was happening, what you said, how you felt. Keep recalling details of the scene until the emotion you had *then* is being felt again by you *right now*.

However you choose to observe an emotion, once the emotion is clearly recognized, stay with it. Keep describing to yourself the changes in quality, intensity, or type of emotion you are feeling.

Ideally, you should observe the feeling until it has significantly changed—in quality or strength—and you have some sense of the wave effect of your emotion. While watching your feeling, you'll also notice thoughts, sensations, and other distractions that try to pull your attention away. This is normal. Just do your best to bring your focus back to your emotion whenever your attention wanders. Just stay with it until you've watched long enough to observe your emotion grow, change, and diminish.

As you learn to mindfully observe a feeling, two important realizations can emerge. One is the awareness that all feelings have a natural life span. If you keep watching your emotions, they will peak and gradually subside. The second awareness is that the mere act of describing your feelings can give you a degree of control over them. Describing your emotions often has the effect of building a container around them, which keeps them from overwhelming you.

Read the instructions before beginning the exercise to familiarize yourself with the experience. If you feel more comfortable listening to the instructions, use your smartphone to record the directions in a slow, even voice so that you can listen to them while practicing this technique. If you record the directions, pause between each paragraph so you can leave time to fully experience the process.

Instructions

Take a long, slow breath and notice the feeling of the air moving in through your nose, going down the back of your throat, and into your lungs. Take another breath and watch what happens in your body as you inhale and let go. Keep breathing and watching. Keep noticing the sensations in your body as you breathe. [Pause here for one minute if you are recording the instructions.]

Now turn your attention to what you feel emotionally. Look inside and find the emotion you are experiencing right now. Or find an emotion that you felt recently. Notice whether the emotion is a good or a bad feeling. Notice whether it is pleasant or unpleasant. Just keep your attention on the feeling until you have a sense of it. [Pause here for one minute if you are recording the instructions.]

Now look for words to describe the emotion. For example, is it elation, contentment, or excitement? Or is it sadness, anxiety, shame, or loss? Whatever it is, keep watching and describing the emotion in your mind. Notice any change in the feeling and describe what's different. If any distractions or thoughts come to mind, do your best to let them go without getting stuck on them. Notice if your feeling is intensifying or diminishing, and describe what that's like. [Pause here for one minute if you are recording the instructions.]

Keep observing your emotion and letting go of distractions. Keep looking for words to describe the slightest change in the quality or intensity of your feeling. If other emotions begin to weave in, continue to describe them. If your emotion changes into an altogether new emotion, just keep observing it and finding the words to describe it. [Pause here for one minute if you are recording the instructions.]

Thoughts, physical sensations, and other distractions will try to grab your attention. Notice them, let them go, and return your focus to your emotion. Stay with it. Continue observing it. Keep going until you've observed your emotion change or diminish.

CONCLUSION

You've now learned some basic mindfulness skills. Hopefully, you have a better understanding of how your mind works and why these skills are important to learn. You should continue using them on a daily basis. In the next chapter, you will build on these skills and learn more advanced mindfulness skills.

CHAPTER 5

Advanced Mindfulness Skills

In the previous chapter, you learned what mindfulness is and you also learned the basic "what" skills of dialectical behavior therapy. This means that you learned to become more mindful of *what* you are focusing on by using these methods:

- Focusing more fully on the present moment

- Recognizing and focusing on your thoughts, emotions, and physical sensations

- Focusing on your moment-to-moment stream of awareness

- Separating your thoughts from your emotions and physical sensations

WHAT YOU'LL LEARN IN THIS CHAPTER

Now, in this chapter, you'll be introduced to the more advanced "how" skills of mindfulness (Linehan, 1993a). These skills will help you learn *how* to be both mindful and nonjudgmental in your daily experiences. In this chapter, you will learn five "how" skills:

1. How to use wise mind

2. How to use radical acceptance to acknowledge your daily experiences without judging them

3. How to do what's effective

4. How to create a mindfulness regimen for yourself in order to live your life in a more aware, focused way

5. How to overcome the hindrances of your mindfulness practice

As in the last chapter, it is important that you do the exercises in this chapter in the order that they're presented. Each of these exercises builds on the one before it.

WISE MIND ⊗

As stated in the last chapter, wise mind is the ability to make healthy decisions about your life. The term "wise mind" has been used previously in Buddhist mindfulness practices (Chodron, 1991). It describes a person's ability to simultaneously recognize two things. First, that he or she is suffering—from ailments, overwhelming emotions, or the results of unhealthy actions. And second, that he or she also wants to be healthy and has the potential to change. Linehan has acknowledged that Zen Buddhist practices greatly influenced the development of dialectical behavior therapy (Linehan, 1993a), so it is not surprising that dialectical behavior therapy also recognizes that a person needs to both accept their pain while simultaneously engaging in actions that help alleviate that pain. And one of the primary tools to achieving this goal in dialectical behavior therapy is also to use "wise mind," the ability to make decisions based on both your rational thoughts and your emotions (Linehan, 1993a). This might sound easy to do, but let's consider the traps that many people often fall into.

For example, Leo was a successful salesman with a new company. He had a happy family and a fairly good future ahead of himself. However, Leo frequently became upset when he couldn't close a deal, and so he often felt depressed and thought of himself as a person who would never be able to fully succeed in his life. Despite the positive feedback he received from his supervisors, Leo couldn't shake the feelings of failure that came from deals he couldn't close. As a result, a few months after starting his job, Leo quit, just like he had quit similar jobs in the past. He went on to take a new job, but similar feelings of failure followed him wherever he went, and he never felt fully satisfied with himself.

Similarly, Takeesha was a popular college professor who always received high ratings from her students and other faculty members. But after a few unsuccessful personal relationships, Takeesha felt very lonely. She eventually stopped trying to meet new people because she anticipated that those relationships would just end in failure too. As a result, she felt unworthy of anyone's love and resigned herself to spending the rest of her life living alone.

Unfortunately, both Leo and Takeesha were overcome by what dialectical behavior therapy calls "emotion mind" (Linehan, 1993a). *Emotion mind* occurs when you make judgments or decisions based solely on how you feel. But keep in mind that emotions themselves are not bad or problematic. We all need emotions to live healthy lives. (You'll learn more about the role of emotions in chapters 7 and 8.) The problems associated with emotion mind develop when your emotions *control* your life. This trap is especially dangerous for people with overwhelming emotions because emotion mind distorts your thoughts and judgments, and then these distortions make it hard to formulate healthy decisions about your life. Consider what happened to Leo and Takeesha: despite their successes, their emotions overwhelmed their lives and led them to make unhealthy decisions.

The balancing counterpart to emotion mind is "reasonable mind" (Linehan, 1993a). *Reasonable mind* is the part of your decision-making process that analyzes the facts of a situation, thinks clearly about what is happening, considers the details, and then makes rational decisions. Obviously, rational thinking helps us solve problems and make decisions every day. But again, as with emotions, too much rational thinking can also be a problem. We all know the story of the very intelligent person who didn't know how to express his or her emotions and, as a result, lived a very lonely life. So here, too, a balance is needed in order to live a fulfilling, healthy life. But for people with overwhelming emotions, balancing feelings and rational thought is often hard to do.

The solution is to use wise mind to make healthy decisions about your life. Wise mind results from using both emotion mind and reasonable mind together (Linehan, 1993a). Wise mind is a balance between feelings and rational thoughts.

Again, let's consider the examples of Leo and Takeesha. Both of them were being controlled by their emotion minds. If Leo had been making decisions with wise mind, before quitting his job he would have balanced his decision with reasonable mind. He should have reminded himself of the facts of the situation: he was already a successful salesman, and he only became upset when he couldn't close a deal. Therefore, was it reasonable that he should quit? Definitely not. What about Takeesha? She received great feedback from both her students and fellow faculty members. So was it reasonable to stop meeting new people after a few failed relationships? Definitely not. This is why using wise mind is so important.

You can develop wise mind by using the mindfulness skills you have already been practicing in chapter 4. Remember that part of what these exercises did was to help you recognize and separate your thoughts from your emotions. So you've already been using both your emotion mind and your reasonable mind. And by practicing those mindfulness skills even more, it will become easier to make healthy decisions based on a balance of what your emotions and your rational thoughts tell you.

WISE MIND AND INTUITION

According to dialectical behavior therapy, wise mind is similar to intuition (Linehan, 1993b). Often, both intuition and wise mind are described as "feelings" that come from "the gut" or the stomach area. The exercise that follows will help you get more in touch with your gut feelings, both physically and mentally. This exercise will help you locate the center of wise mind in your body. This is the spot from which many people report knowing what to do and making sensible, wise-mind decisions about their lives.

Interestingly, this phenomenon of gut feelings might be supported by scientific evidence. Researchers have discovered that a vast web of nerves covers your digestive system. This web of nerves is second in complexity only to the human brain, so some researchers have referred to this area as the *enteric brain*, meaning the brain in the stomach.

Exercise: Wise-Mind Meditation

When you begin using this technique, set a timer for three to five minutes and practice this exercise until the alarm goes off. Then, as you get more accustomed to using this technique, you can set the alarm for longer periods of time, like ten or fifteen minutes. If you feel more comfortable listening to the instructions, use your smartphone to record the directions in a slow, even voice so that you can listen to them while practicing this technique.

Instructions

To begin, find a comfortable place to sit in a room where you won't be disturbed for as long as you've set your timer. Turn off any distracting sounds. If you feel comfortable closing your eyes, do so to help you relax.

Now locate the bottom of your sternum on your rib cage. You can do this by touching the bone at the center of your chest and then following it down toward your abdomen until the bone ends. Now place one hand on your abdomen between the bottom of your sternum and your belly button. This is the center of wise mind.

Take a few slow, long breaths and relax. Now slowly breathe in through your nose and then slowly exhale through your mouth. Feel your abdomen rise and fall as you breathe. Imagine your belly filling up with air like a balloon as you breathe in, and then feel it deflate as you breathe out. Feel the breath moving in across your nostrils and then feel your breath blowing out across your lips, as if you're blowing out candles. As you breathe, notice any sensations in your body. Feel your lungs fill up with air. Notice the weight of your body as it rests on the seat in which you're sitting. With each breath, notice how your body feels, and allow your body to become more and more relaxed.

Now, as you continue to breathe, let your attention focus on the spot underneath your hand. Let your attention focus on the center of wise mind. Continue to take slow, long breaths. If you have any distracting thoughts, just allow those thoughts to leave you without fighting them and without getting stuck on them. Continue to breathe and focus on the center of wise mind. Feel your hand resting on your stomach.

As you focus your attention on your center of wise mind, notice what appears. If you've had any troubling thoughts, problems, or decisions that you have to make in your life, think about them for a few seconds. Then ask your center of wise mind what you should do about these problems or decisions. Ask your inner intuitive self for guidance, and then notice what thoughts or solutions arise out of your center of wise mind. Don't judge whatever answers you receive. Just note them to yourself and keep breathing. Continue to focus your attention on your center of wise mind. If no thoughts or answers come to your questions, just continue breathing.

Now continue to notice your breath rising and falling. Keep breathing and returning your focus to the center of wise mind until the timer goes off. Then when you've finished, slowly open your eyes and return your focus to the room.

HOW TO MAKE WISE-MIND DECISIONS

Now that you've had practice locating your wise-mind center, you can "check in" with that area of your body before you make decisions. This can help you determine whether a decision is a good one. To do this, simply think about the action you are about to take and focus your attention on your center of wise mind. Then consider what your wise mind tells you. Does your decision feel like a good one? If so, then maybe you should do it. If it doesn't feel like a good decision, then maybe you should consider some other options.

Learning to make reliably good decisions about your life is a process that evolves as long as you are alive, and there is no single way to do this. Checking in with your center of wise mind is simply *one* way that works for some people. However, some words of caution are needed here. When you first use wise mind to make decisions about your life, it will probably be difficult to tell the difference between an intuitive gut feeling and a decision made the old way with emotion mind. The difference can be determined in three ways:

1. *When you made your decision, were you being mindful of both your emotions and the facts of the situation? In other words, did you make the decision based on both emotion mind and reasonable mind?*

If you haven't considered the facts of the situation and are being controlled by your emotions, you're not using wise mind. Sometimes we need to let our emotions settle and "cool off" before we can make a good decision. If you've recently been involved in a very emotional situation, either good or bad, give yourself enough time for your hot emotions to cool down so that you can use reasonable mind.

2. *Did the decision "feel" right to you?* Before you make a decision, check in with your center of wise mind and notice how it feels. If you check in with your center of wise mind and you feel nervous, maybe the decision you're about to make isn't a good one or a safe one. However, maybe you feel nervous because you're excited about doing something new, which can be a good thing. Sometimes it's hard to tell the difference, and that's why using reasonable mind to make your decision is also important. Later, when you have more experience making healthy decisions for your life, it will be easier to tell the difference between a good nervous feeling and a bad nervous feeling.

3. *You can sometimes tell if you've used wise mind by examining the results of your decision.* If your decision leads to beneficial results for your life, chances are you used wise mind to make that decision. When you start using wise mind, keep track of your decisions and the results in order to determine whether you're *really* using wise mind. Remember, wise mind should help you make healthy decisions about your life.

(Visit http://www.newharbinger.com/44581 to download How to Make Wise-Mind Decisions.)

RADICAL ACCEPTANCE

Another very important part of wise mind, and mindfulness in general, is a skill called radical acceptance (Linehan, 1993a). (You already explored radical acceptance in chapters 1 and 2, but the following description will help you understand how it relates to mindfulness skills.) Radical acceptance means tolerating something without judging it or trying to change it. Remember the definition of mindfulness that we gave you in the last chapter? Mindfulness is the ability to be aware of your thoughts, emotions, physical sensations, and actions— in the present moment—*without judging or criticizing yourself, others, or your experience.* Radical acceptance is a very important piece of being mindful because if you're judging yourself, your experience, or someone else in the present moment, then you're not really paying attention to what's happening in that moment. In many ways, judgment is the royal road to suffering, because when you judge others, you get angry, and when you judge yourself, you get depressed. So in order to be truly mindful in the present moment, and in order to be fully centered in wise mind, you must practice being nonjudgmental.

Radical acceptance might sound like a difficult skill to master, but it's definitely worth the effort. Consider this example. Thomas struggled with a problem that's very common for people with overwhelming emotions. He divided everyone and everything into two categories: they were either all good or all bad. There was no in-between for him. When people treated him nicely, they were good, but when someone disagreed with him, he considered them to be bad, even if the person had just been on his good side a few minutes before. This quick fluctuation between good and bad led Thomas to make a lot of judgments and critical remarks about himself and others. Over the years, the accumulation of fluctuations and judgments made Thomas very sensitive to situations that could go wrong. He always expected that other people would make mistakes, insult him, or betray him in some way. One time his sister said that she couldn't help him take his car to the repair shop, and Thomas blew up at her. He criticized her for being ungrateful and selfish. However, the truth was that she had to take her own daughter to the doctor, but Thomas never heard her reasoning. He was too wrapped up in his own judgmental thinking to really listen to anyone else. In truth, Thomas had created a pattern in his life where all of his judgments and critical thinking became realities, and this led to a very lonely and distressing life.

When Thomas was finally introduced to the skill of radical acceptance, he was critical of it too. "This is ridiculous," he thought, "This stupid idea isn't going to help me. I don't need this. How can anyone not be critical?" But with the urging of his family, Thomas decided to try using radical acceptance. At first, it was very difficult for him to not make judgments about himself and other people, but he continued using the exercises in this workbook, and, with practice, radical acceptance became easier. Slowly, his thinking began to change. Thomas spent less time obsessing over judgmental thoughts and critical remarks, and he spent less time anticipating that other people would insult or betray him. He also no longer thought of people as either just good or bad. He began to recognize that everyone makes mistakes, and that's okay. He also became more mindful of his thoughts, feelings, sensations, and actions in the present moment, which helped him focus better on his daily experiences and make healthier choices for his life.

As you can see from this example, one of the hardest parts of using radical acceptance is recognizing when you're being judgmental of yourself or others. This takes practice, and the skills in the workbook will help. But recognizing when you're being judgmental also takes time. You're going to make mistakes. When you're first learning to be nonjudgmental, there will be times when you *will* be judgmental. Then you'll recognize what you're doing, and you'll be more critical of yourself for being judgmental. But that's okay too. That's part of the learning process. Learning how to use radical acceptance is a lot like the story of a man who's walking down a city street and falls through an open manhole to the sewer. He climbs out, looks in the hole, and says, "I better not do that again." But the next day, walking down the same street, he steps into the same open manhole, climbs out, and says, "I can't believe I did it again." Then on the third day, he's about to step into the same open manhole when he suddenly remembers what happened on the two previous days, so he avoids the fall. On the fourth day, the man remembers to walk around the open manhole as soon as he starts walking down that street. And on the fifth day, he chooses to walk down a different street in order to avoid the problem completely. Obviously, learning how to use radical acceptance will take you longer than five days, but the process of falling into the same judgmental traps will happen in a very similar way.

Below are several exercises to help you develop a nonjudgmental attitude and to use the skill of radical acceptance. But before you start, let's clarify radical acceptance a little more, because it can often be a confusing concept for many people. To use radical acceptance *does not* mean that you silently put up with potentially harmful or dangerous situations in your life. For example, if you are in a violent or abusive relationship and you need to get out, then get out. Don't put yourself in harm's way and simply tolerate whatever happens to you. Radical acceptance is a skill that is supposed to help you live a healthier life; it is not a tool to fill your life with more suffering.

However, there's no doubt that it will be tough to start using radical acceptance because it will require you to think about yourself, your life, and other people in a new way. But once you start using radical acceptance, you'll find that it actually gives you more freedom. You'll no longer spend as much time judging yourself and others, and so you'll be free to do many other things instead. Radical acceptance is one of the most important tools to learn in dialectical behavior therapy, and it's definitely worth the effort.

Exercise: Negative Judgments ☒

The first step to changing a problem is to recognize when that problem occurs. So to begin changing your judgmental thinking, the first step is to recognize when you're being judgmental and critical. Use the following Negative Judgments Record for the next week. Do your best to keep track of all the negative judgments and criticisms that you make. This includes those you make about things you read in the newspaper or see on television, judgments you make about yourself and other people, and so on. Make photocopies of the Negative Judgments Record if you need to (or visit http://newharbinger.com/44581 to download it), and keep one folded in your pocket so that you can record your judgments as soon as you recognize that you're making them. If you decide that you're only going to write down your negative judgments once a day, such as before you go to sleep, the process of learning radical acceptance will take longer. At the end of the day, you might forget many of the negative judgments that you've made.

In order to remind yourself to write down your negative judgments, it might help to give yourself visual reminders. Some people have found that wearing something special to remind them, like a new ring or a bracelet, prods them to remember and write down their judgments. Other people put up sticky notes around their home and office with the word "judgments" written on them. Do whatever works best for you. Do this exercise for at least one week, or until you recognize that you're starting to catch yourself in the moment when you're making negative judgments. Keep track of *when* you made the judgment, *where* you were, and *what* the negative judgment was. Use the following example to help you.

(NOTE: *When you have completed a Negative Judgments Record, keep it to use in the Judgment Defusion exercise later in this chapter.*)

Example: Negative Judgments Record

When?	Where?	What?
Sunday, 2 p.m.	Home	I thought, "I hate Sundays; they're always so boring."
Sunday, 6:30 p.m.	Home	I told my girlfriend I didn't like the shirt she was wearing.
Monday, 8:30 a.m.	In the car pool on the way to work	I thought about how much I hate the people on the road who always drive like idiots.
Monday, 11 a.m.	Work	I thought about how stupid my coworkers are for asking me the same questions every day.
Monday, 12:30 p.m.	Work	I thought about how much I hate my boss for buying me a computer that's not fast enough to do my work.
Monday, 1:45 p.m.	Work	I got mad at myself for making a mistake and called myself an "idiot."
Monday, 2:30 p.m.	Work	I got mad at the president after reading about his views on foreign policy in the newspaper.
Monday, 4:15 p.m.	Work	I thought about the ugly color they painted the room I'm sitting in.
Monday, 5:15 p.m.	In the car pool on the way home	I told Sandra she was being rude for keeping her car radio turned up too loud.
Monday, 11:30 p.m.	Home	I got upset with myself for staying up so late and not getting enough sleep.

Negative Judgments Record

When?	Where?	What?

RADICAL ACCEPTANCE AND BEGINNER'S MIND ⊠

Now that you've recognized many of your negative judgments, you're closer to using full radical acceptance. Remember, radical acceptance means that you observe situations in your life without judging or criticizing yourself or others. In the previous exercise, you focused on recognizing your *negative* judgments because they are usually the easiest ones to spot. But positive judgments can also be problematic.

Remember the example of Thomas we recently gave you? He divided everyone into two categories: either all good or all bad. He liked people when they were good, but when they did something to upset him, he got angry and labeled them "bad." So do you see how making even positive judgments about people or things can be problematic? When you think of someone (or something) with a rigid and predetermined idea of how that person is going to treat you, then it's easy to become disappointed, because no one (and nothing) is perfect. Presidents sometimes lie, religious people sometimes gamble, things that we like sometimes break, and people we trust sometimes hurt us. As a result, when you put someone into a category of being 100 percent good, trustworthy, saintly, wholesome, or honest, it's very easy to get disappointed.

But this doesn't mean that you should never trust anyone. What radical acceptance says is that you should approach people and situations in your life without judging them to be good or bad, positive or negative. In some forms of meditation, this is called *beginner's mind* (Suzuki, 1970). This means that you should enter every situation and every relationship as if you were seeing it for the very first time. This reoccurring newness prevents you from bringing any old judgments (good or bad) into the present moment, which allows you to stay more mindful. Plus, by keeping the situation fresh, it also helps you stay in better control of your emotions. As a result, it's easy to see why one of the goals of dialectical behavior therapy is to help you stop making any judgments at all, either positive or negative (Linehan, 1993b).

Exercise: Beginner's Mind

In the following exercise, you'll practice using radical acceptance and beginner's mind. This exercise is similar to the last one, but now you will need to be aware of both the positive and the negative judgments that you make. Again, if you need to use visual reminders to help you remember to write down your judgments, use whatever works for you: a bracelet, a ring, a sticky note with the word "judgment" on it, a reminder on your smartphone, and so on.

Do this exercise for at least one week or until you recognize that you're starting to catch yourself in the moments when you're making both positive and negative judgments. Keep track of *when* you made the judgment, *where* you were, and *what* the positive or negative judgment was. As with the last exercise, make photocopies of the Beginner's Mind Record if you need to (or visit http://newharbinger.com/44581 to download it), and keep one folded in your pocket so that you can record your judgments as soon as you recognize that you're making them. The more quickly you record them after they occur, the sooner radical acceptance will become a regular part of your life. Use the example of the Beginner's Mind Record on the following page to help you. The blank Beginner's Mind Record for your use is on the page after that. (*NOTE: When you have completed a Beginner's Mind Record, keep it to use in the Judgment Defusion exercise later in this chapter.*)

Example: Beginner's Mind Record

When?	Where?	What?
Friday, 12 p.m.	Lunch with Laura	I thought, "Laura is an incredibly talented person who never makes any mistakes."
Friday, 2:30 p.m.	Work	I called myself "incompetent," because I'm not going to be able to finish all my paperwork before five o'clock.
Friday, 2:45 p.m.	Work	After talking with my mother on the phone, I thought about what a lousy job she did raising me.
Friday, 5:30 p.m.	At the bar, after work	I was thinking that the bartender looked really nice and was probably the type of person who would make a really good husband.
Friday, 7:30 p.m.	Home	At first I told my boyfriend that he was sweet for making dinner, but when he put too much salt on my food, I told him he was an idiot.
Saturday, 2:30 p.m.	Shopping mall	I found the "perfect" pair of jeans that are going to make me look fantastic.
Saturday, 3:00 p.m.	Shopping mall	I was thinking about how ugly one of the guys in the store looked.
Saturday, 4:15 p.m.	Home	I got upset and called myself an idiot when I realized that the jeans didn't fit.
Saturday, 9 p.m.	Home	I got mad at my boyfriend for not helping me get all my chores completed today.
Saturday, 10:30 p.m.	Home	I was thinking about what a perfect day tomorrow is going to be.

Beginner's Mind Record

When?	Where?	What?

JUDGMENTS AND LABELS

Hopefully, after the last exercise, it's easy to see how putting labels on people, thoughts, and objects—making them either good or bad—can later lead to disappointment. In order to move closer to using radical acceptance, the next exercise will continue to help you monitor the judgments that you make, and then it will help you let go of those judgments.

So far in this chapter, you've already recognized many of the problems associated with making judgments:

- Judgments can trigger overwhelming emotions.

- Judgments can often lead to disappointment and suffering.

- Judgments prevent you from being truly mindful in the present moment.

Obviously, one of the problems with judgments and criticisms is that they occupy your thoughts. In many cases, it can become very easy to start obsessing on a single judgment. Perhaps you've even had the experience of a single judgment occupying your thoughts all day. Maybe it was something bad about yourself or someone else. Or maybe it was something good about yourself or someone else. We've all had this experience. So when your thoughts are occupied by something that happened in the past or by something that might happen in the future, how mindful are you being about the present moment? Probably you're not being very mindful. And when those obsessive thoughts are judgments about yourself or someone else, how easy is it for your emotions to get triggered? Probably it's very easy, especially if you struggle with overwhelming emotions.

Exercise: Judgment Defusion

This Judgment Defusion exercise is designed to help you release or "let go" of your judgments and other obsessive thoughts. In the last chapter, you practiced using the thought defusion technique as a basic mindfulness exercise. This exercise is very similar. Again, the object is to watch your judgments arise and then to let go of them without getting stuck on them.

Like thought defusion, judgment defusion also requires the use of your imagination. The object of this exercise is to visualize your judgments, either as pictures or words, harmlessly floating away from you without obsessing about them or analyzing them. Whichever way you choose to do this is okay. If you used a technique in the last chapter that worked, use it again here. If you need a different visualization technique, here are just a few suggestions that other people have found helpful:

- Imagine sitting in a field watching your judgments float away on clouds.

- Picture yourself sitting beside a stream watching your judgments float past on leaves.

- Picture yourself standing in a room with two doors, then watch your judgments enter through one door and leave through the other.

If one of these ideas works for you, that's great. If not, feel free to create your own. Just make sure that your idea captures the purpose of this exercise, which is to visually watch your judgments come and go without holding on to them and without analyzing them.

Before you begin this exercise, review the records you filled out for the Negative Judgments exercise and the Beginner's Mind exercise, in order to refamiliarize yourself with some of the judgments you've made over the last few weeks. You can even keep these records near you so you can refer to them if you have trouble remembering any of your recent judgments. During the exercise, you will close your eyes and imagine whichever visualization technique you've chosen. Then you'll watch your past judgments (and any new judgments) come into your thoughts and float away, without you getting stuck on them.

Read the instructions before beginning the exercise to familiarize yourself with the experience. If you feel more comfortable listening to the instructions, use your smartphone to record the instructions in a slow, even voice so you can listen to them while practicing this technique. When you are first using judgment defusion, set a timer for three to five minutes and practice letting go of your judgments until the alarm goes off. Then, as you get more accustomed to using this technique, you can set the alarm for longer periods of time, like eight to ten minutes. (For a copy of the instructions below, visit http://www.newharbinger.com/44581 and download How to Do Judgment Defusion.)

Instructions

To begin, find a comfortable place to sit in a room where you won't be disturbed for as long as you've set your timer. Turn off any distracting sounds. Take a few slow, long breaths, relax, and close your eyes.

Now, in your imagination, picture yourself in the scenario that you chose in order to watch your judgments come and go, whether it's by a stream, in a field, in a room, or somewhere else. Do your best to imagine yourself in that scene. After you do, start to become aware of the judgments that you're having, just like in the last exercises in which you wrote down your judgments. Start to observe the judgments that are coming up, whatever they are. Don't try to stop your thoughts, and do your best not to criticize yourself for any of the judgments. Just watch the judgments arise, and then, using whatever technique you've chosen, watch the judgments disappear. If you need to refer to any of the records from the past exercises to remind yourself of recent judgments, feel free to do that. But then close your eyes and watch those judgments float away.

Whatever the judgment is, big or small, important or unimportant, watch the judgment arise in your mind and then let it float away or disappear by whichever means you've chosen. Just continue to watch the judgments arise and disappear. Use pictures or words, whatever works best for you, to represent the judgments. Do your best to watch the judgments arise and disappear without getting hooked into them and without criticizing yourself. If more than one judgment comes up at the same time, see them both arise and disappear. If the judgments come very quickly, do your best to watch them all disappear without getting hooked on any of them. Continue to breathe and watch the judgments come and go until your timer goes off.

When you've finished, take a few more slow, long breaths, and then slowly open your eyes and return your focus to the room.

NONJUDGMENT AND YOUR DAILY EXPERIENCES

The purpose of the previous exercise is to help you let go of your judgments, and the more you practice it, the easier it will get. Then, after you've been practicing it regularly for at least a few weeks, it will become easy for you to let go of your judgments in the present moment. Hopefully, there will come a day, very soon, when a judgment will arise in your thoughts, either positive or negative, and you'll simply let it go. Maybe you'll need to close your eyes for a few seconds, if you're in a place where that's safe, and visualize the thought floating away. Or maybe you'll be in a conversation with someone when a judgment arises in your thoughts, and you'll simply be able to let it go. That is when you truly will be using radical acceptance.

Exercise: Judgments versus the Present Moment

Now that you've practiced being mindful of your thoughts, feelings, and senses in the previous chapter, and you've practiced being mindful of your judgments in this chapter, the next step is to combine the two experiences. In this exercise, you will learn to shift your attention back and forth in a mindful, focused way between your judgments and your physical sensations.

When you spend a lot of time obsessing over your thoughts and judgments, it's easy to get lost in your own fantasies about how the world *should* be. But again, these fantasies often lead to disappointment and suffering. As you continue to practice your mindfulness skills in your life, it will continue to be important to recognize and separate your judgments and fantasies from what's really happening in the moment. One of the easiest ways to do this is to become mindful of your physical senses—what you notice using your eyes, ears, nose, and senses of touch and taste. Often, people refer to this as *grounding* themselves. Grounding yourself in your physical sensations can stop you from obsessing over your judgments, and by doing so, it will also help you become more mindful of what's happening in the present moment.

Read the following instructions before beginning the exercise to familiarize yourself with the experience. Then you can either keep these instructions near you if you need to refer to them while you're doing the exercise, or you can record them in a slow, even voice on your smartphone so that you can listen to them while you practice shifting your focus between your judgments and your present-moment awareness.

Instructions

To begin, find a comfortable place to sit in a room where you won't be disturbed for ten minutes. Turn off any distracting sounds. Take a few slow, long breaths, close your eyes, and relax.

Now, keeping your eyes closed, focus your attention on the weight of your body as it rests on the seat in which you're sitting. Notice the weight of your feet and legs resting on the ground. Notice the weight of your hands and arms resting. Notice the weight of your head resting on top of your neck. Mentally scan your body from head to toe and notice any sensations that you feel. Take your time. [Pause here for one minute if you are recording the instructions.]

Now notice any tension you might be feeling anywhere in your body, and imagine the tension melting away like wax in the hot sun. Again, take your time to scan your body for any tension, and keep taking slow, deep breaths. [Pause here for one minute if you are recording the instructions.]

When you are finished scanning your body, move your focus to your thoughts and judgments. Just notice any thoughts or judgments that arise in your mind, and when they do, allow them to float away by whichever means you found successful in the last exercises. Allow the thoughts and judgments to leave you without getting stuck on them. Take a minute to do this, and keep breathing slow, long breaths. [Pause here for one minute if you are recording the instructions.]

Now redirect your attention to your sense of hearing. Notice any sounds that you can hear coming from outside your room, and note to yourself what they are. Now become aware of any sounds you hear coming from inside the room, and note to yourself what they are. Try to notice even small sounds, such as the ticking of a clock, the sound of the wind, or the beating of your heart. If you become distracted by any thoughts, return your focus to your sense of hearing. Take a minute to do this, and keep breathing. [Pause here for one minute if you are recording the instructions.]

When you are finished noticing any sounds, once again redirect your focus to your thoughts and judgments. Notice any thoughts or judgments that arise in your mind, and when they do, allow them to float away by whichever means you found successful in the last exercises. Allow the thoughts and judgments to leave you without getting stuck on them. Take a minute to do this, and keep breathing slow, deep breaths. [Pause here for one minute if you are recording the instructions.]

Now, once again, redirect your attention. This time, put your focus on your sense of smell. Notice any smells that are in the room, pleasant or otherwise. If you don't notice any smells, just become aware of the flow of air moving into your nostrils as you breathe in through your nose. Try your best to maintain your focus on your sense of smell. If you become distracted by any thoughts, return your focus to your nose. Take a minute to do this, and keep breathing slow, deep breaths. [Pause here for one minute if you are recording the instructions.]

When you are finished noticing any smells, once again redirect your focus to your thoughts and judgments. Notice any thoughts or judgments that arise in your mind, and when they do, allow them to float away by whichever means you found successful in the last exercises. Allow the thoughts and judgments to leave you without getting stuck on them. Take a minute to do this, and keep breathing slow, long breaths. [Pause here for one minute if you are recording the instructions.]

Now redirect your attention to your sense of touch. Notice the sensation of whatever your hands are resting on. Or, keeping your eyes closed, reach out with one of your hands to touch an object that is within reach. Or, if there is no object within reach, touch the chair you're sitting in or touch your leg. Notice what the object feels like. Notice if it's smooth or rough. Notice if it's pliable or rigid. Notice if it's soft or solid. Notice what the sensations feel like on the skin of your fingertips. If your thoughts begin to distract you, simply return your focus to the object that you're touching. Take a minute to do this, and keep breathing slow, long breaths. [Pause here for one minute if you are recording the instructions.]

When you are finished noticing any touch sensations, once again redirect your focus to your thoughts and judgments. Notice any thoughts or judgments that arise in your mind, and when they do, allow them to float away by whichever means you found successful in the last exercises. Allow the thoughts and judgments to leave you without getting stuck on them. Take a minute to do this, and keep breathing slow, long breaths. [Pause here for one minute if you are recording the instructions.]

Now, slowly, open your eyes. Keep breathing slow, deep breaths. Take a few minutes to focus your visual attention on the room you're sitting in. Notice the objects that are in the room. Notice how light or dark the room is. Notice the different colors that are in the room. Notice where you are in the room. Move your head to look around. Take in all the visual information that you can. If your thoughts begin to distract you, simply return your focus to the room you're looking at. Take a minute to do this, and keep breathing slow, long breaths. [Pause here for one minute if you are recording the instructions.]

When you have finished noticing any visual sensations, once again redirect your focus to your thoughts and judgments. But this time, keep your eyes open. Pick a few objects in the room to focus on. But in your mind, continue to notice any thoughts and judgments that arise, and when they do, allow them to float away. Allow the thoughts and judgments to leave you without getting stuck on them. If you need to close your eyes to do this, that's okay. But open your eyes once the thoughts have floated away, and return your focus to the room you're in. Continue to monitor your thoughts and judgments and continue to let them go without getting stuck on them. Take a minute to do this, and keep breathing slow, long breaths. [Pause here for one minute if you are recording the instructions.]

When you've finished, if you still have time left, continue to switch your focus between your thoughts and judgments and what you notice visually. Then, when your timer goes off, take three to five slow, long breaths and return your focus to the room.

SELF-COMPASSION ⊠

To "have compassion" for someone means to recognize that the person is in pain and needs help. Similarly, when we "show compassion" for someone else, we treat them kindly and don't judge them for their situation or feelings—regardless of whose fault it is. Yet, for so many of us human beings, it's often easier to help and forgive others—even complete strangers—rather than to be kind to ourselves. So why is it so much easier to be compassionate toward others and more difficult to be compassionate toward yourself?

- Maybe you think that other people are more deserving of help and respect than you are.

- Maybe you think you've done so many things wrong that no one can forgive you and you don't deserve to be treated compassionately.

- Maybe you're afraid of acknowledging that you are in pain because you're afraid of being overwhelmed by it.

- Maybe you think that forgiving yourself is the same as excusing your behavior and avoiding consequences.

- Or maybe no one has ever treated you compassionately in the past, so you think there's something wrong with you.

In fact, none of these statements is true. Imagine if one of your most beloved friends or family members came to you and said, "I don't deserve compassion because I [fill in one of the statements above]." You would likely disagree with them and try to convince them otherwise. Similarly, now is the time to start practicing compassion for yourself, and to acknowledge that you deserve kindness and help just like everyone else. (If you already believe this, skip to the self-compassion meditation below to strengthen your belief; otherwise, keep reading.)

Regardless of the beliefs that are keeping you stuck, being compassionate with yourself is one of the most important skills you can learn in this workbook. You need self-compassion in order to make any lasting improvements in your life. Every type of self-help work—whether it's getting help from a therapist or using this workbook—starts with self-compassion. Self-compassion is a belief that you are *deserving* of kindness, forgiveness, and help—just like everyone else!

The truth is that we all make mistakes in our lives, and some of those mistakes unfortunately hurt ourselves or others. However, it doesn't help to keep punishing yourself for the mistakes you've made; that only makes the situation worse. In many ways, self-compassion requires the use of radical acceptance. Remember, radical acceptance is the skill of letting go of judgments and acknowledging what is actually occurring in your life due to a long chain of events. Self-compassion requires the same thing. It's time to acknowledge that you are the person you are, with a history of unchangeable events, *and* you still deserve peace, safety, health, and happiness. Starting right now, you can radically accept who you are with all of your past mistakes *and* start making healthier, values-based decisions in your life because you deserve happiness and forgiveness, just like everybody else!

There's also one more important reason why you deserve compassion. That's because you have experienced great pain in your life. You have had losses. You have likely experienced rejection or abandonment at some point. You have faced physical pain and illness. And you have likely experienced disappointment when something you desperately wanted didn't happen. It's likely that you also suffered similar hurts and losses in childhood, and memories of those experiences may still even cast shadows on your life. Plus, you have likely suffered with feelings of shame, sadness, and fear—and these same painful feelings continue to show up in your life now. You deserve compassion because you've had to face your share of pain and struggle. Wouldn't you feel compassion for another human being who's suffered like this—even a stranger? So, shouldn't you extend the same amount of compassion to yourself?

Use the meditation below to develop and reinforce your sense of self-compassion. Practice it regularly and throughout the day look for opportunities to express compassion toward yourself, like forgiving yourself, making healthy decisions, and doing nice things for yourself.

Exercise: Self-Compassion Meditation ⊠

Use the self-compassion meditation below to develop and strengthen your ability to show kindness and acceptance toward yourself (adapted from McKay & Wood, 2019). To begin, use mindful breathing to help yourself relax and focus. Read the instructions before beginning the exercise to familiarize yourself with the experience. If you feel more comfortable listening to the instructions, use your smartphone to record the directions in a slow, even voice so that you can listen to them while practicing this technique.

Instructions

Find a comfortable place to sit in a room where you won't be disturbed. Turn off any distracting sounds. If you feel comfortable closing your eyes, do so to help you relax.

To begin, take a few slow, long breaths, and relax. Place one hand on your stomach. Now slowly breathe in through your nose and then slowly exhale through your mouth. Feel your stomach rise and fall as you breathe. Imagine your belly filling up with air like a balloon as you breathe in, and then feel it deflate as you breathe out. Feel the breath moving in across your nostrils, and then feel your breath blowing out across your lips. As you breathe, notice the sensations in your body. Feel your lungs fill up with air. Notice the weight of your body resting on whatever you're sitting on. With each breath, notice how your body feels more and more relaxed. [Pause here for thirty seconds if you are recording the instructions.]

Now, as you continue to breathe, begin counting your breaths each time you exhale. You can count either silently to yourself or aloud. Count each exhalation until you reach 4 and then begin counting at 1 again. To begin, breathe in slowly through your nose, and then exhale slowly through your mouth. Count 1. Again, breathe in slowly through your nose and slowly out through your mouth. Count 2. Repeat, breathing in slowly through your nose, and then slowly exhale. Count 3. Last time—breathe in through your nose and out through your mouth. Count 4. Now begin counting at 1 again. [Pause here for thirty seconds if you are recording the instructions.]

Now bring your awareness inside your own body, noting the world of sensation there at this very moment. You live in this body—allow yourself to be aware of your breath, your life force. As you hold that awareness, slowly repeat the following phrases (either silently or aloud) on each exhalation of your breath:

"May I be peaceful."

"May I be safe."

"May I be healthy."

"May I be happy and free from suffering."

Now repeat the phrases two or three more times, allowing their meaning to deepen each time. Allow yourself to feel and accept your own sense of compassion. [Repeat the phrases two or three more times if you are recording the instructions.]

Finally, when you are done, take a few additional slow breaths, rest quietly, and savor your own sense of goodwill and compassion.

MINDFUL COMMUNICATION WITH OTHERS ⊠

As you continue to practice mindfulness skills by yourself, it's also very important that you begin to incorporate these skills into your interactions with others. Mindful communication is often the key to a successful relationship. If you're constantly making judgmental statements to someone, the chances are good that you'll lose that relationship. In the chapters on interpersonal effectiveness skills, you will learn how to ask others for what you need in a healthy way. But for now, let's look at how to be more mindful of the messages you send to other people.

Consider the following statements:

- "You make me mad."

- "You're such a jerk, I could scream."

- "Sometimes you make me so upset I just want to end it all."

- "I know that you did that to me on purpose just to hurt me."

What do all of these statements have in common? It's true that they all express some kind of emotion, such as anger, distress, and sadness. But more importantly, they're all judgments of the other person. Each of the statements blames the other person for the way the speaker feels. Now consider how you would feel if someone said one of these statements to you. What would you do? Maybe you would say something just as angry back to the person, which would lead to a big fight. The result would be that nothing gets resolved. Or maybe you would just shut down emotionally, stop listening, or walk away. Again, nothing would get resolved. Judgmental statements like these stop any form of effective communication. So what can you do instead?

One of the solutions is to turn "you" statements into mindful "I" statements.

- Mindful "I" statements are based on your own mindful awareness of how you feel.

- Mindful "I" statements are a more accurate description of how you feel.

- Mindful "I" statements let a person know how you feel in a nonjudgmental way.

- Mindful "I" statements evoke greater empathy and understanding from the other person, which allows the person to meet your needs.

Let's look at the four previous examples and turn them from "you" statements into mindful "I" statements.

Instead of saying, "You make me mad," say, "Right now, I feel very mad." Doesn't that sound less judgmental and blaming? If someone said the alternative statement to you ("I feel very mad"), wouldn't you be more willing to discuss the situation? Wouldn't you feel less angry?

Look at the second sentence. Instead of saying, "You're such a jerk, I could scream," say, "I feel so angry right now I could scream." Do you hear the difference it makes to change a "you" statement into an "I" statement? The other person no longer feels blamed and will be more willing to listen.

Let's look at the third sentence. Instead of saying, "Sometimes you make me so upset I just want to end it all," say, "I feel so upset and hopeless sometimes that I get very depressed."

And finally, look at the last sentence. Instead of saying, "I know that you did that to me on purpose just to hurt me," say, "I felt very hurt when you did that."

Again, mindful "I" statements are more accurate about how you feel, they are less judgmental, the other person will probably be more willing and able to listen to you if you use them, and, most importantly, you are more likely to get your needs met if you use them.

Exercise: Mindful "I" Statements

Now let's look at some more judgmental "you" statements and have you practice turning them into mindful "I" statements. Write your alternative mindful "I" statement in the space below the judgmental statement.

1. "You make me feel horrible."

    _____

2. "I know you're doing this on purpose to make me go crazy."

    _____

3. "Why do you keep making me feel so angry?"

    _____

4. "You're being insulting."

    _____

5. "Stop fooling around; you're getting on my nerves."

    _____

6. "If you don't listen to what I'm telling you, I'm not going to talk to you anymore."

    _____

7. "You're being a jerk, stop it."

    _____

8. "You're such a @%&!*#!, I can't believe it."

    _____

9. "Why do you keep doing that to me?"

    _____

10. "Sometimes I feel like you're being too inflexible."

    _____

How did you do? Did it get harder to think of mindful "I" statements as the exercise progressed? Some of the later sentences probably required extra thinking. Let's look at some possible answers.

The first sentence was easy. The message is that the speaker feels horrible. So an alternative mindful "I" statement could be "I feel horrible" or "I feel horrible sometimes, when you (say that, do that, and so on)."

In the second sentence, the speaker feels crazy, anxious, or upset. So an alternative mindful "I" statement could be "I feel crazy/anxious/upset when you do that."

In the third sentence, the speaker feels angry. So an alternative mindful "I" statement could be "I feel angry right now."

In the fourth sentence, the speaker feels insulted or foolish. So an alternative mindful "I" statement could be "I feel like an idiot when you do that."

In the fifth sentence, the speaker feels anxious, tired, or angry. So an alternative mindful "I" statement could be "I feel anxious/tired/angry when you tease me like that."

In the sixth sentence, the speaker feels insulted, unheard, and ignored. But he or she also probably feels upset about being ignored. So an alternative mindful "I" statement could be "I feel upset when you ignore me."

In the seventh sentence, the speaker might feel many things. Usually, when you ask someone to stop doing something, it's because the action hurts. So maybe the speaker feels hurt, and an alternative mindful "I" statement could be "I feel hurt when you do that."

The eighth sentence is trickier. The speaker calls the other person some insulting expletive. This also usually indicates that the speaker's feelings have been hurt. So an alternative mindful "I" statement could be similar to the last sentence: "I feel very hurt when you do that."

The ninth sentence is phrased as a question, but it's really a statement about how the speaker feels. Again, the implication is that the speaker feels hurt, insulted, belittled, or something similar. So an alternative mindful "I" statement could be any version of these: "I feel very hurt (or insulted, or whatever) when you do that to me."

And lastly, the tenth sentence is the trickiest because the speaker uses the word "feel." Maybe you were tricked into thinking that this sentence didn't need to be changed. But this sentence is really a hidden judgment about the other person. What the speaker really means is "I *think* you're too inflexible." But people often exchange the word "think" for "feel" in order to hide their criticism or make their judgment sound less harsh. However, now you know better, so don't fall into the same trap. In this case, something about the other person's inflexible actions make the speaker feel uncomfortable or trapped. Maybe the other person never considers other points of view before he or she makes decisions. So an alternative mindful "I" statement could be "I feel uncomfortable when you don't consider my point of view."

Mindful "I" statements are clearly a more effective way of communicating how you feel and what you need, but they depend on your mindful awareness of your own feelings. Hopefully, after practicing the exercises in the last two chapters, you've become more skilled at recognizing your own emotions and you can start using mindful "I" statements to let others know how you feel.

DOING WHAT'S EFFECTIVE ⊠

Using successful communication skills, such as mindful "I" statements, is a part of what dialectical behavior therapy calls "doing what's effective" (Linehan, 1993b). This means that you do what's appropriate and necessary in the present moment—to resolve a problem, cope with a situation, or reach your goal—even if what you do feels unnatural, uncomfortable, or goes against what you are experiencing emotionally. For example, you're probably not comfortable making statements like the ones you made in the last exercise, where you speak directly to the other person about how you feel. But sometimes in order to get what you want, you have to modify what you feel like doing, especially if you struggle with overwhelming emotions. Here are some other examples of doing what's effective:

- You're in the grocery store shopping for your weekly supply of food, but, unfortunately, so are many other people. After shopping for an hour and waiting in line for fifteen minutes, you feel exhausted. You're so tired and annoyed that you think about leaving your shopping cart and just walking out. But if you did walk out, then you'd be without groceries for a week or you'd just have to start all over again at some other supermarket. So you stay in line and just get it over with.

- You're driving down the freeway and the car in front of you is driving below the speed limit in the left-hand lane. You feel so angry that you think about smashing into the car to push it out of the way. But if you did, you and the other driver would be seriously injured, and chances are you'd also get arrested. So you patiently wait for a chance to pass the driver, or you wait for your exit and then get off the freeway.

- You and your romantic partner get into a big argument. Both of you are yelling. You feel so hurt and upset that you think about walking out the door and ending the relationship. But in the back of your mind, you also recognize that this is the best relationship you've had in a long time, and you wish that it would work out. So, instead of leaving, you take a deep breath and use mindful "I" statements to let your partner know how you're feeling.

- Your boss gives you a new task even though you're already burdened with more work than you have time for. You feel insulted, angry, and taken advantage of. You're so mad that you think about screaming at your boss, telling him off, quitting, and walking out the door. But if you did, then you'd be without a paycheck for a long time. So you decide to bite your tongue for now until you can speak to your boss more calmly at some point in the near future, and you do the best you can.

- You ask your friend to take you shopping because she has a car and you don't. But your friend says she can't because she's busy doing something else. You feel annoyed and angry because you help her all the time when she asks you. You want to yell at her and tell her what a lousy friend she is. But if you did, you might lose her friendship completely. So instead of yelling, you call a different friend to ask for a ride.

As you can see, doing what's effective sometimes means *not* doing what you feel like doing or *not* doing what you've been habitually doing for many years. This is why mindfulness is such an important part of doing what's effective. If you're going to change the way you behave in the present moment, you have to be aware of what you're thinking, feeling, and doing in the present moment so that you can choose to do what's effective.

Doing what's effective also depends on not making judgments. You already know that making both positive and negative judgments can lead to disappointment and suffering. But making judgments about situations and your actions can also prevent you from doing what's effective. Here's an example: Judith had a math teacher who assigned homework that Judith thought was too hard. "This is ridiculous," she thought to herself. "How unfair of him to give us these assignments. This is wrong; he shouldn't be allowed to do this. I'm not going to do the homework." So she didn't. But as a result, she failed the class. Judith's judgments about what was "right" and "wrong" prevented her from doing what was effective. Clearly, it would have been more beneficial to her if she had remained mindful of her thoughts and feelings, avoided judging the assignments, and just done the best that she could.

Doing what's effective *is* doing what is necessary in a given situation in order to get a resolution to a problem. Doing what's effective *isn't* "selling out," "giving up," or "caving in."

Doing what's effective is a skill, just like acting. Sometimes in order to get what you want, you have to behave in a certain way. Sometimes you have to act as if you are competent, skilled, or satisfied in order to reach your goal, even if you don't feel that way. And that's what effective actions are designed to do—to help you reach your goals. In the example above, Judith's goal was to get a satisfactory grade in her math class. But she allowed her judgments and feelings to prevent her from reaching that goal.

Remember, in order to do what's effective, you have to do the following:

- Be mindful of your thoughts and feelings.

- Avoid judging the situation or your actions.

- Choose actions that are appropriate and necessary to reach your goal.

- Do the best you can.

BEING MINDFUL IN YOUR DAILY LIFE ⊠

Now that you've almost completed these two chapters on mindfulness skills, you probably recognize the benefits of being mindful in your daily life. But to be realistic, no one is mindful all the time. There will certainly be moments in your life when you'll forget to be mindful. So what should you do?

In his book *Living the Mindful Life: A Handbook for Living in the Present Moment*, psychologist Charles Tart (1994, p. 13) remarks, "It does not take a really strenuous effort to make yourself become mindful and more present. The effort is very small. The problem is remembering to do it! We forget all the time. It is not hard, but we just do not remember to do it." So how should you remember to be mindful? Throughout his book, Dr. Tart uses a bell that rings at random times to remind the reader to be mindful of how he or she is thinking and feeling. But if you don't want to use a random bell, there are other ways to remind yourself. In some of the exercises in this chapter, you might have used a special ring or bracelet to remind yourself. Or maybe you used sticky notes or an app on your smartphone. If those tools helped you, continue to use them to remind yourself to stay mindful.

However, the best way to continue to stay mindful in your daily life is to practice being mindful. The more you practice, the more you will remember to stay mindful. As part of the last exercise in this section, we have designed a simple daily mindfulness regimen to help you continue practicing your skills. It's very important that you continue to use these skills, and to practice other mindfulness exercises that you think are necessary, even as you move on to learning other dialectical behavior skills in this workbook. Mindfulness skills are so important to the overall effectiveness of dialectical behavior therapy that they have been labeled "core" skills (Linehan, 1993a). If you are using the DBT Skills Card Deck, this practice corresponds to card #25 Do Tasks Mindfully.

DAILY MINDFULNESS REGIMEN

Your daily mindfulness regimen will consist of three skills that you've already learned:

1. Mindful breathing

2. Self-compassion meditation

3. Wise-mind meditation

and one you'll learn in a few pages:

4. Doing tasks mindfully

Mindful breathing is a skill you learned in chapter 4, Basic Mindfulness Skills. Remember, to breathe mindfully, you need to focus on three parts of the experience:

1. You must count your breaths. This will help you focus your attention, and it will also help you calm your mind when you're distracted by thoughts.

2. You need to focus on the physical experience of breathing. This is accomplished by observing the rising and falling of your breath as you slowly inhale and exhale.

3. You need to be aware of any distracting thoughts that arise while you are breathing. Then you need to let the thoughts float past without getting stuck on them, as you did in the Thought Defusion exercise. Letting go of the distracting thoughts will allow you to refocus your attention on your breathing and help you further calm yourself.

Practice breathing mindfully for three to five minutes a day at a minimum. But if you want to practice it longer, do it for as long as you can. Remember, the more frequently you practice mindfulness skills, the calmer you will feel and the more control you will have over your present-moment experiences. Refer to the Mindful Breathing exercise in chapter 4 if you need to review the instructions.

Then, at the conclusion of your mindful breathing exercise, reinforce your sense of kindness and forgiveness for yourself by practicing the self-compassion meditation for two to three minutes. To begin, bring your awareness inside your own body, and note the sensation of your breath moving there. Then, as you hold that awareness, slowly repeat the following phrases on each exhalation (either silently or aloud):

"May I be peaceful."

"May I be safe."

"May I be healthy."

"May I be happy and free from suffering."

Then repeat the phrases two or three more times, allowing their meaning to deepen each time.

The wise-mind meditation is a skill you learned earlier in this chapter. It will help you focus your attention on your center of wise mind, which is also sometimes called your center of intuition or "gut feelings." Remember, wise mind is just one decision-making process that many people find helpful. It incorporates using both your emotion mind and your reasonable mind, meaning that wise-mind decisions require you to reflect on how you feel as well as the facts of a situation. This skill also helps you make intuitive decisions that "feel" right to you. Wise-mind meditation will help you make decisions based on the way your body reacts to a decision and your own inner knowledge (what you know to be "true" for you). Again, practice the wise-mind meditation for at least three to five minutes a day, or longer if you want to.

And finally, your daily mindfulness regimen will include doing tasks mindfully. This might sound like a new skill to you, but you've already practiced doing all the steps that are necessary. Doing tasks mindfully means doing all the things you normally do in your life, like talking, walking, eating, and washing, while also staying focused on your thoughts, emotions, physical sensations, and actions in the present moment, and without judging what is happening. In effect, this is the exercise where all the skills you've learned in the last two chapters finally come together. (Visit http://www.newharbinger.com/44581 to download How to Do Tasks Mindfully.)

How to Do Tasks Mindfully

To do tasks mindfully, you need to do the following:

- Focus and shift your attention between your thoughts, feelings, physical sensations, and actions in order to be mindful of your present-moment experience.

- Let go of distracting thoughts and judgments by allowing them to float past without getting stuck on them so that you don't get distracted from what's happening in the present moment.

- Use radical acceptance to remain nonjudgmental.

- Use wise mind to make healthy decisions about your life.

- Do what's effective in order to accomplish your goals.

Some people find it helpful to use a memory device—like the following one—to remind themselves to do tasks mindfully:

"Mindfulness Is Like a FLAME"

Focus and shift your attention to be mindful of the present moment.

Let go of distracting thoughts and judgments.

Use radical **A**cceptance to remain nonjudgmental.

Use wise **M**ind to make healthy decisions.

Do what's **E**ffective to accomplish your goals.

Let's look at some examples of doing tasks mindfully, using all the skills you've learned in this chapter and chapter 4.

After reading these two chapters, Loretta began approaching many of her tasks mindfully. At night, she would even brush her teeth mindfully. First, she focused her attention on how the toothbrush felt in her hand and how the tube felt as she squeezed out the paste. She was also aware of how her body felt, standing in front of the bathroom mirror, and how the weight of her body felt as she stood in front of the sink. Then, as she began to brush, she became aware of the taste in her mouth, the feel of the bristles on her gums, and the movement of her arm as she brushed. When distracting thoughts arose, such as things she did earlier in the day, she imagined the thoughts floating down a river on a leaf. If judgments arose about people she knew, she did the same thing and watched the judgments float away. Then she continued to shift her focus every few moments to her breathing, feeling it rise and fall. Loretta did a good job being as aware as possible of simply brushing her teeth in that moment. At other times throughout the day, she had similar experiences with other activities. When she washed the dishes, she paid attention to how the water felt and to the smell of the dish soap. While she was cooking, she was very aware of the heat from the stove, the sensation of hunger in her stomach, the sound of the water boiling, and her distracting judgments, which usually concerned whether or not her husband would like the meal. She did her best to let those judgments go and to be as fully present in the moment of cooking as she could be.

Similarly, Scott did his best to be mindful throughout the day. As he walked, he focused his attention on how his feet felt as they touched the pavement. Sometimes, he was even aware of how his feet felt moving in his socks. Then he would shift his focus to what he was seeing. He visually scanned what was around him as he walked, and he made mental notes to himself: "Right now, I'm seeing a woman, a tree, a building," and so on. When distracting thoughts arose, he imagined the thoughts coming in one door and leaving through another. If he saw someone on the street whom he didn't like and judgments arose, he would also let those judgments go. Similarly, if positive judgments arose about people or places he liked, he did his best to let those go too. For example, once he caught himself thinking, "Oh look, there's Mike. He's the guy that loaned me twenty dollars that time. He's the greatest guy in the world. I wish I could be more like him." Scott knew that he couldn't stop those judgments from arising, but instead of getting stuck on them, he would let them go. And if the judgments came back, he would let them go again.

But clearly, the greatest challenge to using mindfulness skills is when you are interacting with someone else. Talking or arguing with someone and being mindful at the same time is often difficult. But it is also the most important time to be mindful, especially for someone struggling with overwhelming emotions. Here's an example:

Claire had been practicing her mindfulness skills for a few weeks when she went shopping for a new dress with her friend Laura. Sometimes, Claire worried that Laura really didn't like her. As a result, when Laura made suggestions, Claire did whatever Laura wanted because she was afraid of losing Laura's friendship. However, Claire didn't like the fact that Laura pushed her into doing things.

On the way to the store, Claire drove, and she did her best to remain mindful of what she was doing. She felt the steering wheel in her hands. She felt the weight of her body resting in the seat. She felt her breath rising and falling as she breathed. She was also very aware of what she was seeing, especially the other cars. But she was also very aware of Laura talking to her as she drove. Naturally, judgments about Laura came up while Claire was driving, and she did her best to just let them go. However, some judgments were easier to let go of than others.

When they got to the shopping mall, Claire also had opportunities to use radical acceptance. There were certain stores she liked and certain stores she didn't like. At first, she was positive that she would find the "perfect" dress in the store she really liked because they always had the "best" clothes. But quickly, Claire recognized the positive judgments she was making, and she let them go. That was lucky too, because none of the stores she liked had the dress she was looking for. In the past, she would have been crushed and gotten upset. But because of radical acceptance, her neutrality and her nonjudgmental attitude allowed her to cope with the situation in a healthier way.

Later, the two women found themselves in a higher-end store looking at dresses that were more expensive than what Claire could afford. However, both she and Laura found a dress that they loved. Immediately, Laura began pressuring Claire to buy it. "Don't worry about how much it costs," Laura said. Claire looked at herself in the mirror and fell in love with the dress, regardless of the price tag. Claire was about to buy the dress when she remembered to use wise mind to help her make her decision. Her emotion mind loved the dress, but her reasonable mind reminded her that she already had a hefty credit card bill and this dress was far too expensive. In the dressing room, Claire took a few slow, deep breaths and put her hand on her center of wise mind. Her abdomen felt very nervous and unhappy. Instantly, she knew it was a very bad idea to buy the expensive dress, so she gave it back to the salesclerk and left the store.

Claire was proud of herself for making the right decision, but the drama didn't end there. Laura began making fun of Claire for being "too cheap" to buy the dress. Again, Claire's mind began to fill with judgments about Laura. She did her best to let them go, but as Laura continued to ridicule her, Claire's only goal became leaving the mall and dropping Laura at home. Internally, Claire wanted to scream at Laura, but she knew that would end up in a big fight. Claire thought about doing what was effective in that moment. She knew that she just had to get home as quickly and safely as possible without getting into a fight that she might later regret.

Claire drove home silently, listening to Laura's criticisms. She was relieved when she finally let Laura off at her house. Later, when Claire was feeling less angry, she even found the courage to call Laura to discuss what happened. Claire did a great job using mindful "I" statements such as "I felt hurt when you teased me." Laura understood and said she was sorry. Claire was proud of herself for handling the situation in a new, healthier way.

BE MINDFUL OF YOUR MINDFULNESS ACTIVITIES

Obviously, it will take lots of practice to become as mindful as Claire was in that situation. But hopefully, you see the benefits of using mindfulness in all of your daily tasks.

In the beginning of chapter 4, Basic Mindfulness Skills, you learned that there were three main reasons why you should learn mindfulness skills:

1. They will help you focus on one thing at a time in the present moment, and by doing this you can better control and soothe your overwhelming emotions.

2. They will help you learn to identify and separate judgmental thoughts from your experiences.

3. They will help you develop wise mind.

Unfortunately, there is no shortcut to becoming instantaneously and permanently mindful. But as Dr. Charles Tart said, learning how to be mindful isn't a strenuous activity; you simply have to remember to do it. So, however you need to remember to be mindful, we hope it works for you. One way is to use the Weekly Mindfulness Activities Record on the following page. This will help you remember to follow your daily mindfulness regimen. To record how often you use mindful breathing, self-compassion meditation, wise-mind meditation, and do tasks mindfully, make photocopies of the Weekly Mindfulness Activities Record for each week or download it at http://www.newharbinger.com/44581.

Under the headings of "Mindful Breathing," "Wise-Mind Meditation," and "Self-Compassion Meditation," record the length of time you spend doing each exercise. This will help you keep track of your improvement doing these exercises. Under the heading of "Doing Tasks Mindfully," record what it was that you did mindfully and where you were when you did it.

Then, under the headings labeled "Other Mindful Exercise," record any further mindfulness exercises that you do during the week.

Remember, these mindfulness skills are "core" skills in dialectical behavior therapy (Linehan, 1993a). So, continue to use them even as you move on to using the other skills in this workbook.

Weekly Mindfulness Activities Record

For the week of _____

Day	Mindful Breathing	Wise-Mind Meditation	Self-Compassion Meditation	Doing Tasks Mindfully	Other Mindful Exercise	Other Mindful Exercise
Monday	Time:	Time:	Time:	What: Where:		
Tuesday	Time:	Time:	Time:	What: Where:		
Wednesday	Time:	Time:	Time:	What: Where:		

Day	Mindful Breathing	Wise-Mind Meditation	Self-Compassion Meditation	Doing Tasks Mindfully	Other Mindful Exercise	Other Mindful Exercise
Thursday	Time:	Time:	Time:	What: Where:		
Friday	Time:	Time:	Time:	What: Where:		
Saturday	Time:	Time:	Time:	What: Where:		
Sunday	Time:	Time:	Time:	What: Where:		

RESISTANCES AND HINDRANCES TO MINDFULNESS PRACTICE

It is common to encounter inner resistance and difficulties as you practice mindfulness and develop skills. What many people do not know is that there are some hindrances to mindfulness that are so common that they have been recognized by meditation teachers and practitioners for thousands of years!

This final section of the chapter will help you identify five common hindrances to mindfulness meditation and suggest ways you can work skillfully with each one.

The Five Hindrances

Desire, aversion, sleepiness, restlessness, and *doubt* are the five hindrances long recognized as common obstacles to meditation (and mindfulness) practice.

These energies appear as obstacles when they take you out of the present moment or cause you to become lost in thoughts and feelings that interfere with your mindfulness practice of observing accurately and without judgment. However, they do not have to be obstacles. In truth, they can become your wisest teachers if you are willing to recognize, observe, and learn from them.

- *Desire* refers to the wish for things to be different—right now! This can be a wish for a different sense experience (to "feel better" or "feel happy or peaceful," for example) or to become someone or something different than what you experience yourself as now (become the "perfect person" or "perfect meditator," for example).

- *Aversion* means having anger for or ill will toward what is here. Aversion includes other forms of resistance to present-moment experience, such as feeling bored or afraid. Often, the very activity of judgment or judgmental thinking is an expression of aversion.

- *Sleepiness* means just that—feeling sleepy, heavy, and dull. It is important to note that the causes of sleepiness can include physical fatigue, but, also, a second kind of sleepiness is actually a resistance to something happening in the mind and body that may be frightening or painful. Learning to distinguish between these two is very helpful.

- *Restlessness* is the opposite of sleepiness. It can be very uncomfortable. It is a "storm" of thoughts, feelings, and sensations that demand movement and are quite distracting.

- *Doubt* is that inner voice that says, "I can't handle this. I don't know how to do it. What good is this? This definitely is *not* for me." Doubt is often expressed as words in your mind and feelings of fear and resistance to what is happening.

Working Wisely with the Hindrances

The first and most potent way to handle any of the hindrances is to make the *experience* of the hindrance itself a focus for your mindfulness. Acknowledge what is happening without fighting it. Gently place attention on desire, aversion, sleepiness, restlessness, or doubt, and look deeply, allowing the energy to reveal itself in all of its forms. Patiently return your soft and curious attention time and again, as often as necessary, to the hindrance energy, naming it and learning what it has to teach you. The lessons can come in many ways, including thoughts, memories, feelings, and body sensations. For example, maybe when focusing on your feeling of restlessness, you'll be reminded of childhood memories when you were criticized for being "lazy" or "idle." Or, maybe when focusing on your feeling of sleepiness, you'll be reminded of your need to rearrange your priorities in life in order to get more rest. Lessons like these can help you cope with the hindrances more successfully in the future.

In addition, you may find benefits in the following specific suggestions for each hindrance:

- *For desire, recall that no matter how many times you get what you desire, you always want more.* Let this wisdom empower you to resist the temptation of desire and learn from it instead. Keep noticing and naming desire without acting on it.

- *For aversion, recognize anger and ill will as some of your strongest teachers.* Resolve to learn from them. At times, it also helps if you can work to balance them by developing thoughts of compassion, kindness, and forgiveness.

- *For sleepiness, know it as a powerful condition that demands your full attention.* It can help to sit up straight, even stand. Splash water on your face. Take a break and do something active, walking mindfully, for example.

- *For restlessness, besides making it the object of mindfulness, it can be very helpful to sharpen your concentration.* Take a more narrow or smaller focus, for example, placing attention at the tip of your nose for practicing mindful breathing, or relaxing and counting your breaths from 1 to 10 and back to 1 until the restlessness subsides.

- *For doubt, especially when your mind is racing everywhere, it can help to concentrate attention in the present moment with some resolve and steadiness.* Other remedies for doubt can be conversations with mindfulness teachers and others who follow this path, and inspirational readings related to how others handle doubt.

Finally, remember to take a kind and interested nonjudging attitude toward the hindrances when they appear. When you can treat them as teachers, not obstacles, they will cease to be hindrances!

CHAPTER 6

Exploring Mindfulness Further

MINDFULNESS AND MEDITATION

The mindfulness skills that are at the core of the dialectical behavior therapy approach are actually linked directly to a much larger and more ancient tradition of meditation. In that larger tradition is a significant body of experience and wisdom related to developing and practicing mindfulness. This experience and wisdom has much to offer anyone interested in mindfulness, whether they seek improved psychological or physical health, personal enrichment, or even spiritual growth.

This chapter invites you to explore mindfulness further by trying some additional practices adapted from the ancient tradition of meditation and now appearing in many clinical settings that teach mindfulness-based approaches for a variety of health-related conditions.

The intention and hope is that you will develop an even deeper appreciation for the power of mindfulness to support you, promote your happiness, and lead you increasingly to rest in wise mind.

Marsha Linehan, who developed dialectical behavior therapy, has noted this larger context for mindfulness in commenting that the mindfulness skills central to dialectical behavior therapy are "psychological and behavioral versions of meditation practices from Eastern spiritual training." Linehan goes on to say that in developing dialectical behavior therapy, "I have drawn most heavily from the practice of Zen, but the skills are compatible with most Western contemplative and Eastern meditation practices" (Linehan, 1993b, p. 63).

In the past twenty-five years or so, many health care professionals have become interested in mindfulness and its applications in treating a wide variety of health-related conditions ranging from stress to chronic pain to anxiety and depression to cancer. In bringing mindfulness forward in Western health care settings, the ancient teachings and wisdom of various contemplative and meditative traditions have provided much valuable insight.

Although many (like Linehan) have drawn upon these older traditions for guidance, the actual practices used for purposes of health and healing do not require adherence to any specific faith or religious beliefs, nor do they carry any specific cultural requirements. The practice of mindfulness is truly something for all human beings. The practices you will find in this chapter also apply equally to any interested person.

First, you will learn about the role of "heartful" qualities of kindness and compassion and how they are actually embedded attitudes in any activity of mindfulness.

Next, you will learn how mindfulness can deepen, breath by breath in the present moment, by attention to and the support of the dimensions of spaciousness and stillness.

Kindness, compassion, spaciousness, and *stillness*—this chapter invites you to bring attention more consciously to these qualities and discover their power to support and deepen your practice of mindfulness.

ENHANCING YOUR MINDFULNESS SKILLS USING KINDNESS AND COMPASSION

In dialectical behavior therapy, a core "how" skill is being nonjudgmental. In mindfulness-based stress reduction, a mindfulness approach to stress reduction developed by Jon Kabat-Zinn and others, *nonjudging* is the first of seven attitudes considered to be the foundation of mindfulness practice. The others are *patience, beginner's mind, trust, nonstriving, acceptance,* and *letting go* (Kabat-Zinn, 1990, p. 33).

Yet you may have noticed that it is *not* always so easy to be nonjudging. In fact, the habits of judging and criticizing are deeply ingrained in nearly everyone, for a wide variety of reasons.

Because of this deep-habit energy of judging, meditation teachers have long taught the importance of building a foundation for mindfulness upon attitudes of kindness and compassion.

For example, the well-respected meditation teacher Christina Feldman has observed that "attention, awareness, understanding, and compassion form the basic skeleton of all systems of meditation." She goes on to say, "Compassion is a fundamental principle of meditation. Meditation is not a narcissistic, self-interested path. It provides the foundation for love, integrity, compassion, respect, and sensitivity" (Feldman, 1998, p. 2).

In recent years, health psychologists have begun to look more deeply at "positive" emotions and attitudes and their role in promoting health. The rich tradition of positive mental health inquiry builds on the work of psychologists Gordon Allport and Abraham Maslow in the 1960s and continues strongly today. It is motivated in large part by an interest in developing an expanded vision of human capacity and potential. Of particular interest on this theme is that expanded human potential has been one of the primary goals of meditation training since ancient times.

Contemporary health psychologists and researchers Shauna L. Shapiro and Gary E. R. Schwartz have written about the positive aspects of meditation. They point out that mindfulness is about *how* one pays attention. In addition to the seven attitudinal qualities identified by Kabat-Zinn, Shapiro and Schwartz suggest that an additional five qualities be incorporated to address the affective (or "heart") dimension of mindfulness. The five "heart" qualities they name are *gratitude, gentleness, generosity, empathy,* and *loving-kindness* (Shapiro & Schwartz, 2000, pp. 253–273).

Loving-kindness deserves special mention. It has been popularized by the meditation teacher Sharon Salzberg (1995; 1997; 2005). As health care professionals learn more about loving-kindness, this form of meditation is gaining popularity in a variety of health care settings as a meditation practice that supports mindfulness and also carries healing potential of its own.

Loving-kindness is variously described as deep friendliness and welcoming or as a quality embodying compassion and cherishing, filled with forgiveness and unconditional love. It is a deep human capacity, always present, at least potentially. It can be seen when one observes a mother tenderly caring for her child.

Loving-kindness can be a powerful aid to your mindfulness practice. All you need to do is to admit and allow feelings of kindness and compassion into your way of paying attention mindfully. Resting in kindness this way, *with compassion and affection embedded in your attention,* can protect you from the deep habits of judging and criticism and support you in the "how" dialectical behavior therapy skill of being truly nonjudgmental.

Exercise: Meditation Practice for the Loving-kindness of Yourself and Others

The following is a brief meditation practice to cultivate loving-kindness for yourself and for others. Practice it whenever and for as long as you like. Try it as a "lead-in" to any of your formal mindfulness practices. If you feel more comfortable listening to the instructions, use your smartphone to record the directions in a slow, even voice so that you can listen to them while practicing this technique.

Instructions

Take a comfortable position. Bring your focus mindfully to your breath or body for a few breaths. Open and soften as much as feels safe to you as you allow yourself to connect with your natural inner feelings of kindness and compassion for others. [Pause here for a minute if you are recording the instructions.]

Now shift your attention to yourself. It could be a sense of your whole self or some part that needs care and attention, such as a physical injury or the site of an illness or a feeling of emotional pain.

Imagine speaking gently and quietly to yourself, as a mother speaks to her frightened or injured child. Use a phrase like "May I be safe and protected" or "May I be happy" or "May I be healthy and well" or "May I live with ease" or make up one of your own. Let the phrase you pick be something anyone would want (safety, ease, joy, and so on). Pick one that works for you. It can be a single phrase. Then put all your heart into it each time you speak to yourself. Let kindness and compassion come through you. [Pause here for a minute if you are recording the instructions.]

Practice by repeating your phrase to yourself silently as if singing a lullaby to a baby. Practice for as long as you like. It may help to practice for just a few minutes at a time at first and later build up to a longer practice.

When you like, you can shift your attention and focus to a friend or someone you know who is troubled. You can also focus on groups of people, such as "all my friends" or "all my brothers and sisters." [Pause here for a minute if you are recording the instructions.]

When you wish, you can experiment with difficult people in your life. Try sending them kindness and your wish that they might be happy, and watch your inner response. In doing loving-kindness for a difficult person, you are *not* allowing them to abuse or hurt you but are making an attempt to see that they, too, are human beings who seek happiness. This can change your relationship to the situation and release you from resentment you may be holding.

Please note that in doing loving-kindness meditation, you are likely to experience many different feelings! Some may even be disturbing, such as sadness, grief, or anger. If this happens, you have *not* made a mistake. It is common for deeply held feelings to be released as one practices loving-kindness. This release is actually a kind of healing in itself. Just pay attention to all of your feelings, honoring each one, and continue your practice.

ATTENTION TO SPACIOUSNESS AND STILLNESS DEEPENS MINDFULNESS

The core dialectical behavior therapy skill of mindfulness includes the "what" skill of observing and the "how" skill of nonjudging. But old habits of attention can often make it difficult to observe fully or to really be nonjudging. When it seems especially difficult to be mindful, observe closely, or be nonjudging, you simply may not be relaxing enough or resting in your wholeness. Instead, you are very likely overly identified with some active and present smaller part or parts of yourself.

Meditation teachers often use the metaphor of an ocean when illustrating your wholeness compared to identification with a smaller part of yourself (your thoughts and judgments or your feelings of anger or fear, for example). In this metaphor, it is noted that the waves and the ocean are not separate. Although the waves are varied and can be intense and dramatic, they still are made of water and are part of the greater ocean, even down to the deepest depths. It is said that your wholeness (sometimes called *big mind* or some similar term) is like the ocean, while the parts (feelings, thoughts, stories in your mind) are like the waves—constantly rising and falling, appearing and disappearing, while their essence, the ocean, is always present.

The tendency to *identify* with the wave and to lose your feeling of connection with the larger ocean of who you are is very strong. Practicing mindfulness, learning to recognize the reasoning mind and the emotional mind when they arise, can offer freedom from rigid identification with your smaller parts, as you have discovered.

And by shifting your focus at times, on purpose, to experiences often not noticed or taken for granted, you can become much more flexible in your attention, more mindful, and more able to break the habitual identification with old habits of thinking and feeling.

Choosing *space* and *stillness* (or *silence*) as your objects of mindfulness can be a very potent practice for gaining this flexibility and freedom from the habits of identifying with the "waves" of your mind (thoughts or feelings that are deep and intense).

Exercise: Meditation Practice for Mindfulness of Space, Inside and Outside of You

The following two meditation practices offer you a means to cultivate awareness of space (inner and outer) and of stillness and silence.

Try these practices with a sense of curiosity and playfulness. You don't have to make anything special happen or become anyone or anything other than who you already are!

In fact, it is helpful to consider the possibility that *you actually already have vast spaciousness and stillness available to you (like the vast ocean depths) and all that is required is to allow space and stillness to reenter your awareness.* Let the spaciousness and stillness within you "come back in," so to speak. There is no work you have to do—none whatsoever! Just bring kind attention to what is already here. If you feel more comfortable listening to the instructions for these two meditations, use your smartphone to record the directions in a slow, even voice so that you can listen to them while practicing these techniques.

Instructions

Take a comfortable position. Collect attention by focusing mindfully on your breath sensations for a few breaths. [Pause here for a minute if you are recording the instructions.]

When you feel steady and focused, widen the focus to include all sounds, letting them come to you without adding or subtracting anything. Focus on the direct experience of sound without being caught in the name or story about any sound. [Pause here for a minute if you are recording the instructions.]

Practice mindfulness of breath sensations and sounds for a few more breaths. [Pause here for a minute if you are recording the instructions.]

Now bring your attention to the spaces between the breaths, there between in-breath and out-breath, and there, at the end of the out-breath before the next in-breath. Let your attention rest there, in the spaces between each breath. Come back to the space whenever your attention wanders. [Pause here for a minute if you are recording the instructions.]

When you notice that sounds draw your attention, first notice the sound, then notice the spaces between the sounds. Notice how one sound is louder, another softer, one closer, one farther, and how all have space between and around them. Notice how all the sounds exist within a larger container of space. Let your attention rest in the space that holds all the sounds, allowing them to come and go. [Pause here for a minute if you are recording the instructions.]

When you wish, open your eyes. Look around at what is before you. What do you see? Objects, of course, but do you see the space between the objects? Look more closely. See the space and the shape of the space between objects near and far. Can you see the vast space that holds all the objects you are viewing? Relax and look deeply. [Pause here for two to three minutes if you are recording the instructions, before ending the exercise.]

Whenever you like, practice noticing space, either as a formal meditation practice (as suggested above with breath sensations, sounds, or viewed objects) or more informally, just paying attention in different situations as you go about your day.

You may even want to experiment with noticing the space that contains your thoughts and feelings. Can you relax, observe, and allow thoughts and feelings to arise, change, and leave the space of the present moment?

Exercise: Meditation Practice to Turn Toward Stillness and Silence

Instructions

Take a comfortable position. Establish and steady your attention in the present moment by focusing mindfully on your breath sensations for a few breaths. [Pause here for a minute if you are recording the instructions.]

When you notice that your attention moves to something else, thoughts or sounds, for example, you don't have to fight that and you don't have to follow it. Just let the breath sensations return to your awareness, with patience and kindness. [Pause here for a minute if you are recording the instructions.]

As you practice mindfulness of your breath, you may begin to notice that a sense of inner stillness arises. It may appear only in brief flashes at first, but don't be discouraged. Just let it come. Continue noticing any feelings of stillness you experience. Relax in them, and allow them to come to you. Initially, you may notice the stillness in your body as a feeling of calm and ease. Then, it will become easier to experience the stillness in your mind when your thoughts quiet down. [Pause here for a minute if you are recording the instructions.]

Sometimes the stillness appears more clearly as silence. When you notice any sense of silence, between sounds or between thoughts, for instance, let your attention rest there. Let it return there when it wanders. [Pause here for a minute if you are recording the instructions.]

Listen carefully to all sounds as they come and go. Don't focus on any one sound, but instead focus on the silence and space between the sounds. As your attention steadies, notice how the sounds arise from silence and return to silence. Let your attention rest in the silence as you listen for the next sound. [Pause here for two to three minutes if you are recording the instructions, before ending the exercise.]

CONCLUSION

In practicing mindfulness, you are joining a vast and ancient tradition, cultivated by countless human beings for thousands of years. Many teachers have pointed out that practicing mindfulness includes the attitudes of kindness and compassion in the way you pay attention. As you become more mindful, a growing sense of wholeness, including spaciousness and stillness, becomes brighter and can help transform your experience of living. This chapter invites you to draw upon some valuable teachings from the tradition of mindfulness meditation—by focusing on kindness and compassion and spaciousness and stillness—in order to discover more about your own amazing and powerful resources for healing and enriching your life.

CHAPTER 7

Basic Emotion Regulation Skills

YOUR EMOTIONS: WHAT ARE THEY?

To put it simply, emotions are signals within your body that tell you what's happening. When something pleasurable is happening to you, you feel good; when something distressing is happening to you, you feel bad. In many ways, your emotions are like an instant news service that gives you constant updates about what you're doing and what you're experiencing.

Your initial reactions to what is happening to you are called *primary emotions*. These are strong feelings that come on quickly, that don't involve having to think about what's happening. For example, if you won a contest, you might instantaneously feel surprised. When someone you care about dies, you quickly feel sad. When someone does something that offends you, you might immediately feel angry.

But in addition to experiencing primary emotions, it's also possible to experience *secondary emotions*. These are emotional reactions to your primary emotions. Or to put it another way, secondary emotions are feelings about your feelings (Marra, 2005). Here's a simple example. Erik yelled at his sister because she did something that made him feel angry. His feeling of anger came on very quickly. But a little later he felt guilty about getting so angry with her. Anger was his primary emotion, and guilt was his secondary emotion.

However, it's also possible that you can experience numerous secondary emotions in response to a single primary emotion. Here's a more complicated example. Shauna became anxious when she was asked to make a future presentation at work. As the day drew closer, she became depressed as she thought about how anxious she was getting, and then she started to feel worthless that she couldn't make a simple presentation. Then, the day after the presentation, she started to feel guilty that she had made such a big deal about it in the first place. You can see how a person's emotions can get very complicated very quickly. Anxiety was Shauna's primary emotion, and depression, worthlessness, and guilt were all her secondary emotions in response to her anxiety.

It's possible that your primary emotional reaction to a situation can set off a limitless chain reaction of distressing secondary emotions that cause you much more pain than your original emotion does. For this reason, it's important that you try to identify what your original primary emotion is in a distressing situation so that you can learn to cope with that feeling before the avalanche of secondary emotions overwhelms you. This is where emotion regulation skills can be helpful. Emotion regulation skills are an important part of dialectical behavior therapy because they will help you cope with your distressing primary and secondary feelings in new and healthier ways (Dodge, 1989; Linehan, 1993a).

These skills are especially useful because without them, people often choose to deal with their primary and secondary emotions in ways that only cause them more suffering. In Shauna's example, it's easy to imagine that she could have chosen to use alcohol or drugs to deal with her feelings of anxiety, cutting or self-mutilation to deal with her feelings of depression, and binge eating to deal with her feelings of guilt. These are all harmful coping strategies that are often used by people with overwhelming emotions. For this reason, it's extremely important that you learn the emotion regulation skills in this workbook so that you can cope with your primary and secondary emotions in healthier ways and avoid the prolonged suffering that often accompanies them.

Emotion regulation skills are also important for dealing with another problem called *ambivalence*. Ambivalence occurs when you have more than one emotional reaction to the same event and each emotion pulls you in a different direction or makes you want to do something different. For example, Tina had grown up without her father in her life. Then one day when she was twenty-five, her father contacted her and wanted to see her. Tina felt excited about the opportunity of forming a new relationship with him, but she was equally angry with him for abandoning her family. Clearly, Tina's emotions were split, and they pulled her in two different directions about what to do.

If you've been dealing with overwhelming emotions for a long time, it's easy to understand that you might feel frustrated and hopeless about controlling your emotional reactions. But remember: although it might be difficult to control your primary emotional reaction, there's still hope that you can learn to control your secondary emotional responses as well as how you choose to cope with your emotions. And it could be that later on, when you start using all the skills in this workbook, especially the mindfulness skills, you might even gain some control over your primary emotional responses too.

HOW DO EMOTIONS WORK?

Emotions are electrical and chemical signals in your body that alert you to what is happening. These signals often begin with your senses of sight, touch, hearing, smell, and taste. Then the signals travel to your brain, where they are processed in an area called the *limbic system*, which specializes in observing and processing emotions so that you can respond to emotional situations. The limbic system is also connected to the rest of your brain and body so that it can tell your body what to do in response to an emotional situation.

Your emotions are extremely important for many reasons, especially your survival. Here's an example. Louise was walking down Main Street when suddenly a very large and angry dog began barking viciously and running toward her. In that instant, an emotional signal was sent from her eyes and ears to her brain. Her limbic system then processed the information without Louise having to think about what to do. This type of response is called *fight, flight, or freeze*, and it determined whether Louise was going to stay to fight the dog, run away, or freeze and hope that the dog didn't see her. Wisely, she chose to run away, and she escaped without being harmed. Her emotions helped her survive and avoid any pain.

Now let's suppose that two weeks later she was once again walking through town when she started to turn down Main Street. Very quickly, she began to feel afraid. This is called a *conditioned response*. Louise's limbic system was trying to protect her by helping her remember the dangerous dog on Main Street. Sensibly, she chose to walk down a different street to avoid the dog. In this example, Louise's emotions initially helped her escape danger and pain, and later, they also helped her avoid potential harm.

Here's another example of how emotions work. Sheila was walking through town when she suddenly saw Courtney, a good friend from many years before. Immediately, Sheila felt happy. When Courtney saw Sheila, she smiled right away. Sheila noticed her smile and thought, "She must be happy to see me too." So Sheila smiled as well. The two women quickly reconnected and made plans to do something together in the near future. The encounter made both women feel happy that they'd met accidentally after so many years.

In this example, the smile was an act of communication for both women. It helped each person recognize how the other person was feeling. If Courtney had frowned and looked the other way when she saw Sheila, Sheila would have recognized the expression as one of disgust and would probably have avoided contact with her. Every person, no matter what their culture, has the ability to express emotions in the same way and to recognize emotional expressions in other people. A smile is a smile no matter where you were born.

These are just two very simple examples, but you can see that emotions serve many purposes. Emotions are signals that help you do the following:

- Survive ("fight, flight, or freeze")

- Remember people and situations

- Cope with situations in your daily life

- Communicate with others

- Avoid pain

- Seek pleasure

WHAT ARE EMOTION REGULATION SKILLS?

As you've already learned, emotion regulation skills will help you cope with your reactions to your primary and secondary emotions in new and more effective ways. (Remember, you can't always control what you feel, but you can control how you react to those feelings.) These are some of the most important techniques to learn in dialectical behavior therapy, so you might not be surprised that you've already been practicing some of them in the chapters on distress tolerance and mindfulness skills. The four skill groups in dialectical behavior therapy (distress tolerance, mindfulness, emotion regulation, and interpersonal effectiveness) overlap and reinforce each other because this helps you learn the skills more easily and to remember them more quickly.

In dialectical behavior therapy, there are nine emotion regulation skills that will help you gain control of your emotions and the behaviors associated with them (Linehan, 1993b). These skills are as follows:

1. Recognizing your emotions

2. Overcoming the barriers to healthy emotions

3. Reducing your physical vulnerability

4. Reducing your cognitive vulnerability

5. Increasing your positive emotions

6. Being mindful of your emotions without judgment

7. Emotion exposure

8. Doing the opposite of your emotional urges

9. Problem solving

This chapter will cover the first five emotion regulation skills, and the next chapter will cover the last four skills. As in the previous chapters, the exercises in these two chapters will build on each other, so make sure that you do the exercises in order.

RECOGNIZING YOUR EMOTIONS ⊠

Learning how to recognize your emotions and their effect on your life is the first step to controlling your high-intensity emotional reactions. Very often, people spend their lives paying little attention to how they feel. As a result, there are a lot of important things happening inside them that they know little about. The same holds true for people struggling with overwhelming emotions, but it occurs in a different way. Very often, people struggling with this problem recognize the tidal wave of distressing emotions that overcomes them (such as sadness, anger, guilt, shame, and so on), but by the time they recognize the tidal wave, it's too late to do anything about it.

To control your overwhelming emotional reactions, it's first necessary to slow down the emotional process so that it can be examined. And then, after it's examined, you can make healthier decisions. This exercise will help you begin this process by examining an emotional situation that has already occurred in the past. It will require you to be as honest with yourself as possible. The purpose of this exercise is to discover what emotions you were feeling (both primary and secondary emotions) and then figure out how those emotions affected your actions and feelings later on.

Let's consider an example. Ling struggled with overwhelming emotions that often got out of control. One evening, she came home from work and found her husband drunk on the sofa again. He refused to go to psychotherapy and he didn't consider himself an alcoholic, so he wouldn't go to a meeting of Alcoholics Anonymous. Ling immediately felt angry, so she started screaming at her husband, calling him a "worthless drunk." But he just lay there without arguing or moving. She wanted to hit him, but she didn't. After a few minutes, Ling started to feel hopeless and ashamed too. She had tried everything to help her husband, but nothing seemed to work. She didn't feel like she could stay in her marriage any longer, but she also didn't believe in divorce. Ling went to the bathroom and locked herself in. She thought about killing herself, to end the pain she was feeling. But instead, she took out a razor and started cutting herself on her leg just enough to make herself bleed. That night she forgot to set her alarm because she was too upset, so she missed the first few hours of work and got reprimanded by her manager.

Ling's story is common for many people. Using this story, let's follow the six-step process that will help you recognize your emotions (Linehan, 1993b).

1. *What happened?* This is your opportunity to describe the situation that led to your emotions. In this example, Ling comes home and once again finds her husband drunk. He refuses to get help or to talk about his problem.

2. *Why do you think that situation happened?* This is an opportunity for you to identify the potential causes of your situation. This is a very important step because the meaning that you give to the event will often determine what your emotional reaction is to that event. For example, if you think someone hurt you on purpose, you will react very differently than if you think someone hurt you by accident. Here, Ling believes that her husband is an alcoholic who hates her and regrets marrying her in the first place, so he has just given up on his life to hurt her.

3. *How did the situation make you feel, both emotionally and physically?* Try to identify both primary and secondary emotions if you can. Learning how to identify your emotions will take practice, but it will be worth the effort that you make. If you need help finding words to describe how you feel, see the List of Commonly Felt Emotions in chapter 4. Also, try to identify how you were feeling physically. Emotions and physical sensations, especially muscle tension, are strongly related. In this example, Ling's primary emotion is anger (after seeing her husband drunk), and then she feels the secondary emotions of hopelessness and shame. Physically, she notices that all the muscles in her face and arms become very tense, and she feels sick to her stomach.

4. *What did you want to do as a result of how you felt?* This question is very important because it identifies your *urges*. Often, when a person is overwhelmed with emotions, he or she has the urge to say or do something that is drastic, painful, or extremely dangerous. However, the person doesn't always do these things; sometimes the urges are just thoughts and impulses. When you start to notice what you *want* to do and compare it with what you *actually* do, the results can be cause for hope. If you can control some urges, chances are good that you can control other urges too. In this example, Ling had the urge to do two things that would have been very dangerous and deadly: hit her husband and kill herself to end her pain. Thankfully, she didn't do either one, which later gave her hope that she could control other urges as well.

5. *What did you do and say?* This is where you identify what you actually did as a result of your emotions. In this example, Ling locks herself in her bathroom and begins to mutilate herself. She also yells at her husband and calls him a "worthless drunk."

6. *How did your emotions and actions affect you later?* Here you can identify the longer-term consequences of what you felt and did. In Ling's example, she oversleeps for work the next morning because she forgets to set her alarm, and she is disciplined by her boss, which puts her job at risk.

Exercise: Recognizing Your Emotions

On the next page is an example of the Recognizing Your Emotions Worksheet with Ling's experience filled in. On the following page, there's a blank worksheet for you to fill in an example from your own life. Before you use the blank worksheet, make photocopies of it so that you can continue to use it in the future. Or simply write the headings on a clean sheet of paper to make your own worksheet. Or, if you prefer, visit http://www.newharbinger.com/44581 to download the Recognizing Your Emotions Worksheet.

For now, use the worksheet to examine an emotional incident from your recent past. Pick a situation that you can clearly remember. Do your best to identify your primary and secondary emotions. And remember, be as honest as you can with yourself. No one has to see this worksheet except for you.

Then, for at least the next two weeks, pick a situation that happens to you each day and examine it using the Recognizing Your Emotions Worksheet. Remember, you need to practice examining past situations so that you can later learn how to identify your emotions and their consequences *while they are happening.*

Example: Recognizing Your Emotions Worksheet

Questions	Your Responses
When did the situation happen?	Last night.
What happened? (Describe the event.)	I came home and my husband was lying on the sofa drunk again. He still refuses to go to therapy or AA. I yelled at him and called him a "worthless drunk." But he just sat there, without saying anything. So I went in the bathroom and cut myself.
Why do you think that situation happened? (Identify the causes.)	My husband is an alcoholic who hates me and regrets marrying me. I also think he's given up on his own life and just does things like this to hurt me on purpose.
How did that situation make you feel, both emotionally and physically? (Try to identify both the *primary* and the *secondary* emotions.)	Primary emotions: Anger Secondary emotions: Hopelessness and shame Physical sensations: Face and arms became tense, sick to my stomach
What did you want to do as a result of how you felt? (What were your urges?)	I wanted to hit my husband, and I had the urge to kill myself to end my pain.
What did you do and say? (What actions or behaviors did you engage in as a result of how you felt?)	I locked myself in the bathroom and started cutting myself. Then I went to bed by myself because I was so angry. I yelled at my husband and called him a "worthless drunk."
How did your emotions and actions affect you later? (What short-term or long-term consequences were there as a result of your actions?)	I was so angry when I went to bed that I forgot to set my alarm. So I woke up late for work. When I got in, my boss yelled at me again. He said that if I'm late one more time, he'll have to fire me.

Recognizing Your Emotions Worksheet

Questions	Your Responses
When did the situation happen?	
What happened? (Describe the event.)	
Why do you think that situation happened? (Identify the causes.)	
How did that situation make you feel, both emotionally and physically? (Try to identify both the *primary* and the *secondary* emotions.)	Primary emotions: Secondary emotions: Physical sensations:
What did you want to do as a result of how you felt? (What were your urges?)	
What did you do and say? (What actions or behaviors did you engage in as a result of how you felt?)	
How did your emotions and actions affect you later? (What short-term or long-term consequences were there as a result of your actions?)	

Exercise: Emotional Record ⊠

To help you recognize your emotions, it's often helpful to say how you're feeling out loud. This method of labeling might sound silly at first, but the act of saying how you feel out loud will highlight your emotions for you and help you pay extra attention to what you're experiencing. Describing your emotions aloud, especially your overwhelming emotions, can also help deflate your distressing feelings. So the more you can talk about an emotion, the less urge you might have to do something about it. You do not have to scream how you feel; it might be enough to say your emotion quietly to yourself. Just find what works best for you. Say to yourself, "Right now I feel…" And remember to pay attention to your pleasant and joyful emotions too. The more you're able to recognize them and say them out loud, the more fully you'll be able to enjoy those feelings.

Then, in order to further reinforce the experience, record your emotions in your Emotional Record, following. Use the example worksheet to help you. Recording your feelings throughout the week will help you recognize, label, and describe your emotions. (Visit http://www.newharbinger.com/44581 to download the Emotional Record.)

Example: Emotional Record

When Did It Happen and Where Were You?	How Did You Feel? ("Right now, I feel...")	Did You Say How You Felt Out Loud?	What Did You Do After You Recognized How You Felt?
Thursday night, at home	I feel angry.	Yes	I went to the kitchen and had a glass of wine.
Thursday night, at home	I feel sad.	No	I tried to go to sleep, but I kept thinking about how sad I was.
Friday morning, on the bus	I feel agitated.	Yes	I tried to calm down by distracting myself and reading the newspaper.
Friday morning, at work	I feel pissed off.	Yes	I went outside and had a cigarette.
Friday afternoon, at work	I feel jealous.	No	I continued to ignore my friend who's dating a woman that I like.
Friday night, at home	I feel lonely.	Yes	I decided to go to the movies by myself and have a good time.
Saturday afternoon, at the park	I feel happy.	Yes	I stayed at the park with my friends.
Saturday night, at Ben's house	I feel cheerful.	Yes	I didn't say much to anyone because I didn't want to mess up my feelings.

Emotional Record

When Did It Happen and Where Were You?	How Did You Feel? ("Right now, I feel...")	Did You Say How You Felt Out Loud?	What Did You Do After You Recognized How You Felt?

OVERCOMING THE BARRIERS TO HEALTHY EMOTIONS ⊠

Now that you've started to recognize your emotions more fully, hopefully you're also noticing how your emotions can influence your behaviors and thoughts. Please look carefully at the following diagram.

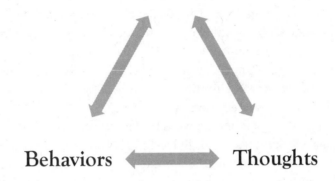

This diagram depicts how your emotions can *influence* your thoughts and behaviors and also how your emotions can be *affected by* your thoughts and behaviors. For example, Jim lost his favorite watch (a behavior). He felt sad (an emotion), and then he thought to himself, "I'm so absentminded; I'm an idiot" (a thought). But this thought just made him feel more depressed (an emotion), so he went home and got drunk (a behavior) and later felt ashamed (an emotion). Do you see how your emotions can be both the result and the cause of your thoughts and behaviors?

This can become a vicious cycle for your emotions if you get caught in self-destructive behaviors or self-critical thinking. But this cycle can also lead to more fulfilling emotional experiences if you engage in healthy behaviors and self-affirming thoughts. For example, maybe after Jim lost his watch (a behavior) and felt sad (an emotion), he could have used a coping thought like "Mistakes happen; nobody's perfect." Then he might have been able to forgive himself for his mistake (another thought) and continue his day, feeling at ease (an emotion). Or after feeling sad about losing his watch, maybe he could have gone for a long walk (a behavior), which would have made him feel refreshed (an emotion). There were many coping thoughts and behaviors Jim could have used to prevent getting caught in a cycle of distressing emotions.

EMOTIONS AND YOUR BEHAVIORS

Clearly, your emotions and your behaviors are strongly linked, and, not surprisingly, stronger emotions often lead to bigger behavioral reactions. As a result, many people with overwhelming feelings also struggle with out-of-control behaviors. Sometimes people with overwhelming emotions do self-destructive things when they feel angry, depressed, or anxious. For example, they cut or mutilate themselves, manipulate others (which often leads to fights and destructive relationships), overeat, undereat, drink alcohol excessively, or use excessive drugs. Obviously, these types of behaviors are harmful to everyone who's involved. Yet people who engage in these behaviors often do them repeatedly. So the question remains: why do people do these types of things? The answer lies in emotions.

Let's start with the basics: many behaviors are repeated because they are rewarded. A person goes to work for the reward of a paycheck. A student goes to school for the reward of a degree. People play sports for the reward of competing. A musician plays an instrument for the reward of creating music. And a gardener plants flowers for the reward of seeing them blossom. All of these rewards *reinforce* these behaviors and make them more likely to be repeated in the future. If you didn't get a paycheck for going to work, you wouldn't go anymore. If your teachers told you that there was no chance for you to graduate, you'd probably drop out. And if you only got weeds every time you planted a garden, you'd probably stop doing that too.

In the same way, your emotions can serve as rewards that reinforce your behavior. Here's a simple example of how pleasurable emotions can reinforce a behavior: Phil helped his friend Stefan move into a new apartment (a behavior). Stefan was very grateful, which made Phil feel happy about helping him (an emotion). So the next time Stefan asked for a favor, Phil was happy to help him again (another behavior) because it would make him feel good again (another emotion).

However, emotions can reinforce self-destructive behaviors as well. Consider this example: Teresa, who struggled with overwhelming emotions, once said, "If I feel bad, I want my husband to feel bad too." Logically, this doesn't make sense, but thoughts, emotions, and behaviors aren't always logical. As a young girl, Teresa had never been taught how to cope with her distressing emotions. When she was in emotional or physical pain, she suffered alone without anyone's help. No one paid attention to how she felt.

Then, as an adult, she realized that someone would give her and her pain attention if she hurt the other person too, usually by making them feel upset. For example, when Teresa felt upset at work, she would go home and pick a fight with her husband about something unimportant (her behavior), and he would feel miserable as well. Then he would finally recognize how Teresa felt and talk to her about her feelings (which was her emotional reward). Teresa may not have been consciously aware that she was hurting her husband on purpose, but that didn't matter. At some point in her life, her thoughts had become automatic: "I feel bad, so I have to make someone else feel bad; then I'll feel better." And because her behavior was consistently rewarded with a positive (although illogical) emotional experience—validation from her husband—her behavior was reinforced and repeated in the future.

The Basics	Teresa's Experience
Emotion or thought	"I feel sad."
↓	↓
Behavior	She starts a fight with her husband.
↓	↓
Behavior is rewarded	Her husband recognizes how she feels.
↓	↓
Behavior is repeated	There are more fights in the future.

However, the way Teresa coped with her distressing feelings only made her feel better for a very limited amount of time. In the long term, her marriage suffered at the expense of her emotional validation. Teresa and her husband had frequent fights as a result of her behaviors, and these fights always made her feel even worse.

The emotional rewards that reinforce self-destructive behaviors are important to understand. Two types of self-destructive behaviors that people with overwhelming emotions often engage in are cutting/self-mutilation and manipulating others. Both of these behaviors offer short-term rewards that make them likely to be repeated, but both types of behaviors are also followed by long-term damage. (A little later in this chapter, in the section "Reducing Your Physical Vulnerability to Overwhelming Emotions," you'll learn about self-destructive eating and substance-use behaviors too.)

Cutting/Self-Mutilation

Many people who cut, burn, or scar themselves say that their actions make them feel better or that their actions relieve some of their pain. To a certain degree, they're right. Cutting and other types of self-mutilation can cause the body to release natural painkillers called *endorphins* that help heal the wound. These painkillers can make a person feel physically and emotionally better for a very short amount of time. Yet as temporary as these rewards are, these physical and emotional feelings reinforce self-mutilation in the future. But remember, these behaviors can be dangerous and possibly lead to death or infection. And while the pain relief is temporary, the scars, the memories, and the guilt that often accompany these actions still remain.

If you engage in any cutting or self-mutilating behaviors, identify what those behaviors are in the space below. Then identify what the temporary rewards might be. And finally, identify what the long-term cost and dangers are, due to those behaviors.

The cutting and self-mutilating behaviors that I engage in are _____

_____

_____

The temporary rewards for my behaviors are _____

_____

_____

The long-term costs and dangers of my behaviors are _____

_____

_____

Manipulating Others

In the earlier example, you saw why Teresa picked fights with her husband when she was feeling upset. Her actions, though damaging to her marriage, made her feel better for a short amount of time. Her behavior was rewarded with emotional validation, so it was repeated in the future. But, the frequent fights with her husband made her feel even worse in the long run.

Similarly, other forms of manipulation can have short-lived emotional rewards that lead to repetition. When you force someone into doing what you want, maybe you feel satisfied or in control. These can all be strong emotional rewards, especially considering that many people with overwhelming emotions feel like their own lives are out of control. But, again, even these emotional rewards are temporary.

Here are some examples. Whenever Brandy felt bored, she liked to "mess with people," just to give herself pleasure. Often she would lie to her friends and tell them phony rumors she claimed to have heard about them. Then, when her friends would get upset, Brandy would pretend to comfort them. This made her feel powerful, until her friends discovered the truth and then stopped talking to her. Similarly, Jason was very controlling of his girlfriend, Patricia. When they would go out for dinner, he would order for her, even if she wanted something different. He also wouldn't let her spend time with her friends; he was constantly calling her on her cell phone to see where she was; and he told her that if she ever left him, he'd kill himself. Patricia really cared about Jason, and she didn't want to see him get hurt, but, eventually, Jason's manipulative behaviors wore her out. So, despite his suicidal threats, Patricia broke up with him.

Remember, no one likes to be manipulated. Eventually, the person who is being manipulated gets tired of being controlled and puts up resistance. Then the relationship becomes confrontational and unrewarding and often ends very painfully. This is usually the worst possible result for a person struggling with overwhelming emotions because he or she is often extremely afraid of being abandoned by others. In fact, all the manipulative behaviors are usually attempts to cope with this fear of being left alone and to force people to stay with them. But when the relationships fail, the fear of being abandoned becomes a reality, and this can set off even more incidents of self-destructive behaviors.

If you engage in any manipulative behaviors, identify what those behaviors are in the space below. Then identify what the temporary rewards might be. And finally, identify what the long-term cost and dangers are due to those behaviors.

The manipulative behaviors that I engage in are _____

_____

_____

The temporary rewards for my behaviors are _____

_____

_____

The long-term costs and dangers of my behaviors are _____

_____

_____

REDUCING YOUR PHYSICAL VULNERABILITY TO OVERWHELMING EMOTIONS ⊠

In addition to recognizing how your thoughts and behaviors can influence your emotions, it's also important that you recognize how other health-related issues influence how you feel. Here are some examples.

Food

Your body needs the nutrients it gets from food in order to keep functioning properly, just as a car depends on gasoline to keep running. As a result, the food you eat affects how you feel directly, both emotionally and physically.

Different foods can affect the way you feel, as can the amount of food you eat. For example, foods with a lot of fat in them, like ice cream and pastries, can temporarily make you feel pleased and satisfied. But if you eat too much of them, you might start to feel heavy and sluggish. Over time, if you eat an excessive amount of food with high levels of fat or sugar, you'll also gain weight. This often makes people feel sad or unhappy about themselves, and it can also lead to health problems like diabetes and heart disease. Other foods with high sugar content, like candy and soda, can quickly make you feel energized. But as the effect wears off, these foods can leave you feeling very tired or even depressed.

Just as eating too much of certain foods can make you feel ill, eating too little food can also make you feel unhealthy. Getting too few nutrients in your diet can make you feel dizzy or light-headed because you're not getting the energy you need to keep functioning.

It's recommended that you eat a moderate amount of a wide variety of healthy foods every day, including fruits, vegetables, grains, and proteins. If you are curious about your diet or need help creating a healthy diet, contact a medical professional or a certified dietician for advice. Or visit a reputable nutrition website where you can find recommendations and guidelines for eating a healthy, well-balanced diet.

In the space below, record any thoughts you have about how your own eating habits affect how you feel, and then write at least two ways you can improve your eating habits in order to feel better.

My eating habits affect how I feel because _____

_____

_____

I can improve my eating habits by

1. _____

_____

2. _____

_____

Overeating and Undereating

Also, be aware that some people with overwhelming emotions use food in self-destructive ways, either by drastically overeating or undereating. Sometimes people overeat because the food makes them feel emotionally calm, or even numb, for a short amount of time. And, again, these feelings lead to the person's behavior being repeated in the future. Equally dangerous is the fact that some people try to control their overeating by engaging in purging activities like vomiting. Frequent purging can lead to a very dangerous eating disorder called *bulimia* that can have devastating effects on your body.

Drastic undereating can also make a person feel good for a short amount of time. Undereating can serve as a form of self-control. Many times, people with overwhelming emotions feel like their lives are out of their own control, and undereating gives them a sense of power over their lives that makes them feel better. However, this desire for control can be dangerous because excessive undereating can lead to *anorexia*, an extremely unhealthy and potentially life-threatening eating disorder characterized by a person's drastically reduced weight.

If you engage in any overeating or undereating, identify what those behaviors are in the space below. Then identify what the temporary rewards might be. And finally, identify what the long-term costs and dangers are due to those behaviors.

The overeating or undereating behaviors that I engage in are _____

_____

_____

The temporary rewards for my behaviors are _____

_____

_____

The long-term costs and dangers of my behaviors are _____

_____

_____

Drugs and Alcohol

Like food, anything else you put in your body will affect how you feel. Alcohol and drugs often make a person feel temporarily happy, numb, excited, or just different. Naturally, these feelings can lead to repeated use of these substances, especially after the temporary feelings have worn off. However, the excessive use of alcohol, recreational drugs, or abused prescription drugs can lead to many health complications, addiction problems, legal issues, financial difficulties, and relationship problems.

For example, alcohol is a depressant that makes you feel tired, sluggish, and sad. Many people don't believe this because they say alcohol makes them feel more energized and social. However, alcohol actually makes them feel less self-conscious, so they're more willing to do or say things that they normally wouldn't. But with enough alcohol in anyone's body, he or she will start to feel sad and tired.

The use of recreational drugs and certain prescription drugs can have similar effects. Certain drugs, such as cocaine and methamphetamines, can initially make a person feel "good" or "energized." But after the effects of the drug wear off, the person may also start to feel depressed, anxious, or paranoid. The same is also true of many other recreational drugs, such as marijuana, "bath salts," and heroin. Certain prescription drugs can also make you feel depressed and anxious, so be sure to check with the medical professional who prescribed them if you're feeling any distressing side effects.

Nicotine from tobacco products and caffeine are also considered to be drugs, although they are legal and very prominent in our society. Nicotine is a stimulant that activates a person's muscles, regardless of the fact that some people say that smoking makes them feel more relaxed. In these cases, what the person is actually experiencing is a temporary sense of relief from his or her body, which has been craving more nicotine. Nicotine is a highly addictive substance that makes people want to smoke more cigarettes or continue vaping, and that craving can make a person feel very irritated until he or she smokes again.

Caffeine is also a stimulant that is found in coffee, tea, many sodas, sports drinks, and some painkillers. If you drink too much caffeine, you will start to feel jittery, shaky, and irritated. You can also become addicted to caffeine, and if you don't get enough of it in your body after you're addicted, you can become irritated and possibly develop headaches and other physical symptoms.

With the regular use of alcohol, recreational drugs, and many prescription drugs, you may crave more of the substance just to feel the same effect it once gave you or to feel "normal." This is called *tolerance*. If you notice you are having this experience with any substance, including prescribed drugs, you should speak with a medical professional. You should also speak with a medical professional if you have a history of alcohol or drug abuse and you want to stop. Withdrawal from alcohol and some other drugs can be potentially dangerous.

In the space below, identify what the temporary rewards might be for your behavior and identify possible long-term costs and dangers. Then record any thoughts you have about how your own alcohol and drug use affects how you feel, and write at least two ways you can improve your habits in order to feel better.

The alcohol or drug-using behaviors that I engage in are _____

_____

_____

The temporary rewards for my behaviors are _____

_____

_____

The long-term costs and dangers of my behaviors are _____

_____

_____

My alcohol and drug use affects how I feel because _____

_____

_____

I can improve my alcohol and drug habits by

1. _____

_____

2. _____

_____

Physical Exercise

The human body is designed for motion and activity. Because of this, it's important that everyone engage in some amount of regular exercise in order to keep their bodies healthy and functioning properly. Without exercise, your body won't burn up the extra energy it stores from the food you eat. As a result, you might start to feel sluggish, you might start to gain weight, and you may even feel a little depressed. It's recommended that everyone engage in approximately thirty minutes of moderate or vigorous exercise most days of the week. This can include walking, jogging, swimming, biking, weight training, or any other activity that makes your body work harder than it usually does. Regular exercise is especially important to keep your heart healthy.

Even if your movement is limited or if you've never exercised before, there's always something that you can do that's within your safety limits. Be sure to check with a medical professional or a physical fitness trainer before engaging in any type of strenuous activity, like weight lifting. And talk with your medical professional if you experience any abnormal pain when you exercise.

In the space below, record any thoughts you have about how your own exercise habits (or lack of exercise) affect how you feel, and then write at least two ways you can improve your habits in order to feel better.

My exercise habits affect how I feel because _____

_____

_____

I can improve my exercise habits by

1. _____

_____

2. _____

_____

Sleep

Getting enough sleep is one of the most important things you can do to feel healthy. The average adult needs approximately seven or eight hours of sleep each night. Children and some adults need slightly more. If you're not getting enough sleep each night, you probably feel sluggish and tired all day, and you probably also find it hard to think clearly. It's no wonder that a lack of sleep is often the cause of accidents and poor decision-making ability.

No amount of caffeine can make up for the sleep you missed the night before. In fact, caffeine, alcohol, and other drugs can all interfere with your ability to sleep at night. Your body needs a proper amount of rest because it uses the time when you are asleep to repair itself. If you're not sleeping, your body can't heal itself properly.

If you wake up many times throughout the night, if you snore excessively, or if you wake up gasping for breath, these can all be signs of sleep disorders, and you should talk to a medical professional.

Do your best to develop proper sleep habits in order to get the rest that you need. Refer to the Guide to Sleep Hygiene on the following page to help you develop healthy sleep habits. Then, in the space below, record any thoughts you have about how your own sleep habits affect how you feel, and write at least two ways you can improve your sleep habits in order to feel better.

My sleep (or lack of sleep) affects how I feel because _____

_____

_____

I can improve my sleep habits by

1. _____

_____

2. _____

_____

Illness and Physical Pain

Obviously, if you're experiencing any illness or physical pain, this will affect how you feel emotionally. Your physical feelings and your emotional feelings are directly connected, and sometimes it's hard or impossible to feel emotionally healthy if you aren't also feeling physically healthy. Therefore, it's critical that you get medical help for any illness or physical pain you might be experiencing. Furthermore, it's also extremely important for you to follow the advice of the medical professional who is treating your illness and to follow the prescription plan for any medications you might be given.

To prevent possible illness and physical pain in the future, if you aren't already experiencing them now, use the guidelines in this section to create a healthier life based upon proper nutrition, plenty of exercise, avoidance of alcohol and nonprescribed drugs, and plenty of necessary sleep.

In the space below, record any thoughts you have about how your own illness or physical pain affects how you feel, and then write at least two ways you can treat any illness or pain in order to feel better.

My illness or pain affects how I feel because _____

_____

_____

I can treat my illness or pain by

1. _____

_____

2. _____

_____

Guide to Sleep Hygiene ⊗

Proper sleep habits are essential for any healthy lifestyle. Use the following suggestions if you have trouble falling asleep or staying asleep. (Visit http://www.newharbinger.com/44581 to download the Guide to Sleep Hygiene.)

- Avoid caffeine for at least six hours before going to sleep.

- Avoid alcohol, nicotine, and recreational drugs before going to sleep and throughout the night.

- Avoid bright lights, including television and computer screens, before going to sleep because they are stimulating to your brain and might keep you awake.

- Don't exercise or eat a heavy meal shortly before going to sleep.

- Avoid napping during the day because it will make you less tired at night.

- Make your bedroom as comfortable as possible. Keep the temperature at a cool, comfortable level, keep your room as dark as possible (use a sleep mask if you need one), and minimize as much noise as possible (use earplugs if you need them).

- Only use your bed for sleeping and sexual activity, not for working, reading, or watching television. This way, your body will associate your bed with sleep, not with activity.

- If you have trouble falling asleep or if you wake up in the middle of the night and can't fall back to sleep, get out of bed and do something soothing until you feel tired enough to go back to sleep. Don't lie in bed thinking about other things; this will just make you feel more aggravated and make it harder to get back to sleep.

- Go to bed at the same time every night and wake up at the same time every morning. Create a regular pattern of sleeping and waking that your body can predict.

- Use some kind of relaxation method before going to sleep in order to calm your body and mind: take a bath, meditate, pray, write down your thoughts, use relaxation skills, and so on.

- If your sleep problems persist, if you can't stay awake during the day, or if you're feeling depressed, contact a medical professional for advice.

Physical Tension and Stress

If you experience physical tension on a regular basis, you also probably feel emotionally stressed out, anxious, drained, or irritated. Muscle tension, like an illness, directly affects your emotions. Similarly, if you feel anxious, your emotions can often lead to muscle tension, especially in the neck and shoulders, as well as stomach ailments and skin problems.

There are many situations in modern life that can make you feel physically tense and stressed: long working hours, a job you don't like, commuting to work, difficult relationships, a demanding family schedule, what's happening in the world news, politics, and so on. As a result, it's very important that you find healthy ways to cope with tension and stress so that they don't lead to further illness.

Many good coping skills are found in this book in the mindfulness and distress tolerance chapters. The Mindful Breathing exercise is very effective for helping you relax, as are many of the self-soothing exercises. Go back to those chapters, if you need to, to find exercises that work for you.

In the space below, record any thoughts you have about how your physical tension and stress affect how you feel, and then write at least two ways you can cope with your stress and tension in order to feel better.

My tension and stress affect how I feel because _____

_____

_____

I can treat my tension and stress by

1. _____

_____

2. _____

_____

Exercise: Recognizing Your Self-Destructive Behaviors

Now that you've learned about different forms of self-destructive behaviors and physical vulnerabilities, make photocopies of the following Recognizing Your Self-Destructive Behaviors Worksheet (or download it at http://www.newharbinger.com/44581) to observe your own self-harming actions for the next two weeks. This worksheet is very similar to the Recognizing Your Emotions Worksheet found earlier in this chapter. However, this exercise asks you to observe your self-destructive behaviors and then to identify what the emotional rewards were for your behavior and why those rewards were only temporary. Use the following example worksheet to help you.

Example: Recognizing Your Self-Destructive Behaviors Worksheet

Questions	Your Responses
When did the situation happen?	Tonight
What happened? (Describe the event.)	My girlfriend and I got into a fight. I asked her to come over, but she said she was too busy. Then I told her I didn't know what I would do to myself if she didn't come over, so she did.
Why do you think that situation happened? (Identify the causes.)	She's selfish sometimes. But I also know she's tired when she gets home from work. She's also studying for some classes she's taking. We were both in bad moods.
How did that situation make you feel, both emotionally and physically? (Try to identify both the *primary* emotions and the *secondary* emotions.)	Primary emotions: Anger Secondary emotions: Hopeless, annoyed, afraid that she might leave me Physical sensations: My face became hot, my hands clenched.
What did you want to do as a result of how you felt? (What were your urges?)	I wanted to scream at her and tell her how selfish she is. I also thought about scarring my arm, like I've done in the past.
What did you do and say? (What self-destructive behaviors did you engage in as a result of how you felt?)	I told her she had to come over if she really loved me, or I didn't know what I would do. Then I hung up the phone without waiting for her reply. I went in the kitchen and ate a half-gallon of ice cream while I waited for her to come over. I didn't sleep all night.
What was the emotional reward for your self-destructive behavior? (Identify how the emotional reward was temporary.)	By manipulating her, I got her to come over, which made me feel good. But when she came over, we fought. The ice cream also made me feel good for a little while, but I've been putting on too much weight lately, which makes me feel guilty. Not sleeping another night just made me feel worse the next morning.

Recognizing Your Self-Destructive Behaviors Worksheet

Questions	Your Responses
When did the situation happen?	
What happened? (Describe the event.)	
Why do you think that situation happened? (Identify the causes.)	
How did that situation make you feel, both emotionally and physically? (Try to identify both the *primary* emotions and the *secondary* emotions.)	
What did you want to do as a result of how you felt? (What were your urges?)	
What did you do and say? (What self-destructive behaviors did you engage in as a result of how you felt?)	
What was the emotional reward for your self-destructive behavior? (Identify how the emotional reward was temporary.)	

OBSERVING YOURSELF WITHOUT JUDGING YOURSELF ⊠

As you can see from the previous exercise, self-destructive behaviors can only offer you temporary relief. In the long run, they are all more damaging to yourself and others. For this reason, it's important that you begin to notice what the rewards are for all of your behaviors, but especially the self-destructive ones.

But at the same time, also remember that you shouldn't criticize or judge yourself if you discover unhealthy rewards reinforcing your behaviors. Remember that the principle on which dialectical behavior therapy is based states that two apparently contradictory things can both be true. The most important *dialectic* is accepting yourself without judgment while simultaneously changing destructive behaviors so you can live a healthier life (Linehan, 1993a). It's not wrong to admit that some of your behaviors need to be changed; you can still be a good, kind, and loving person. Your behaviors probably exist as they do because you were never taught how to deal with your overwhelming and distressing emotions in any other way. If you had been shown a healthier way to deal with your emotions, you'd probably do it, wouldn't you? That's what the skills in this workbook are all about—teaching you healthier ways to cope with your feelings.

REDUCING YOUR COGNITIVE VULNERABILITY ⊠

You've already learned how your thoughts influence how you feel. Remember Jim who lost his watch? He originally thought, "I'm so absentminded; I'm an idiot," which just made him feel worse about what he had done. This type of thought is called a *trigger thought* (McKay, Rogers, & McKay, 2003) because it triggers, or causes, emotional pain and suffering. If you frequently dwell on trigger thoughts, you probably experience overwhelming emotions more frequently than other people. However, we all have trigger thoughts that pop up from time to time. The goal of developing emotion regulation skills is to learn what to do with those thoughts when they do come up. Some of these thoughts are criticisms that we were told when we were children by our parents, guardians, teachers, and others. But other trigger thoughts are self-criticisms that we use to insult ourselves or make our lives more difficult.

Below are several trigger thoughts that often cause a person to feel emotionally distressed. Check (✓) any of them that you use, and then write any additional trigger thoughts in the space provided. If you have trouble remembering a trigger thought that you use, think of the last time you felt upset, angry, sad, depressed, worried, or anxious, and then remember the thoughts you had that made you feel worse. These are your trigger thoughts. Here are some examples:

- ☐ "I'm an idiot/jerk/moron."

- ☐ "I can't do anything right."

- ☐ "I'm a failure."

- ☐ "I'm incompetent."

- ☐ "No one's ever going to love me."

- ☐ "I'm unlovable."

- ☐ "There's something wrong with me."

☐ "I'm broken."

☐ "No one cares about me."

☐ "Everyone always leaves me."

☐ "People always hurt me."

☐ "I can't trust anyone."

☐ "I'm going to be alone forever."

☐ "I can't make it in life without the help of _____."

☐ "I don't deserve to be happy/successful/loved."

☐ Other ideas: _____

_____

Obviously a trigger thought can be a powerful negative force in your life if it constantly comes to your attention and leads to distressing emotions. But remember, in addition to trigger thoughts, Jim also used a coping thought, "Mistakes happen; nobody's perfect," and then he was able to feel more at ease. Coping thoughts can be an equally powerful force if you know how to use them. In this section, you'll learn three cognitive skills to help you deal with trigger thoughts and overwhelming emotions: thought and emotion defusing, coping thoughts, and balancing your thoughts and feelings.

Exercise: Thought and Emotion Defusion

Thought defusion (Hayes et al., 1999) is a practice that was already taught in chapter 4, Basic Mindfulness Skills, but it's so important as an emotion regulation skill that it deserves to be repeated here too. Thought defusion is a skill that helps you "unhook" from your thoughts and overwhelming emotions. This is a skill that requires the use of your imagination. The purpose is to visualize your thoughts and emotions either as pictures or words, harmlessly floating away from you, and without obsessing about them, analyzing them, or getting stuck on them.

Typically, people find that imagining their thoughts and emotions floating away in one of the following ways is helpful. But if you've already been using a different means of visualization, or if you want to create something similar, do what works best for you. Here are some examples:

• Imagine sitting in a field watching your thoughts and emotions floating away on clouds.

• Picture yourself sitting near a stream watching your thoughts and emotions floating past on leaves.

• See your thoughts and emotions written in the sand, and then watch the waves wash them away.

Remember to continue using the concept of radical acceptance while doing this exercise. Let your thoughts and related emotions be whatever they are, and don't get distracted by fighting them or criticizing yourself for having them. Just let the thoughts and emotions come and go.

For the purposes of learning emotion regulation skills, you can use one of two variations of this Thought and Emotion defusion exercise. You can start the exercise without any preconceived thoughts and simply watch whatever thoughts and related emotions arise, and then let them come and go without getting stuck on any of them. Or you can begin this exercise by first focusing on one of your trigger thoughts. Recall a recent distressing memory in which your trigger thoughts arose. Notice how you feel emotionally and physically, and then begin the thought defusion exercise. In this case, many memories from that event (and the trigger thought itself) will come to your thoughts automatically. As they do, continue as usual to watch those thoughts and emotions come and go without analyzing them or getting stuck on them.

Read the instructions before beginning the exercise to familiarize yourself with the experience. If you feel more comfortable listening to the instructions, use your smartphone to record the instructions in a slow, even voice so that you can listen to them while practicing this technique. When you are first using thought defusion, set a timer for three to five minutes and practice letting go of your thoughts and related emotions until the alarm goes off. Then, as you get more accustomed to using this technique, you can set the alarm for longer periods of time like eight or ten minutes. But don't expect to be able to sit still that long when you first start.

Do this exercise as often as possible. Then, when you feel comfortable with the skill, you can begin letting go of trigger thoughts and distressing emotions in your daily life by briefly closing your eyes and imagining the thoughts and emotions floating past.

Instructions

To begin, find a comfortable place to sit in a room where you won't be disturbed for as long as you've set your timer. Turn off any distracting sounds. Take a few slow, long breaths, relax, and close your eyes.

Now, in your imagination, picture yourself in the scenario that you chose to watch your thoughts come and go, whether it's by the beach or a stream, in a field or a room, or wherever. Do your best to imagine yourself in that scene.

After you do, also start to become aware of the thoughts that you're having. Start to observe the thoughts that are coming up, whatever they are. Don't try to stop your thoughts, and do your best not to criticize yourself for any of the thoughts. Just watch the thoughts arise, and then, using whatever technique you've chosen, watch the thoughts disappear.

If any of your thoughts is a trigger thought, just note to yourself that you're having a trigger thought, observe any emotion that it brings up, and then let the thought and emotion go past, by whatever means you've chosen, without getting stuck on them and without analyzing them. [Pause here for a minute if you are recording the instructions.]

Whatever the thought or emotion is, big or small, important or unimportant, watch it arise in your mind and then let it float away or disappear by whichever means you've chosen. [Pause here for a minute if you are recording the instructions.]

Keep breathing slowly, in and out, as you watch your thoughts and emotions float away.

When you notice distressing emotions arising in you because of your thoughts, let them float past in your imagination. [Pause here for a minute if you are recording the instructions.]

Just continue to watch the thoughts and feelings arise and disappear. Use pictures or words to represent your thoughts and feelings, whatever works best for you. Do your best to watch the thoughts and related feelings arise and disappear without getting hooked into them and without criticizing yourself. [Pause here for a minute if you are recording the instructions.]

If more than one thought or feeling comes up at the same time, see them both arise and disappear. If the thoughts and feelings come very quickly, do your best to watch them all disappear without getting hooked onto any of them.

Continue to breathe and watch the thoughts and feelings come and go until your timer goes off. [Pause here for a minute if you are recording the instructions.]

When you've finished, take a few slow, long breaths, and then slowly open your eyes and return your focus to the room.

Using Coping Thoughts

Coping thoughts are designed to soothe your emotions when you're in a distressing situation. They are statements that remind you of your strength, your past successes, and some commonly held truths. Do you remember what happened to Jim when he lost his watch? Originally, he thought, "I'm so absentminded; I'm an idiot," which made him feel depressed. But then he used the coping thought "Mistakes happen; nobody's perfect," and he was able to feel more at ease. You already learned about using self-encouraging coping thoughts in chapter 2, Advanced Distress Tolerance Skills, but they're so important for helping you regulate your emotions that they need to be repeated here. In the following List of Coping Thoughts, you'll find many coping thoughts that you can use to remind yourself of your strength and your past successes when you find yourself in a distressing situation.

Find a few coping thoughts that you consider powerful and motivating, or create your own. Then write them on a note card and keep them with you, or use a note app in your smartphone to record them. Then remind yourself of your coping thoughts when you're in a distressing situation. Also, try putting them on sticky notes and post them in spots where you can see them on a regular basis, like on your refrigerator or mirror. The more often you see these soothing and self-affirming thoughts, the quicker they'll become an automatic part of your thought process.

Here's a list of some coping thoughts that many people have found to be helpful (McKay, Davis, & Fanning, 1997). Check (✓) the ones that might be helpful for you and then create your own.

List of Coping Thoughts

☐ "Mistakes happen; nobody's perfect."

☐ "This situation won't last forever."

☐ "I've already been through many other painful experiences, and I've survived."

☐ "This too shall pass."

☐ "My feelings are like a wave that comes and goes."

☐ "My feelings make me uncomfortable right now, but I can accept them."

☐ "I can be anxious and still deal with the situation."

☐ "I'm strong enough to handle what's happening to me right now."

☐ "This is an opportunity for me to learn how to cope with my fears."

☐ "I can ride this out and not let it get to me."

☐ "I can take all the time I need right now to let go and relax."

☐ "I've survived other situations like this before, and I'll survive this one too."

☐ "My anxiety/fear/sadness won't kill me; it just doesn't feel good right now."

☐ "These are just my feelings, and eventually they'll go away."

☐ "It's okay to feel sad/anxious/afraid sometimes."

☐ "My thoughts don't control my life; I do."

☐ "I can think different thoughts if I want to."

☐ "I'm not in danger right now."

☐ "So what?"

☐ "This situation sucks, but it's only temporary."

☐ "I'm strong and I can deal with this."

☐ Other ideas: _____

_____

_____

Balancing Your Thoughts and Feelings ⊠

As you've already learned, overwhelming emotions can be caused by many events. But you can also be overwhelmed by your emotions when you only pay attention to part of what's really happening. This type of thinking is called *filtering* (Beck, Rush, Shaw, & Emery, 1979). If you are using the DBT Skills Card Deck, this practice corresponds to card #34 See the Big Picture. Here are some examples:

- Zeva was a straight-A student, she always made the honor roll, and she had already received a full scholarship to her first choice of colleges. But when she got a poor grade on her math test she broke down. "I'm such a loser," she thought to herself, and, very quickly, she felt overwhelmed, upset, and angry.

- Antonio asked his girlfriend if she could come over at three o'clock. She said that she was busy until seven, and she'd come over then. Antonio immediately got angry and accused her of abandoning him.

- Jennifer grew up in a typical middle-class family in a fairly good neighborhood. Most often, her parents were kind and supportive, and they always tried to do their best for her. However, one day when Jennifer was five, her father punished her for talking back to him, and she was grounded for a week. Later, as an adult, whenever Jennifer thought about her young life, she only remembered that incident, and she got upset whenever she thought about it.

Do you see the filtering in each person's thought process? Zeva was devastated by one less-than-perfect grade because she filtered out all of her past successes. Antonio filtered out the fact that his girlfriend said she would come over at a different, more convenient time. And Jennifer filtered out all of her positive childhood experiences and only focused on the one hardship she'd experienced.

Imagine living your life with dark sunglasses on all the time so that it's impossible to see the colors of the world. Think about what a limited, dreary life you might have. Similarly, when you filter your experience and only focus on the distressing elements of your life, you're also choosing to live a limited, unfulfilling life.

In order to begin balancing your thoughts—and therefore your emotions as well—it's necessary to examine the evidence that supports both sides of an emotion-stimulating event:

- Evidence supporting your self-criticisms versus evidence that you're a good person

- Evidence that only bad things happen to you versus evidence that good things happen too

- Evidence that no one cares about you versus evidence that people do care about you

- Evidence that you never do anything right versus evidence of your past successes

- Evidence that the current situation is awful versus evidence that it's not as bad as you think

- In general, evidence for the bad versus evidence for the good

Seeing the "big picture" is the opposite of filtering. This can be hard to do if you've spent your life narrowly focusing on just the negative evidence in your life. But you can learn to see the big picture by examining the evidence that goes against your distressing thoughts and feelings. These facts, which are often ignored by people with overwhelming emotions, fill out the rest of the big picture and can often change how you feel about a situation. Then, with practice, you'll filter less of your experiences and become less overwhelmed by your emotions.

In order to see the big picture, use the following guidelines. Whenever you find yourself in a situation in which you feel overwhelmed by your emotions, ask yourself these questions:

1. What happened?

2. As a result, what did you think and feel? (Be specific.)

3. What evidence *supports* how you think and feel?

4.   What evidence *contradicts* how you think and feel?

5.   What's a more accurate and fair way to think and feel about this situation?

6.   What can you do to cope with this situation in a healthy way?

Naturally, when you start to feel overwhelmed by a situation, first ask yourself what happened. This is the best place to start. Identify what it is that's making you feel upset. Using Zeva as an example, she would have noted that she got a poor grade on her math test.

Second, identify your thoughts and feelings. Remember, your thoughts greatly influence how you feel. But if your thoughts about a situation are being filtered and you're not seeing the big picture, your thoughts are more likely to cause overwhelming, distressing emotions. In Zeva's example, she thought, "I'm such a loser," and then she felt overwhelmed, upset, and angry.

Third, ask yourself what evidence supports how you're thinking and feeling about the situation. This is usually an easy question to answer. If you've spent your life filtering your experiences so that you only see the negative, distressing facts, it's easy to think of lots of reasons why you feel so distressed and overwhelmed. After all, this is what you usually do. Zeva could easily identify why she was feeling so upset: she had studied hard, as she always did, but had gotten a poor grade on her test, which was her lowest score all year.

The fourth question, however, is usually new and challenging for people struggling with overwhelming emotions. Asking yourself to identify the evidence that contradicts how you think and feel about a situation requires that you view the situation in a new and deeper way. For instance, imagine how much different the world must look to a person standing on the street when compared to a person flying above in an airplane. They're both looking at the same landscape, but the person in the plane has a better view of the whole landscape—the big picture.

Similarly, you need to examine more of the facts and evidence that affect your situation and make up your big picture. As you saw earlier in the examples, people often filter out the positive elements of their lives and ignore the facts that might change the way they feel about a situation. If you really want to stop being overwhelmed by your emotions, you'll have to look at all those facts. Remember what Zeva filtered out? She's a straight-A student, she's on the honor roll, and she got a full scholarship to her first choice of colleges. Now consider how that information contradicts what she thought ("I'm a loser") and how she felt (overwhelmed, upset, and angry). Obviously, Zeva filtered out some very important pieces of her big picture.

Remember, because this question is new for you, it often takes some time to think of an answer. So give yourself a few minutes to think about the possible facts before saying, "There is no contradictory evidence." Be fair and kind to yourself. There's always evidence for and against any topic. And even if the contradictory evidence is minor, it still adds to your big picture. Consider Zeva's example. Even if her example was different and she was a B student or a hardworking student, these facts still could have changed the way she felt about the poor grade. No fact or contradictory piece of evidence is too small to be overlooked.

Next, keeping in mind the new evidence that contradicts the trigger thought, ask yourself whether there is a more accurate and fair way to think and feel about this situation. This is a good time to be mindful of your emotions and to use radical acceptance. Remember, this exercise is designed to help you look at your emotional reactions in a new way; it is not designed to criticize you. Therefore, don't be critical of yourself. Try to be accepting of yourself and your emotions as you continue to see your emotions in a new way. In this step, add the new evidence to your big picture and try to create a more accurate and fair way to think and feel about this situation. In reality, this might not change how you feel right now, but it will help you notice how you could feel about this situation in the future. Using these skills, Zeva's answer could have been something like, "It's okay to feel disappointed because I studied a lot and I didn't do well. But this is just one bad grade. I mostly get As, and I'm doing well in general."

Finally, Zeva would have asked, "What can I do to cope with this situation in a healthy way?" Here is where you should draw from all the skills and techniques you've learned in this workbook, including the REST strategy to help you relax, evaluate, set an intention, and take action. For example, Zeva could have used some of the distress tolerance and self-soothing skills to calm her emotions, like talking to a friend or listening to some relaxing music. She could also have used her mindfulness skills, like mindful breathing or thought defusion. Or she could have used a coping thought, like "Nobody's perfect; everyone makes mistakes."

Obviously, using the questions in this exercise isn't going to magically change the way you feel right away. But asking yourself these questions will help you recognize the facts that you've been filtering out, and it will also show you the possibilities of how you might react to a similar situation in the future. Then, with practice, you'll start reacting to those similar situations in a new, healthier way.

Seeing the big picture will also give you hope for your future. Many people who filter their experiences feel hopeless and desperate because they're only seeing the problems and the difficulties in their lives. But looking for contrary evidence opens up their perspectives and lets them see that their lives do include some positive experiences. Looking for evidence against overwhelming emotions is like taking off those dark sunglasses so that you can see the variety of colors in your life, and that's a hopeful experience.

Use the following evidence log to help you recognize the evidence for and against the ways you think and feel. Make photocopies of the Big-Picture Evidence Log (or download it at http://www.newharbinger .com/44581) and keep one with you. Then, when you're in a situation in which you feel overwhelmed, use the log to help you see the big picture. Use the following example of Zeva's experience to help you.

Example: Big-Picture Evidence Log

Questions	Your Responses
What happened?	I got a poor grade on my math test.
As a result, what did you think and feel? (Be specific.)	Thoughts: "I'm such a loser." Feelings: Overwhelmed, upset, and angry
What evidence *supports* how you're thinking and feeling?	I studied as hard as I could, like I usually do, and I still only got a poor grade. That's my lowest grade in class all year.
What evidence *contradicts* how you're thinking and feeling?	I'm a straight-A student. I'm on the honor roll. And I got a full scholarship to my first choice of colleges.
Considering all the evidence, what's a more *accurate and fair* way to think and feel about this situation?	It's okay to feel disappointed because I studied a lot and still didn't do well. But this is just one bad grade. I mostly get As, and I'm doing well in general.
What can you do to cope with this situation in a healthier way?	Talk to my friends. Listen to music I like. Use thought defusion. Use mindful breathing. Use my coping thought: "Nobody's perfect; everybody makes mistakes."

Big-Picture Evidence Log

Questions	Your Responses
What happened?	
As a result, what did you think and feel? (Be specific.)	
What evidence *supports* how you're thinking and feeling?	
What evidence *contradicts* how you're thinking and feeling?	
Considering all the evidence, what's a more *accurate and fair* way to think and feel about this situation?	
What can you do to cope with this situation in a healthier way?	

INCREASING YOUR POSITIVE EMOTIONS ⊠

Before you picked up this workbook for the first time, you were probably an expert on distressing emotions and you understood what a life filled with them could feel like. Now, however, you understand that many people with overwhelming emotions discount their pleasurable emotions, filter them out, or never take the opportunity to experience them in the first place. As a result, they focus only on their distressing emotions, such as anger, fear, and sadness, and they rarely notice their pleasurable emotions, such as happiness, surprise, and love.

Maybe that's what you did before, but now you know that it's very important for you to begin noticing your pleasurable emotions. As you continue to use dialectical behavior therapy to improve your life, you'll want to find more ways of experiencing pleasurable emotions, if you don't have enough of them in your life already. This doesn't mean that you'll never experience another distressing feeling. That's impossible. We all have distressing emotions at different points in our lives. But your life doesn't have to be dominated by them.

One very reliable way of focusing on pleasurable emotions is to create pleasurable experiences for yourself. Again, this is a skill that you've already learned in chapter 1, Basic Distress Tolerance Skills, but it deserves to be repeated here. To begin building a more balanced, healthier life for yourself, take some time out of each day to create a pleasurable experience for yourself, and make note of how you felt and what you thought as a result of that experience.

If you need help thinking of pleasurable experiences, use The Big List of Pleasurable Activities found in chapter 1. Then use the following Pleasurable Activities Log and the example to record what you did, how you felt, and what you thought about the experience. Remember, try to do something pleasurable for yourself every day. You deserve it. (Visit http://www.newharbinger.com/44581 to download the Pleasurable Activities Log.)

Example: Pleasurable Activities Log

When?	What Did You Do?	How Did You Feel?	What Did You Think?
Wednesday night	I took a hot bath.	Very relaxed and calm	"I should do this more often."
Thursday afternoon	I treated myself to a delicious lunch at work.	Satisfied and happy	"I enjoy good food even if I can't always afford it."
Thursday night	I turned off my phone and watched a movie.	Very good; laughed a lot	"I don't watch enough comedies."
Friday night	I went to dinner with my boyfriend.	Excited, nervous, happy	"I wish we went out like that more often."
Saturday morning	I went to temple for religious services	Holy, special, calm	"I should come more often."
Saturday afternoon	I went for a walk at the lake.	Calm and peaceful	"The lake was beautiful."
Saturday afternoon	I went out for ice cream after the walk.	Happy, like I used to when I was younger	"I miss being this happy."
Saturday night	I stayed at home and read.	Relaxed and quiet	"Sometimes it's nice to do quiet things."
Sunday morning	I slept late.	Very rested	"I don't get enough sleep during the week."
Sunday night	I took another bubble bath.	Very relaxed	"I should do this every night."

Pleasurable Activities Log

When?	What Did You Do?	How Did You Feel?	What Did You Think?

CHAPTER 8

Advanced Emotion Regulation Skills

In this chapter, you will learn four advanced emotion regulation skills:

1. Being mindful of your emotions without judgment

2. Emotion exposure

3. Doing the opposite of your emotional urges

4. Problem solving

In chapter 4, Basic Mindfulness Skills, you learned how to mindfully recognize and describe your emotions. Learning to be mindful of your emotions without judging them decreases the chance that they will grow in intensity and become even more painful. Now, in this chapter, emotion exposure will further help you practice two very important things. First, you will learn to observe the natural life cycle of your emotions, watching them rise and fall, shift and change as new emotions replace old ones. Second, you'll learn that you can endure your strong feelings without avoiding or resisting them. You'll get practice staying "in" the emotion, even though you want to run away from it or turn the feeling into harmful actions (such as shouting, hitting, or breaking things). Emotion exposure is a crucial process for learning *not to fear your feelings*, and it will strengthen your emotion regulation skills. The more you practice this exposure work, the more confident you'll become as you face tough emotional challenges.

In addition to being mindful of your emotions without judgment and using emotion exposure, you'll learn a behavioral technique called *doing the opposite of your emotional urges*. This will help you change the way you usually behave when you have a particularly strong emotion. When you have a strong emotion, it usually affects your behavior in two ways. First, you change your facial expression and body language to reflect how you're feeling. For example, if you're angry, you may begin to frown and tighten your fists; or if you're scared, your eyes may open wide while you hunch your shoulders. The second way that a strong emotion affects your behavior is the way in which it causes you to have powerful urges that are often hard to resist. Anger, for example, may produce urges to shout or hit, while fear might push you to cower or back away. "Doing the opposite of your emotional urges" is a strategy that blocks these ineffective, emotion-driven responses while also helping you soften the feeling itself.

The next important steps that you will learn in this chapter are behavior analysis and problem-solving skills to help you deal more effectively with high-emotion situations. You'll identify what causes your emotional responses and learn how to develop alternative strategies to cope with these emotion-triggering events.

The last thing we'll do in this chapter is introduce you to an exercise regimen called the Weekly Regulator. It will help you keep practicing the key emotion regulation skills you've learned here.

BEING MINDFUL OF YOUR EMOTIONS WITHOUT JUDGMENT ⊗

Learning to be mindful of your emotions without judging them decreases the chance that they will grow in intensity and become even more overwhelming or painful.

Exercise: Being Mindful of Your Emotions Without Judgment

This technique begins with the mindful awareness of your breath. Focus on the feeling of the air moving in through your nose, your chest expanding and contracting, and the sense of your abdomen rising and falling with each breath. After four or five slow, long breaths, you can do one of two things: (1) observe whatever current emotion you may be feeling, or if you can't identify an emotion, (2) visualize a recent event in your life when you experienced an emotional reaction. If you visualize a scene, notice as many details as possible. Try to remember what was said and how you and others acted.

Read the instructions before beginning the exercise to familiarize yourself with the experience. If you feel more comfortable listening to the instructions, use your smartphone to record the directions in a slow, even voice, so that you can listen to them while practicing this technique.

Instructions

While breathing slowly and evenly, bring your attention to where you are feeling the emotion in your body. Is it a feeling in your chest or stomach, in your shoulders, or in your face or head? Are you feeling it in your arms or legs? Notice any physical sensations connected with the emotion. Now be aware of the strength of the feeling. Is it growing or diminishing? Is the emotion pleasant or painful? Try to name the emotion or describe some of its qualities. [If you're recording the instructions, pause here for a minute.]

Now try to notice your thoughts. Do you have thoughts about the emotion? Does the emotion trigger judgments about others or about yourself? Just keep watching your emotion and keep observing your judgments. [If you're recording the instructions, pause here for a minute.]

Now imagine that each judgment is one of the following:

- *A leaf floating down a stream, around a bend, and out of sight*

- *A computer pop-up ad that briefly flashes on the screen and disappears*

- *One of a long string of boxcars passing in front of you at a railroad crossing*

- *A cloud cutting across a windy sky*

- *A message written on a billboard that you approach and pass at high speed*

- *One of a procession of trucks or cars approaching and passing you on a desert highway*

Choose the image that works best for you. The key is to notice the judgment, place it on a billboard or leaf or boxcar, and let it go. [If you're recording the instructions, pause here for a minute.]

Just keep observing your emotion. When a judgment about yourself or others begins to manifest, turn it into a visualization (leaf, cloud, billboard, and so on) and watch while it moves away and out of sight. [If you're recording the instructions, pause here for a minute.]

Now it's time to remind yourself of the right to feel whatever you feel. Emotions come and go, like waves on the sea. They rise up and then recede. Whatever you feel is legitimate and necessary, no matter how strong or painful. Take a slow breath and accept the emotion as something that lives in you for a little while—and then passes. [If you're recording the instructions, pause here for a minute.]

Notice your judgmental thoughts. Visualize them and then let them pass. Let your emotions be what they are, like waves on the sea that rise and fall. You ride your emotions for a little while, and then they leave. This is natural and normal. It's what it means to be human. [If you're recording the instructions, pause here for a minute.]

Finish the exercise with three minutes of mindful breathing, counting your out-breaths (1, 2, 3, 4) and focusing on the experience of each moment as you breathe. [If you're recording the instructions, pause here for three minutes.]

Looking back on this exercise, you may have found it to be hard work. Watching and letting go of judgments may feel very foreign, very strange. But you are doing something important—you are learning to observe rather than be controlled by judgmental thoughts. We encourage you to do this exercise three or four times before going on to the next step.

Remember, the key steps to the practice of observing your emotions without judging them are as follows:

- Focus on your breath.

- Focus on the emotion (current or past).

- Notice physical sensations connected to emotion.

- Name the emotion.

- Notice judgments (about self, others, or the emotion itself) and let them go. Use "leaves on a stream" or another image.

- Watch the emotion; emotions are like waves on the sea.

- Remind yourself that you have a right to your feelings.

- Continue to notice and let go of judgments.

- Finish with three minutes of mindful breathing.

EMOTION EXPOSURE ⊠

Facing your emotions instead of avoiding them is a major goal of dialectical behavior therapy. Emotion exposure helps you develop the capacity to accept feelings and be less afraid of them.

Step 1 is to begin keeping an Emotion Log so you can become more aware of specific emotional events and how you cope with them. Make photocopies of the log below or download the Emotion Log at http://www.newharbinger.com/44581. For the next week, keep a record in your Emotion Log for every significant emotion you experience. Under "Event," write down what caused your feeling. The triggering events could be internal—such as a thought, memory, or another feeling—or they could be external, such as something you or someone else said or did. Under "Emotion," write a word or phrase that sums up your feeling. Under "Coping or Blocking Response," write what you did to try to push the emotion away. Did you try to suppress or hide it? Did you act on it by picking a fight or avoiding something scary? This record of your coping or blocking response will help you identify emotions for doing emotion exposure later in this chapter.

Example: Emotion Log

Linda, who had been struggling with anger and feelings of rejection, kept the following Emotion Log during the week before Christmas. Neither of her divorced parents had invited her for the holiday.

Linda's Emotion Log

Date	Event	Emotion	Coping or Blocking Response
12/18	My brother calls, wants to know if I'm going to Dad's house for Christmas. But I wasn't invited.	Hurt, rejected, angry	Said "No" in a very dismissive voice. Changed the subject. Criticized him for being stupid and still trying to be part of the family. Told him Dad doesn't even like him.
12/18	Stuff I said to my brother.	Guilty	Turned it into anger. Sent my father an e-mail, telling him he was a jerk for not inviting me.
12/19	Called my mother, but she was too busy to talk.	Rejected, angry	Thought about what a lousy mother she was. Sent an e-mail not to bother "taking time from her busy schedule" to call me back.
12/20	Saw a beautiful castle in a toy store window. Remembered the crappy after-thought Christmas presents I used to get.	Rejected, sad	Got an ice cream and watched all the "stupid ants" running around, doing their Christmas shopping, slaves to the season.
12/21	Bought my father a leather briefcase.	Angry, guilty	Hoping he opens it at his party and feels crappy he didn't invite me. Wrote a phony note saying "Thanks for being a great dad," and apologizing for my e-mail.
12/22	My mother called back.	Rejected, angry	Very cold to her. Told her I was busy when she invited me for a pre-Christmas dinner.

Emotion Log

Date	Event	Emotion	Coping or Blocking Response

As you look back over your Emotion Log, we'd like you to pay attention to two things. First, identify the emotions that seem chronic, that show up over and over. Second, notice what coping or blocking mechanisms you typically use and their outcome. Do they work? Do you feel better or worse a few hours after you use them?

Emotions that show up repeatedly or have blocking strategies that create more pain than they relieve will be good targets for emotion exposure. Emotions with ineffective or destructive blocking strategies require exposure because you need practice facing and feeling them—without your traditional methods of avoidance. Those types of strategies don't work and often just get you in more trouble.

Linda, after reviewing her log, realized that the things she did to cope with feelings of rejection (such as attacking or criticizing people, as well as being cold and rejecting) were only digging her into a deeper emotional pit. She ended up with overwhelming feelings of guilt and self-hate and seemed even more alienated from her family.

Linda needed to learn how to *be* with her feelings and how to observe them without the traditional avoidance strategies. Emotion exposure would prove to be a tremendously important skill for her. Here's how it works.

Exercise: Emotion Exposure

As soon as you start feeling the emotion you've chosen to work on, do the following procedure. You can either read the instructions to yourself or record them on your smartphone and listen to them.

Instructions

Take three or four slow diaphragmatic breaths. Notice how the breath feels moving into your body, as it fills your lungs, and as it stretches your chest and abdomen. While breathing slowly, notice how you feel inside your body, particularly your abdomen and chest. Also notice how your neck, shoulders, and face feel. [If you're recording the instructions, pause here for a few seconds.]

Now notice how you feel emotionally. Just keep your attention on the feeling until you have a sense of it. Describe that feeling to yourself. Label it. Notice the strength of the feeling. Find words to describe the intensity. Notice whether the emotion is growing or diminishing. If the emotion were a wave, at what point on the wave are you now—ascending on the leading edge, on the crest, or beginning to slide down the far side? [If you're recording the instructions, pause here for a few seconds.]

Now notice any changes in the feeling. Are there other emotions beginning to weave into the first one? Describe to yourself any new emotions that have appeared. Just keep watching and looking for words to describe the slightest change in the quality or intensity of your feelings. [If you're recording the instructions, pause here for a few seconds.]

As you continue to watch, you may notice a need to block the emotion, to push it away. That's normal, but try to keep watching your emotions for just a little while longer. Just keep describing to yourself what you feel and noticing any changes. [If you're recording the instructions, pause here for a few seconds.]

Notice what it's like not to act on your feelings, not to blow up or avoid, not to hurt yourself. Just be aware of the feeling without action, watching but not doing. [If you're recording the instructions, pause here for a few seconds.]

Remind yourself that this is a wave that passes, like countless other emotional waves in your life. Waves come and go. There are many times when you've felt good. Soon this wave will pass, and you will feel, again, a period of calm. Watch the wave and let it slowly pass. [If you're recording the instructions, pause here for a few seconds.]

If judgment—about yourself or another—arises, notice it and let it go. If you have a judgment about feeling this emotion, notice it and let it go. As best you can, try to accept this feeling. It is just one of life's struggles. [If you're recording the instructions, pause here for a few seconds.]

Stay aware of your emotions just a little longer. If they are changing, let them change. Describe to yourself what you feel. Keep watching until the emotion either changes or diminishes. [If you're recording the instructions, pause here for a few seconds.]

Finish the exercise with a few minutes of mindful breathing—counting your breaths and focusing on the experience of each breath. [If you're recording the instructions, pause here for two minutes.]

We encourage you to do emotion exposure for brief periods at first—perhaps as little as five minutes. As you become more used to focusing on feelings, you will be able to tolerate emotion exposure for longer periods. Always be sure to end exposure with mindful breathing because it will soften high-intensity feelings and help relax you. It will also strengthen mindfulness skills and increase your confidence in your effectiveness.

Remember, the key steps to doing the Emotion Exposure exercise are:

- Focus on your breathing.

- Notice how you feel inside your body.

- Notice and describe your emotion.

- Notice whether the feeling is growing or diminishing; see it like a wave.

- Describe any new emotions or changes in quality.

- Notice any need to block the emotion, but keep watching.

- Notice impulses to *act* on your emotion, but keep watching without acting.

- Notice judgments (about self, others, or the emotion itself), and let them go.

- Keep watching until the emotion either changes or diminishes.

- Finish with a few minutes of mindful breathing.

(Visit http://www.newharbinger.com/44581 to download the key steps of the Emotion Exposure exercise.)

Example: Using Mindfulness of Your Emotions and Emotion Exposure

Adam had struggled for more than five years with feelings of hurt and anger regarding his ex-wife. They were now coparenting Adam's seven- and ten-year-old children, with the kids spending half the week at each parent's home. Virtually every time they had contact, Adam's ex-wife said something that enraged him. And it didn't end there. He seethed for days afterward, plotting what he might say or do to get revenge in the future.

The Being Mindful of Your Emotions Without Judgment exercise seemed daunting to Adam, but he was exhausted with the constant emotional upheaval, and his medical doctor had recently warned him about borderline hypertension. He started by focusing on current emotions—nothing to do with his ex-wife. To his surprise, he often felt sad rather than angry.

As Adam observed his sadness, he became conscious of a heavy feeling in his abdomen and shoulders. He had a sudden image of himself carrying a great weight. Judgments came up—he should be stronger, he wasn't a good father, he had screwed up his life. He noticed these thoughts and let them go, imagining them as a string of boxcars passing before him.

Adam didn't fight the sadness—he watched it swell and recede like an ocean wave. He gave himself the right to be sad. Noticing the judgments and letting them go became easier after a few experiences with the exercise. And Adam gained confidence in his ability to calm himself with mindful breathing.

Emotion exposure was more challenging. For this exercise, Adam chose to work on feelings that came up around his ex-wife. His first emotion exposure incident followed a phone call where she accused him of being "cheap and never voluntarily spending anything on the kids."

Adam began by noticing the effect of these words on his body. He felt hot, with a disturbing sense of pressure in the chest and neck. (He wondered if it was his blood pressure.) Now he described the anger to himself. It felt hard and sharp, surging up with deep disgust. There was something else too—a sense of helplessness that seemed almost like despair. It was a feeling that things would never be better, never be different.

As the despair got stronger, Adam noticed an impulse to turn it off, to block it. He wanted a beer, and he started planning the responses he would make to his ex-wife. With an effort, Adam continued to observe his emotions, not trying to hold on to any particular feeling but keeping his attention on *whatever* he felt.

Adam was also aware of impulses to act on the despair. He wanted to get angry instead, to call his ex and shout that she was poisoning his relationship with his kids. Then he had images of getting in his car and driving into a tree—half for revenge and half to end all the pain he was feeling.

While Adam observed his feelings, judgments kept coming up: "My ex is evil...I was stupid to marry her... She destroyed my life...This is too messed up to go on living." It took effort, but he put every thought on a boxcar and let it roll away.

After a time, Adam noticed something that surprised him. The despair feeling began to fade if he didn't hold on to judgments. It softened to a feeling closer to regret.

Adam now returned the focus to his breathing, counting and observing each breath. Three minutes later he felt a dark sort of calm—not the greatest feeling in the world but something he could live with.

DOING THE OPPOSITE OF YOUR EMOTIONAL URGES ⊗

There are usually good reasons for feeling whatever it is you feel. Even when they are painful, your emotions are legitimate and valid. The larger problem is emotion-driven behavior, because acting on emotions often creates destructive outcomes. For example, letting your anger cause you to attack other people with words can disrupt your relationships, while letting fear drive you to avoid critical tasks and challenges can interfere with your duties at work.

A second problem with acting on emotion-driven impulses is that they *intensify* your original feeling. Instead of getting relief, you may get even more consumed with the emotion if you act on your destructive urges. This is where *opposite action* comes in. Rather than fueling your emotion, opposite action helps regulate and change it. Here are some examples of opposite action.

Example: Opposite Action

Emotion	Emotion-Driven Behavior	Opposite Action
Anger	Attack, criticize, hurt, shout.	Validate, avoid or distract, use soft voice.
Fear	Avoid, hunch shoulders.	Approach what you fear, do what you've been avoiding, stand tall.
Sadness	Shut down, avoid, be passive, slump, hang your head.	Be active, get involved, set goals, stand straight.
Guilt/shame	Punish yourself, confess, avoid, shut down.	If unfounded guilt, continue doing whatever is triggering guilt; if guilt is justified, atone and make amends.

Notice that opposite action changes both body language—your posture and facial expression—as well as your actual behavior. Opposite action isn't about denying or pretending an emotion isn't happening. Rather, it is about *regulation*. You acknowledge the emotion but use the opposite behavior to reduce it or encourage a new emotion.

There are six steps to creating opposite action:

1. Start by acknowledging what you feel. Describe the emotion in words.

2. Ask yourself if there's a good reason to regulate or reduce the intensity of this emotion. Is it overpowering you? Does it drive you to do dangerous or destructive things?

3. Notice the specific body language and behavior that accompany the emotion (see the "Emotion-Driven Behavior" column in the table above). What are your facial expression and your posture?

What are you saying and how are you saying it? What specifically do you do in response to the emotion?

4. Identify your opposite action. How can you relax your face and body so it doesn't scream "I'm angry" or "I'm scared"? How can you change your posture to convey confidence and vitality rather than depression? How can you move toward, not away from, what scares you? When you are angry, how can you acknowledge or ignore rather than attack? Make a plan for opposite action that includes a *specific* description of your new behavior.

5. Fully commit to opposite action, and set a time frame to work at it. How long will you maintain the opposite behavior? As you think about making a commitment, keep in mind why you want to regulate your emotions. What's happened in the past when you gave in to emotion-driven behavior? Were there serious costs to you or to others?

6. Monitor your emotions. As you do opposite action, notice how the original emotion may change or evolve. Opposite action literally sends a message to the brain that the old emotion is no longer appropriate—and it helps you shift to a less painful emotion.

Now it's time to do some advance planning. You're going to identify some "frequent flyer" emotions and commit to opposite-action strategies that can help you regulate them.

Filling out the Opposite-Action Planning Worksheet is simple but potentially very important. In it you'll identify emotions you can expect to feel in the future and prepare a radically different response than you've had in the past. (Make photocopies of the Opposite-Action Planning Worksheet or download it at http://www.newharbinger.com/44581.)

Here's an example. Remember Linda and the Emotion Log she filled out just before Christmas? When she began working on her Opposite-Action Planning Worksheet, she identified several opposite actions that she thought might help with her anger, feelings of rejection, and guilt. Here's what she decided.

Example: Linda's Opposite-Action Planning Worksheet

Emotion	Emotion-Driven Behavior	Opposite Action	Time Period	Outcomes
Feeling rejected, angry	1. Withdrawing 2. Attacking 3. Little revenges	Say what hurt me in a soft, nonattacking voice. Be civil; end the conversation quickly. Do something for myself rather than planning revenge.	As long as the conversation lasts	My conversations were calmer, they didn't escalate into fights. I expressed how I felt in a civil way.
Guilt	1. Being "phony nice" 2. Attacking	Apologize straight up, but let people know I don't like how I was treated.	As long as the conversation lasts	People appreciated my honesty. I expressed how I felt in an honest way.

Over several weeks, Linda monitored her opposite-action outcomes to see how the new behavior worked. What she found was that her anger passed more quickly when she followed her opposite-action plan. Using a quiet voice and saying out loud what hurt her seemed to soften the upset. At first, she had been afraid to acknowledge her feelings of rejection because it made her more vulnerable. But after trying it several times (for example, telling her father she was sad not to be with him on Christmas Day), Linda found that her anger often shifted to something less sharp and less painful. She also spent less time ruminating about the ways in which she felt victimized.

Opposite action isn't easy. We won't pretend that it is. But with practice, opposite action can soothe and soften overwhelming emotions. Fear often turns to empowerment, sadness to engagement, anger to detachment, and shame and avoidance to willingness. Planning opposite-action strategies can give you an incredibly effective tool for emotion regulation.

Opposite-Action Planning Worksheet

Emotion	Emotion-Driven Behavior	Opposite Action	Time Period	Outcomes

PROBLEM SOLVING ⊠

Sometimes emotion regulation has to start *before* the overwhelming feelings even begin. Problem solving focuses on identifying the triggering event and finding new, more effective ways to respond in the future. The first step to problem solving is to learn behavior analysis.

Behavior Analysis

Problem solving begins with something called *behavior analysis*. Basically, this amounts to tracing the sequence of events that led up to a problematic emotion. The Behavior Analysis Worksheet will take you step by step through the process. Make photocopies of the Behavior Analysis Worksheet or download it at http://www.newharbinger.com/44581.

EXAMPLE: BEHAVIOR ANALYSIS WORKSHEET

Sam often found himself struggling with overwhelming anger, especially when he had to interact with his mother-in-law. When he did a behavior analysis of his anger reactions, Sam found multiple internal triggers he hadn't expected to find.

Sam's Behavior Analysis Worksheet

1. Problematic emotion: Rage at my mother-in-law

2. Precipitating event

    •   External event: My mother-in-law's visit. She looks disgusted when she sees my house.

    •   Thoughts: My house needs paint. My yard is full of weeds and run-down looking. This place is a dump.

3. Secondary events

    a. Emotion: Sadness

        Thought: I hate this place.

    b. Emotion: Shame

        Thoughts: Why do I spend my life in dumps like this? Why can't I do better than this? I know why—because I'm a loser who can't make any money.

        Behavior: Accused my mother-in-law of not helping us when we needed it, of not caring about our problems, and when she disagreed, I blew up emotionally at her.

Notice that the external event—the mother-in-law's visit—is only one step in a series. And most of the steps leading to the rage are internal—both thoughts and other painful feelings. If Sam is going to better regulate his anger, he may need to identify which steps in the triggering process he wants to change and then use problem solving to plan a different response.

The point here is that you *can* change or soften overwhelming emotions by changing what you do *before* the emotion sweeps you away. The first step, after completing your behavior analysis, is to decide which of the precipitating or secondary events you want to alter. This must be (1) an event you have control over (for example, your own thoughts or behavior) and (2) an event, if altered, that's likely to reduce your problematic emotion.

In Sam's case, he decided to do something about his shame-generating thoughts and the verbal attack. Sam realized that all too often over the years, this same pattern had repeated itself prior to his getting angry. He'd start with self-shaming thoughts, which would soon feel intolerably painful. Then he'd try to mask the shame by finding fault with others, which would trigger anger and eventually an attack.

Behavior Analysis Worksheet

1. Problematic emotion: _____

2. Precipitating event (what happened before the emotion)

    •   External event: Did something happen over which you have no control (like losing a job, getting sick, hearing disturbing news, and so on)?

        _____

    •   Thoughts: What thoughts, prior to the emotion, might have triggered or intensified your reaction?

        _____

    •   Emotion: Was there a prior or different emotion that triggered your reaction?

        _____

    •   Behavior: Was something you or someone else did a trigger for your reaction?

        _____

3. Secondary events: Identify what happened immediately after the precipitating event (but before the problematic emotion). Break it down into a series of steps (a, b, c).

    a. Thoughts: _____

        Emotion: _____

        Behavior: _____

        _____

    b. Thoughts: _____

        Emotion: _____

        Behavior: _____

        _____

    c. Thoughts: _____

        Emotion: _____

        Behavior: _____

        _____

When you complete a Behavior Analysis Worksheet, you'll see how emotions are built. Something always triggers your emotions. Sometimes that trigger is internal—like your own thoughts or feelings—and sometimes there are multiple causes, all of which need to be recognized and traced.

Once you've identified the precipitating or secondary event(s) you want to change using your own Behavior Analysis Worksheet, the next step is to use the ABC Problem Solving technique.

ABC Problem Solving

This is the second step of problem solving after you've completed your Behavioral Analysis Worksheet. It will teach you to identify the ABCs of problem solving:

A. *Alternatives.* Brainstorm alternative responses. How could you change precipitating or secondary thoughts or behaviors?

B. *Best ideas.* Evaluate your list and choose one or two of your best ideas to implement.

C. *Commitment to implementation.* Identify the time and place you'll try your new responses. Write out the new thoughts or behaviors that you'll use.

ALTERNATIVES: BRAINSTORMING

Let's go through the problem-solving steps with Sam as an example. Sam had two brainstorming lists—one to replace his shame-triggering thoughts and the other to change his attacking behavior.

Sam's Brainstorming Ideas

Shame Thoughts	Attacking Behavior
Think of things I do right.	Validate the person before saying anything negative.
Remind myself how crazy this makes me, how eventually I get angry.	Never say anything critical if I'm feeling upset or ashamed.
Distract myself; listen to music.	Give written, not verbal, feedback because I often get too upset and say mean things.
Ask my wife for support.	Remember how the other person would feel before saying anything.
Take a drive; take some pictures.	Check with my wife about whether I'm going off the deep end before giving criticism to anyone.

BEST IDEAS: EVALUATION STEP

Sam evaluated the different ideas he'd come up with, and decided to try the following:

1. I'll distract myself with music or get involved in my photography.

2. I'll run things past my wife before getting on anyone's case, and I'll give thought-out, written feedback if I decide to say anything critical.

COMMITMENT TO IMPLEMENTATION

Finally, Sam decided to follow his plan with his mother-in-law for the rest of his visit, particularly whenever he was alone with her and she said something annoying. For example, when his mother-in-law made a critical comment about how old and outdated his kitchen looked, Sam went to his room, put on his headphones, and listened to some music for a few minutes, in order to help himself calm down. Also, after she left, Sam and his wife sent his mother-in-law a thoughtful e-mail asking her to please not be so critical of their home in the future.

Notice that Sam developed specific alternative behaviors to replace key actions that happened before he got angry, and he identified a situation where he was committed to using his new plan.

The most important thing about problem solving is to know *exactly* what you're going to do differently—and when and where you'll do it. The more concrete and specific you are, the better. Now, using your own example from your Behavioral Analysis Worksheet, work through the same steps, writing your ideas on a blank piece of paper, so that you can create a plan you can commit to following.

WEEKLY REGULATOR

Emotion regulation is best achieved when you employ your new skills on a regular basis. The Weekly Regulator Logsheet is essentially a reminder system to help you do that. Here are the skills you'll focus on:

- Managing physical vulnerability

- Managing cognitive vulnerability

- Noticing and remembering positive events

- Watching and accepting emotions

- Practicing opposite action

- Using problem solving

The Weekly Regulator Logsheet should be filled out at the end of every week. Make plenty of photocopies (or download the Weekly Regulator Logsheet at http://www.newharbinger.com/44581) and review the skills you've utilized during the past seven days. Check the appropriate boxes to indicate when you used your skills.

Weekly Regulator Logsheet
Managing Physical Vulnerability

	Mon	Tue	Wed	Thu	Fri	Sat	Sun
Took proactive steps to deal with physical illness/pain.							
Committed to balanced eating.							
Didn't use drugs/alcohol.							
Got enough sleep.							
Exercised.							
Used relaxation or mindfulness to cope with stress/tension.							

Managing Cognitive Vulnerability

	Mon	Tue	Wed	Thu	Fri	Sat	Sun
Observed trigger thoughts.							
Used coping thoughts.							
Noticed at least one positive event.							

Positive Events This Week

Monday

1. _____

2. _____

3. _____

Tuesday

1. _____

2. _____

3. _____

Wednesday

1. _____

2. _____

3. _____

Thursday

1. _____

2. _____

3. _____

Friday

1. _____

2. _____

3. _____

Saturday

1. _____

2. _____

3. _____

Sunday

1. _____

2. _____

3. _____

Watching and Accepting Emotions

	Mon	Tue	Wed	Thu	Fri	Sat	Sun
Watched the emotion.							
Didn't act on the emotion.							
Didn't judge the emotion.							

Coping with Emotions

	Mon	Tue	Wed	Thu	Fri	Sat	Sun
Used opposite action.							
Used behavior analysis.							
Used problem solving.							

CHAPTER 9

Basic Interpersonal Effectiveness Skills

Interpersonal effectiveness skills are a composite of social-skills training (McKay et al., 1983), assertiveness training (Alberti & Emmons, 1990; Bower & Bower, 1991), and listening skills (Barker, 1990; Rogers, 1951) that have been combined by Linehan (1993a) for dialectical behavior therapy. In addition, we've added negotiation skills (Fisher & Ury, 1991) to complete the program.

Relationships are precious, and they are vulnerable. They bring love, companionship, and support. Yet, sometimes in a matter of moments, they can become broken beyond repair. Keeping your relationships healthy and alive requires interpersonal skills that you can learn in this chapter and the next. The most necessary and important of these skills is assertiveness, which is the ability to (1) ask for what you want, (2) say no, and (3) negotiate conflict *without damaging the relationship*. Before learning assertiveness, however, there are some key things you need to know.

MINDFUL ATTENTION ⊠

Relationships require attention. Whether it's a lover, friend, coworker, or merely a carpool companion, maintaining a good relationship depends on *noticing* the other person's feelings and reactions and then watching the communication process between you. Using the mindfulness skills you practiced in chapters 4 through 6, you can observe facial expression, body language, tone of voice, and choice of words during a conversation to get a fix on the mood and state of the relationship. If you are using the DBT Skills Card Deck, this practice corresponds to card #40 Observe Body Language.

Paying attention means staying in the here and now—not thinking about what you want to say next or focusing on some memory. It means remaining present to what you see, hear, and sense emotionally. In the same way that you can breathe, walk, or even do dishes mindfully, you can also relate and communicate with full awareness to the present moment. When you pay attention, you notice trouble coming—before it overwhelms you—and also gain time to ask clarifying questions that can help you correct misconceptions.

Not paying attention—focusing away from the moment between you and others—has a heavy price. You'll end up doing one or more of the following:

- Missing vital cues about the other person's needs and reactions

- Projecting, inaccurately, your fears and feelings on the other

- Blowing up or running away when "surprised" by a negative response you could have seen coming

Mindful attention also involves watching your own experience in relation to others. Do you need something from the other person (for example, more attention or some help)? Do you need to change the process between you (for example, critical comments, demands, intrusive questions)? Do you have feelings that signal something important about what's going on (hurt, sadness, loss, shame, anxiety)? Noticing your feelings can help you figure out what needs to change in a relationship—before you blow up or run away.

In summary, then, the first interpersonal skill you need to cultivate is mindful attention because it helps you read important signals about the state of a relationship.

Exercise: Mindful Attention ☒

In the very next conversation you have, practice being an observer of the moment by attending to the other person's physical and verbal behavior. If you find anything ambiguous or hard to read, ask a clarifying question. Here are some examples:

- How are you feeling? Are you doing okay?

- How are we doing? Are we okay?

- How are things between us?

- I notice _____; is that accurate?

- Is everything okay with you? With us?

Also notice your own needs and feelings in the interaction—do any of these require communication? How could you say it in a way that preserves the relationship?

For example, Bill had noticed his girlfriend, Gina, looking away from him during dinner. When he asked, "How are things between us?" she told him that she'd been hurt when he didn't invite her to his office holiday party. This gave him a chance to explain that he hated company events and only planned to put in an appearance for a few minutes.

COMPASSION FOR OTHERS

In addition to paying mindful attention to your relationships, it's also important to remain compassionate toward other human beings in general. As you learned in chapter 5, showing compassion means that you recognize a person's pain, offer them help, and do so without judgment. In many ways, pain and suffering unite all human beings because we all experience pain and suffering in our lives. In fact, one of the basic principles upon which the Buddhist philosophy is founded states that all conscious beings experience suffering. This doesn't mean that your entire life will include *only* suffering, but it does mean that you and all the rest of us will experience pain, disappointment, loss, and heartbreak. These things are inevitable.

To develop a compassionate attitude also requires you to recognize that we are all doing the best we can in this life—despite the pain and suffering—using whatever coping skills we have. Yet, we often judge others for not performing the way we think they *should* be performing. Or we criticize others for behaving in a way with which we don't agree. But how often do we stop and think about what that other person might be struggling with? Maybe the person who cut you off on the freeway today was going to visit his dying mother in the hospital. Maybe the person who was rude to you on the phone just found out that she has cancer. Or maybe the person you work with who is so angry toward everyone has a history of childhood abuse, so he pushes others away before he can get hurt again. The truth is, we rarely find out about the pain that other people are experiencing.

The meditation below will remind you to extend your compassionate thoughts and feelings toward all human beings, including those you don't like. Again, remember, we are all just doing the best we can, and sometimes even those people we don't like have a reason for behaving the way they do. By extending your compassionate attitude toward all people, (1) you learn to let go of judgments and related negative emotions like anger, (2) you open your heart and mind to other possibilities, and (3) you potentially develop stronger connections with other people.

Exercise: Other-Compassion Meditation

Use the other-compassion meditation below (adapted from McKay & Wood, 2019) to develop and strengthen your ability to show kindness and acceptance toward others. To begin, use mindful breathing to help yourself relax and focus. Read the instructions before beginning the exercise to familiarize yourself with the experience. If you feel more comfortable listening to the instructions, use your smartphone to record the directions in a slow, even voice so that you can listen to them while practicing this technique.

Instructions

First, find a comfortable place to sit in a room where you won't be disturbed. Turn off any distracting sounds. If you feel comfortable closing your eyes, do so to help you relax.

To begin, take a few slow, long breaths, and relax. Place one hand on your stomach. Now slowly breathe in through your nose and then slowly exhale through your mouth. Feel your stomach rise and fall as you breathe. Imagine your belly filling up with air like a balloon as you breathe in, and then feel it deflate as you breathe out. Feel the breath moving in across your nostrils, and then feel your breath blowing out across your lips. As you breathe, notice the sensations in your body. Feel your lungs fill up with air. Notice the weight of your body resting on whatever you're sitting. With each breath, notice how your body feels more and more relaxed. [Pause here for thirty seconds if you are recording the instructions.]

Now, as you continue to breathe, begin counting your breaths each time you exhale. You can count either silently to yourself or aloud. Count each exhalation until you reach 4 and then begin counting at 1 again. To begin, breathe in slowly through your nose, and then exhale slowly through your mouth. Count 1. Again, breathe in slowly through your nose and slowly out through your mouth. Count 2. Repeat, breathing in slowly through your nose, and then slowly exhale. Count 3. Last time—breathe in through your nose and out through your mouth. Count 4. Now begin counting at 1 again. [Pause here for thirty seconds if you are recording the instructions.]

Now bring your awareness inside your own body, noting the world of sensation there at this very moment. You live in this body—allow yourself to be aware of your breath, your life force. As you hold that awareness, bring to mind a person who makes you smile, who naturally brings happiness to your heart. [Pause here for a few seconds.] Let yourself feel what it's like to be in that person's presence. [Pause here for a few seconds.] Now recognize that this person wants to be happy and free of suffering. As you hold that awareness, mentally repeat the following phrases, letting them be a deep wish for that person:

"May you be peaceful."

"May you be safe."

"May you be healthy."

"May you be happy and free of suffering."

Repeat the phrases two or three more times, allowing their meaning to deepen each time. Allow yourself to feel and accept your own sense of compassion toward this person that you like. [Repeat the phrases two or three more times if you are recording the instructions.]

Now bring to mind the image of a person you find difficult or dislike. Remind yourself that this difficult person is also struggling to find their way through life, and in doing so, they are causing you pain. Mentally repeat:

"Just as I want to be peaceful and free from suffering…

May you, too, find peace.

May you be safe.

May you be healthy.

May you be happy and free of suffering."

Again, repeat the phrases two or three more times, allowing their meaning to deepen each time. Allow yourself to feel and accept your own sense of compassion toward this person that you find difficult. [Repeat the phrases two or three more times if you are recording the instructions.]

Finally, when you are done, take a few additional slow breaths, rest quietly, and savor your own sense of goodwill and compassion.

For the next week, make this other-compassion meditation part of your still mind practice. Then, see if you can incorporate the same intentions into your daily interactions with other people. Each time you meet someone, or are affected by someone else, say to yourself:

"Just like me, they want to be happy and free of suffering," or

"Just like me, these people walking past me are caught in the drama and flow of life."

Finally, you may eventually want to abbreviate these mantras into the simple phrase: "Just like me." For example, upon meeting someone you might simply think to yourself, "Just like me," meaning, "Just like me they want to be happy and free of suffering."

PASSIVE VERSUS AGGRESSIVE BEHAVIOR

Ineffective patterns of behavior can have a huge negative impact on your relationships. In particular, there are two kinds of behaviors that frequently interfere with relationships: passive behavior and aggressive behavior. Being passive sometimes seems safe because you just go along with what the other person wants and expects. Long term, however, passivity is the royal road to interpersonal disaster because when you frequently give in to others and abandon your own needs, it creates frustration and resentment that builds inside of you. Eventually, the relationship becomes so painful that you blow up, collapse into depression, or run away. The paradox of being passive is that in the short term, giving in seems to protect the relationship. Long term, however, the relationship takes a shape you can't stand—and you have to destroy it to stop the pain.

In comparison, aggressive behaviors also destroy relationships because they push people away. An aggressive interpersonal style is usually caused by two common false beliefs. The first is a strong sense of the way things *should* be—according to your own opinion. In particular, you are acutely aware of how others ought to behave. You see clearly the right and wrong way to act in each situation, and when others act in a way that violates your sense of what is appropriate or right, you feel a strong need to punish them.

The second source of aggression is a need to control interpersonal events. Things have to go a certain way, and you expect certain outcomes to happen or not happen. So when the other person either violates your sense of what's right or fails to do what you expect, anger starts to build up in you, and you apply more pressure to control what happens. At times, you may feel so determined that you explode—and drive others away.

Both passivity and aggression destroy relationships. Either one of these patterns ends up being very painful for you—and those you care for. The assertiveness skills you'll be introduced to in the next chapter are a middle way. They will give you the tools to seek what you need in relationships, set limits, and negotiate conflicts—all without anger or coercive efforts to control others or the situation.

Exercise: Identify Your Style

Think back over recent interactions in your five most significant relationships. Place a check (✓) next to the statements that reflect your typical behavior:

☐ 1. I go along with something, even if I don't like it.

☐ 2. I push people to do what's right, even if there's an upsetting situation.

☐ 3. I try to be pleasant and easygoing, no matter what people do or say.

☐ 4. I give people a piece of my mind when they deserve it.

☐ 5. I always try to be sensitive to what other people need and feel, even if my own needs get lost in the process.

☐ 6. I know what I want and insist on it, even if it means having to get angry.

☐ 7. When there's a conflict, I tend to give in and let things go the other person's way.

☐ 8. When people don't do what's appropriate or reasonable, I don't let them get away with it.

☐ 9. I'll pull away from a relationship rather than say anything that could be upsetting.

☐ 10. You can't let people continue being selfish or stupid; you have to shake them till they see what they're doing.

☐ 11. I leave people alone, and let them be whatever they are.

☐ 12. If people ignore my needs or insist on things that don't work for me, I get more and more upset until they pay attention.

If you tended to mark *odd* numbers, your predominant style is passive; if you checked *even* numbers, you tend to use an aggressive problem-solving style.

"I WANT–THEY WANT" RATIO

Every relationship consists of two people trying to get what they need. Sometimes they need the same thing—companionship, recreation, calm, and quiet—and it's easy. But when they need different things at the same time, or when one of them needs something the other doesn't want to give, there's trouble. For relationships to succeed you must be able to do the following:

- Know and say what you desire.

- Notice or find out what the other person desires.

- Negotiate and compromise so you can get at least some of what you want.

- Give what you can of what the other person wants.

If the "I want–they want" ratio isn't balanced, your relationship becomes unstable. Paying attention to what each person desires and using assertiveness skills to negotiate conflicts is vital to maintaining healthy relationships.

Exercise: "I Want–They Want"

The following exercise will help you assess the "I want–they want" ratio. Choose one relationship you want to evaluate. In the left-hand column, fill in the things you want and need in that relationship.

Under "Outcome," assess how well those needs are met. In the two right-hand columns, do the same for the other person. Now take a look at the outcomes on each side of the chart. Are more of one person or the other's needs being met? How does the relationship deal with those unmet needs? Are they ignored or negotiated? Are they sources of blame or withdrawal?

"I Want–They Want" Assessment

I Want	Outcome	They Want	Outcome

"I WANT–I SHOULD" RATIO

Every relationship requires keeping a delicate balance between seeking what you want to do and doing what you think you should do (for the good of the relationship or the other person). If most of your focus is directed toward getting and doing what you want with little attention to what must be done for the other, you'll soon earn resentment. If you're overbalanced on the side of "shoulds"—how you *should* act, what you *should* do for the other person—the relationship will begin to feel like a joyless burden, and you'll dream of escape.

For many, "shoulds" can become a controlling tyranny, forcing them to ignore important needs. They're so busy being good and giving that they fail to notice how depressed and desperate they've become. Sooner or later, the pain of denying yourself grows too big, and you have to escape or blow up the relationship.

Exercise: The "Shoulds"

Put a check (✔) next to the items that describe your beliefs or feelings:

- ☐ You should try to give everything that's asked of you in a relationship, even when it means putting your own needs aside.

- ☐ When someone is in pain, you should do anything required to help them.

- ☐ You should be caring and considerate at all times.

- ☐ You shouldn't ask for something if you know the other person doesn't want to give it.

- ☐ There is a right way to act with people, and it should be followed even if it means keeping quiet about your feelings and needs.

- ☐ You shouldn't say no to people; it's impolite.

- ☐ You shouldn't express feelings that might upset someone; it's wrong.

- ☐ You should respond to the needs of others because their needs are a high priority.

- ☐ You should never hurt or offend anyone.

- ☐ You should try not to disappoint others.

The more items you checked, the stronger your beliefs about the right and wrong way to relate with others and the more likely you are to deny your own needs in a relationship. There's nothing wrong with having values about how to treat others, but if those values overpower your ability to ask for what you want, you'll end up feeling helpless in any relationship.

SKILL BUILDING

Improving your interpersonal skills will take hard work. You don't need anyone to tell you how difficult it is to change relationship patterns. But you know why it's important—some relationships you value have blown up because you didn't know how to fix things that went wrong. This chapter and the next will give you new tools to manage how you function in relationships. Sometimes they'll work, sometimes they won't; and sometimes you may forget to use them. But you'll also be amazed how much they can improve a conversation or help to solve a problem.

It's hard, but it's okay if you fall down sometimes—if you blow up or withdraw—because it takes time to learn a new way. Practicing your new interpersonal skills will yield the following results:

- Help you be more effective in your dealings with people

- Improve your ability to get your needs met

- Help you negotiate conflicts without damaging a relationship

- Strengthen your self-respect by giving you alternatives to old, damaging patterns of anger or withdrawal

KEY INTERPERSONAL SKILLS

There are six core interpersonal skills that will change how your relationships feel:

1. *Knowing what you want.* How do you know what you want in a relationship? In some cases, you sense a yearning. Or you're aware of discomfort. The key is to pay attention and look for a way to describe, in your own mind, what you're feeling.

2. *Asking for what you want—in a way that protects the relationship.* The next chapter will give you an effective method and format for doing this. But for the moment, the basic idea is to put your needs into words that are clear, not attacking, and ask for specific behavioral change.

3. *Negotiating conflicting wants.* The willingness to negotiate starts with a clear commitment that there won't be winners or losers. It assumes that each person's needs are valid and understandable, and it draws on a willingness to compromise so that each person gets some of what he or she wants. A simple protocol for negotiating conflicting needs is provided in the next chapter.

4. *Getting information.* One of the most crucial of all interpersonal skills is finding out what the other person needs, fears, hopes for, and so on. The major blocks to getting information are when you (1) falsely assume you know what the other person wants; (2) project your own fears, needs, and feelings on the other person; (3) fear appearing to pry; (4) fear hearing the worst possible answer; and (5) don't know how to ask or what to look for. The next chapter will give you some key strategies for getting information.

5. *Saying no—in a way that protects the relationship.* You can say no in three ways: (1) in a limp, powerless style that just gets overridden; (2) in a hard-edged, aggressive style that alienates people; or

(3) in an assertive style that validates the other person's needs and desires while setting firm boundaries around what you will and won't do. The first two strategies undermine relationships because someone is going to end up feeling controlled and resentful. We'll describe how to implement the third strategy in the next chapter.

6. *Acting according to your values.* Being passive or aggressive in a relationship diminishes both your self-respect and the self-respect of others, because someone is losing out in the relationship—someone's needs and feelings are being ignored. Being clear about how you want to treat others is a critical step to interpersonal effectiveness. Ask yourself, "What type of relationships do I want with other people?" Most likely you want relationships that are loving, trustworthy, and committed. Hopefully, as you've been using the skills and exercises in this workbook, you've begun to think about how you value your relationships. Acting in your relationships according to what you value is another crucial step that will determine the entire nature of your relationships. Don't be surprised when valueless relationships don't work out well. Try setting positive intentions and values for each of your relationships, and act in those relationships according to what you're trying to achieve.

Exercise: Identify Your Interpersonal Values ⊠

On the following lines, list any of your interpersonal behaviors that diminish self-respect. Include anything that emotionally damages you or another person. Also write down sins of omission—things you should have done, but didn't.

Example: *I get angry as soon as someone criticizes me.*

_____

_____

_____

_____

Now, in the space that follows, list your values regarding how people should be treated. These are your basic rules about what you and others are entitled to in a relationship.

Example: *It's important to me to hear that someone I love is hurting.*

_____

_____

_____

_____

When you compare the two lists, assess whether you're using interpersonal strategies that violate your values. Now ask yourself these questions:

Which core values do you disregard most frequently?

_____

_____

How are your relationships impacted when you violate your values?

_____

_____

In the next chapter, you will learn interpersonal strategies that will help you be effective while at the same time will preserve your self-respect.

BLOCKS TO USING INTERPERSONAL SKILLS

Despite how diligent you are about using your new interpersonal skills, there will still be many obstacles along the way that might temporarily block the success of your relationships. But don't worry—identifying these obstacles is half the battle. Once you know what they are, you can prepare to overcome them. Here are some of the most common blocks to using interpersonal skills:

- Old habits—of the aggressive kind

- Old habits—of the passive kind

- Overwhelming emotion

- Failure to identify your needs

- Fear

- Toxic relationships

- Myths

Old Habits—of the Aggressive Kind

In your family of origin, you observed how people solved interpersonal problems, and you began to model your own behavior on what you saw. If members of your family dealt with conflict using anger, blame, or withdrawal, these are the strategies you may have learned to use as well.

Techniques for influencing others that utilize fear, shame, or hurtful psychological pressure are called *aversive strategies*. There are eight of them:

1. *Discounting*: The message to the other person is that his or her needs or feelings are invalid and don't have legitimacy or importance. Here's an example: "You've been watching TV all day; so why do you expect me to come home and cook for you too?"

2. *Withdrawing/abandoning*: The message is "Do what I want or I'm leaving." The fear of abandonment is often so powerful for the person who receives the message that many people will give up a great deal of their own needs to avoid being abandoned.

3. *Threatening*: The message here is "Do what I want or I'll hurt you," or "Do what I want or I'll hurt myself." The most typical threats are to get angry or somehow make the other person's life miserable. Here's an example: "Hey, okay, I won't ask you to help me again. Maybe I'll just go kill myself and then you can live a happier life without me."

4. *Blaming*: The problem, whatever it is, becomes the other person's fault. Because you believe that the other person caused the problem, you also believe that they have to fix it. Here's an example: "The reason we're running up our credit cards every month is because you spend too much on stuff we don't need."

5. *Belittling/denigrating*: The strategy here is to make the other person feel foolish and wrong to have a particular need, opinion, or feeling. Here's an example: "Why do you want to go to the lake all the time? All you ever do is get allergy attacks up there and complain the whole time."

6. *Guilt-tripping*: This strategy conveys the message that the other person is a moral failure, that their needs are wrong and must be given up. Here's an example: "If you don't trust me, that tells me something is very wrong with our relationship."

7. *Derailing*: This strategy switches attention away from the other person's feelings and needs. The idea is to stop talking about them and instead talk about yourself. Here's an example: "I don't care what you want to do, right now I feel hurt and you're not paying attention to me."

8. *Taking away*: Here the strategy is to withdraw some form of support, pleasure, or reinforcement from the other person as punishment for something they said, did, or wanted. Here's an example: "Fine, if you don't want to give me money to go shopping today, then I don't want to go with you next month to visit your parents on their anniversary" (adapted from McKay, Fanning, & Paleg, 1994).

The best way to stop aversive behavior is to observe it closely. After you review this list, ask yourself these questions:

Are there strategies you recognize from your own behavior?

Think back to times you've used aversive tactics—what was the impact on your relationship?

_____

_____

Is this something you want to change? Why?

_____

_____

Old Habits—of the Passive Kind

Some old habits are of the passive rather than aggressive variety. You may have learned in your family how to shut down or surrender when there is a conflict, or simply give in to someone else's demands in order to avoid a conflict. For example, maybe you don't think that you have the right to your own needs. So regardless of whether or not you already have plans, whenever someone asks you to do something for them you just give in and ignore your own wants and needs. For example, "Well, I was planning on going to the movies this afternoon, but I guess I can help you clean your garage instead. What time should I be there?" Or, maybe you don't think that you have a right to your own opinion, or a right to express that opinion, so whenever somebody asks you what you think or what you want, you just surrender to whatever the other person thinks. For example, "I'm not sure what I want to order for dinner. What are you going to get? I'll just get the same thing." But while these passive strategies might appear to be good in the short term, after some time, a person usually becomes frustrated that his or her own needs are not being met, and they get angry and sabotage a relationship in order to get out of it.

The best way to stop passive behavior is to observe it closely. Think back on the way you've handled conflicts in the past and ask yourself these questions:

Are there passive strategies you recognize from your own behavior?

_____

_____

Think back to times you've used passive tactics—what was the impact on your relationship?

_____

_____

Is this something you want to change? Why?

_____

_____

You can use the same Conflict Log (using "Passive Strategy" rather than "Aversive Strategy" in column 4) to track conflicts when you withdraw or shut down.

Exercise: Conflict Log

Use the Conflict Log to help you record and observe both your aggressive and passive interpersonal habits. (Visit http://www.newharbinger.com/44581 to download the Conflict Log.) Then, after using the log for a week or longer, ask yourself these questions:

What kinds of needs or situations trigger your use of aggressive or passive strategies?

_____

_____

Which strategies do you most frequently rely on?

_____

_____

Are you getting what you want using aggressive or passive strategies?

_____

_____

What are the most frequent emotional consequences for using these strategies?

_____

_____

The assertiveness skills in the next chapter will give you more effective alternatives to the aggressive and passive responses you've typically used.

Conflict Log

Date	My Need	My Behavior	Aversive/Passive Strategy	Consequences

Overwhelming Emotion

A third major block to using interpersonal skills is high emotion. Sometimes your best intentions and most carefully laid plans go up in smoke when you're upset. For some people, particularly those who have grown up in abusive homes, getting angry can cause a *dissociative fugue state*. In that frame of mind, they may do or say things that, on later reflection, seem to have been done by someone else. "It didn't feel like me telling my wife to get out," one man insisted. "I felt like I was possessed, in the control of some force outside myself."

There is good evidence that angry, dissociative states are responsible for a lot of emotional and even physical violence. What can you do when overwhelming emotion threatens to unravel your hard-won interpersonal skills? There are two things you can learn to do right now. First, pay attention to the red flags that indicate you're starting to lose control. Different people have different signals, but here are some that are typical:

- Feeling hot or flushed

- Heart pounding

- Short of breath

- Tension in your hands, arms, forehead, or shoulders

- Talking more rapidly or more loudly than usual

- Feeling a strong need to win, to crush someone, to make them feel bad

Exercise: Red-Flag Feelings and Behaviors

Make a list in the following space of red-flag feelings or behaviors that in the past signaled a loss of control:

_____

_____

_____

_____

_____

Now when conflicts arise, watch out for the red flags. If you notice them, you can use a second technique you've already learned: When you first notice that you're beginning to get overwhelmed by your emotions, start using your mindful breathing skills. Take slow, diaphragmatic breaths, and put all of your attention on the physical experience of the breath. This will help calm you and disconnect the old neural pathways that made you feel overwhelmed.

Failure to Identify Your Needs

Interpersonal skills won't do you much good if you don't know what you want in a situation. If you can't clearly articulate your needs, all you're left with is frustration. The first section of the next chapter will offer you strategies for identifying what you want in terms of specific behavioral change from others. Once you can articulate a need to yourself, the sections on assertiveness and making a simple request will give you tools to say it out loud.

Fear

When you feel afraid of something, interpersonal skills often go out the window. You're just too full of catastrophic "what ifs" to think clearly: "What if I'm rejected? What if I lose my job? What if I can't stand this?" Catastrophic thoughts can scare you into using aggressive and aversive strategies. Or they can cause you to avoid a situation altogether. The net result is that you don't function well and aren't effective.

Wise-mind meditation can help you manage in the face of fear, as can mindful breathing. Another thing you can do is directly confront your catastrophic thoughts. There are two steps to this.

Exercise 1: Fear Management—Risk Assessment

Notice that the Fear Management—Risk Assessment/Risk Planning Worksheet on the next page is divided into four columns. In column 1, write down your fear, and in column 2 list all the evidence you have that the fear will occur. Then, in column 3, write down all available evidence that the catastrophe *won't* occur. Now, after reviewing evidence for and against, write your estimate of the percentage of chance that the catastrophe will *actually* happen.

Exercise 2: Fear Management—Risk Planning

In the "Risk Planning" portion of the worksheet, imagine that the catastrophe you fear has actually happened. How would you cope? Do you have resources, family, or friends to help you? Do you have a plan for how you would do your best with the situation? What skills do you have to get you through?

The Risk Assessment/Risk Planning Worksheet is something you may want to photocopy and use again and again—whenever fear threatens to torpedo your relationship skills. (If you prefer, visit http://www.newharbinger.com/44581 to download the Risk Assessment/Risk Planning Worksheet.)

Fear Management—Risk Assessment

My Fear	Evidence Fear Will Occur	Evidence Fear Will Not Occur	Chance (%) of Fear Actually Occurring

Fear Management—Risk Planning

Make a coping plan utilizing your skills and resources in the event your feared scenario comes true.

_____

_____

_____

_____

_____

_____

Toxic Relationships

Relationships where people use aversive strategies on you can make your interpersonal skills very difficult to use. No matter how determined you are to be assertive rather than aggressive or passive, people who blame, threaten, or belittle you can often trip you up and make you want to explode or run away.

The best solution is to get away from these kinds of people. They're not going to change, and you'll never stop being vulnerable to their attacks. However, if these are people you can't avoid—for example, a boss or a family member—there are two things you *must* do to cope. First, you have to calm yourself before dealing with them. Use mindful breathing or wise mind to get centered. Second, based on past experience, you need to anticipate exactly how the toxic individual is likely to act, and then you need to make a specific plan—even a script—to deal with it. Planning ahead and developing a detailed response will keep you from falling back on old, ineffective patterns. See the assertiveness sections in the next chapter for the tools necessary to talk your way out of aversive traps.

Myths

The last of the major blocks to using interpersonal skills is found in the four paralyzing myths of relationship:

1. If I need something, it means there is something wrong or bad about me.

2. I won't be able to stand it if the other person gets mad or says no.

3. It's selfish to say no or ask for things.

4. I have no control over anything.

Each of these myths inhibits you from saying what you need and setting limits. Let's look at each of them.

- *Myth #1.* Every human being needs things from other human beings—whether it's attention, support, love, help, or just plain kindness. We are not sufficient unto ourselves, and our whole lives are spent negotiating with others for everything we require to survive—physically and emotionally. So needing things can't be shameful or wrong; it is basic to the human condition. In contrast to this myth, a healthy alternative coping thought is "*I have a right to want things.*"

- *Myth #2.* Hearing an angry refusal hurts. Sometimes it hits so hard and suddenly that it takes your breath away. But is it true you can't stand it? Think of the rejections you've suffered in your life—they were difficult, but you survived them. Refusals hurt, there's no doubt about it, but the worst thing is living with years of pain because you never asked for what you want. In contrast to this myth, a healthy alternative coping thought is "*I have a right to ask for things—even if the other person won't give them.*"

- *Myth #3.* You may feel that it's selfish to ask for things because of messages in your early family that said your needs didn't count or that your needs were less important than the needs of others. When you examine it, is this really true? Is there something flawed or wrong with you that makes your needs relatively unimportant? The truth is that everyone's needs are valid, and equally important. It isn't selfish to ask for things or set limits. It's normal. It's healthy and necessary. Our survival as individuals depends on knowing and saying what we want. Because if we don't, folks don't pay attention. A helpful coping thought is *"It's normal and healthy to ask for things."*

- *Myth #4.* Control is relative. You can't control the behavior of others, even though some folks go nuts trying. What can be controlled is *your* behavior. Passive or aggressive styles often have bad outcomes. People ignore your needs or get angry and resist you. That's why you feel helpless—the strategies you're using aren't effective. Assertive behavior gets better results. People—more often than not—listen and respond positively. In contrast to this myth, a helpful alternative coping thought is *"I can choose to behave in more effective ways."*

CHAPTER 10

Advanced Interpersonal Effectiveness Skills

This chapter contains all the applied skills of interpersonal effectiveness. Learning and practicing these skills will change your life because you'll have far less conflict and far more rewards in your relationships. Your connections to people will feel different—more satisfying than frustrating and more supportive than depriving. In this chapter, you'll learn the following specific skills:

- Knowing what you want

- Modulating intensity

- Making a simple request

- Making basic assertiveness scripts

- Using assertive listening skills

- Saying no

- Coping with resistance and conflict

- Negotiating

- Analyzing problem interactions

KNOWING WHAT YOU WANT

Interpersonal effectiveness has to begin with self-knowledge. You need to be clear about what you feel and want. Chapters 7 and 8 on emotion regulation will give you words for the nuances of what you feel and techniques to classify the emotion. For our purposes here, you can identify emotions through a simple decision-making process called a *decision tree*. It starts with the basic questions—is the feeling good or bad, painful or pleasurable? If the feeling is good, is it more like satisfaction, excitement, sexual attraction, love/affection, contentment, joy, pleasant anticipation, interest, or satiety? If the feeling is bad, is it more like anxiety, fear, anger, resentment, sadness, grief/loss, hurt, anger or disgust with oneself, embarrassment/shame, guilt, yearning/deprivation, or loneliness/emptiness? The decision tree looks like this:

EMOTIONS

Good	**Bad**
Satisfaction	Anxiety (for the future)
Excitement	Fear (of something now)
Sexual attraction	Anger
Love/affection	Resentment
Contentment	Sadness
Joy	Grief/loss
Pleasant anticipation	Hurt
Interest	Anger or disgust with oneself
Satiety	Embarrassment/shame
	Guilt
	Yearning/deprivation
	Loneliness/emptiness

Allan, for example, was aware that something felt wrong in his relationship with his father. When he looked at the list of feelings, the one that seemed closest was hurt—with a little bit of resentment. Allan could tell it somehow related to his father's planned visit. The man was coming to town with his new wife. Yet, in five days of sightseeing, his dad had scheduled just a single dinner with Allan.

Once you can put words to what you feel, the next question becomes, what does this emotion make you want to change? And, more specifically, what is the behavior of others that you want to modify? Do you want them to do more or less of something? Do you want something to stop? Do you want new behavior that could make a difference in how you feel?

Now think about the behavior change in specific terms. When and where do you want to see this change? How often? What exactly would the new behavior look like?

Now let's condense this process into a series of steps.

Exercise: Knowing What You Want

Think of a recent experience where you had a bad feeling during an interaction. Getting from the feeling to a clear statement of desire would involve the following process:

1. Put the feeling into words: _____

_____

2. What do you want the other person to change?

   • More of _____

   • Less of _____

   • Stop doing _____

   • Start doing _____

   • When _____

   • Where _____

   • Frequency _____

Now put all this information into one or more clear sentences: _____

_____

_____

_____

A woman whose sister frequently criticized how she parented a difficult child wrote this description of what she wanted changed: "I'd like Brenda to stop talking about Mike [my son] and stop talking about my 'needing a backbone' with him. I'd like her to stop it, in particular, when we're around people we know. Instead, I'd rather she ask me about other things—work, my photographs, my writing."

The problem with getting clear and specific about your desires is that it brings up anxiety. Do you deserve to ask for things? Do you dare trouble people with your needs? Are you allowed to disappoint, to annoy, to push people to make an effort on your behalf? The answer is yes. And the reason is that you are a human being who feels, who yearns for things, who hurts, who struggles with moments of pain. All of this entitles you to be heard.

Unfortunately, many people grow up in families that invalidate their needs. And all their lives they feel afraid to ask for things—as if they were bad or undeserving, as if their feelings and pain had no importance.

To remind you of your value and importance as a human being, we'd like you to review the following list of legitimate rights (adapted from McKay et al., 1983). (Visit http://www.newharbinger.com/44581 to download Your Legitimate Rights.)

YOUR LEGITIMATE RIGHTS ⊠

1. You have a right to need things from others.

2. You have a right to put yourself first sometimes.

3. You have a right to feel and express your emotions or your pain.

4. You have a right to be the final judge of your beliefs and accept them as legitimate.

5. You have a right to your opinions and convictions.

6. You have a right to your experience—even if it's different from that of other people.

7. You have a right to protest any treatment or criticism that feels bad to you.

8. You have a right to negotiate for change.

9. You have a right to ask for help, emotional support, or anything else you need (even though you may not always get it).

10. You have a right to say no; saying no doesn't make you bad or selfish.

11. You have a right not to justify yourself to others.

12. You have a right not to take responsibility for someone else's problem.

13. You have a right to choose not to respond to a situation.

14. You have a right, sometimes, to inconvenience or disappoint others.

Put the rights that are most important or liberating to you on a file card, and tape it someplace where you'll see it frequently, like your bathroom mirror, in order to remind yourself.

MODULATING INTENSITY

How you ask for things depends on the situation. The intensity and level of insistence can vary based on two major factors:

1. How urgent is my need?

    Low urgency   1   2   3   4   5   6   7   8   9   10   High urgency

2. How vulnerable is the other person or the relationship?

    Very vulnerable   1   2   3   4   5   6   7   8   9   10   Not vulnerable

Notice that you can assess each of these variables with a ten-point scale. The higher the total number, the more forceful it's appropriate to be. The lower the number, the more moderate and gentle you should be.

Exercise: Modulating Intensity

Think of some recent situations where you've needed another person to change. Evaluate them using these two key questions and the scoring method: What can you learn about the appropriate level of intensity and pressure? Did you use too much—or too little—in certain situations? Imagine what might have happened if you'd adjusted the intensity of your request based on (1) the urgency of need and (2) the level of vulnerability criteria.

Ask yourself these two questions during every situation where you need to express yourself. While you may not always have the time or inclination to use the 1 to 10 rating system, remembering "how urgent?" and "how vulnerable?" can help you make split-second decisions about how much strength, hardness, and volume to put into your voice.

During this exercise, Rachel evaluated some problematic discussions with her husband. One, in particular, had been very frustrating because she wanted him to attend a parent-teacher conference that was scheduled for 3:00—a time when he'd have to miss work. Her husband refused. But their son was having reading problems, and Rachel rated the urgency at an 8, while her husband's vulnerability was rated 7—not very vulnerable. Rachel realized that her gentle, easygoing approach had been a mistake. So next time, when a similar situation occurred, Rachel was more forceful in her request and her husband gave in and attended the meeting.

MAKING A SIMPLE REQUEST ⊠

The skill of making a request is necessary to taking care of yourself. Asking for directions, asking to change tables at a restaurant, asking your mechanic to show you the parts he replaced on your car, asking someone not to smoke in your house—these requests are all about self-protection and quality of life. If you have trouble making such requests, you can easily end up feeling helpless or resentful.

There are four components to a brief request:

1. A *brief justification (optional)*. Explain in one sentence what the problem is. "It's hot in here…These bags are heavy…It's a long way to walk…These seem a little tight." Many situations don't need any justification; when they do, keep it simple.

2. A *softening statement*. This is an important piece because it establishes you as a reasonable person who's polite and nondemanding. Softening statements often start like this.

    *   "Would you mind if…"

    *   "It would be helpful if you could…"

    *   "I'd appreciate it if you would…"

    *   (Said with a smile) "Could I have…"

    *   "Hi, I was wondering if…"

    Notice that these openers are disarming. They're far less likely to encounter resistance than a hard-edged demand.

3. A *direct, specific question*. You say what you want clearly and exactly. Leave any charge or emotion out of your voice. Say what you want in a flat, matter-of-fact way. Don't blame or imply that anything's wrong with the other person. Present your request as normal and reasonable—something that anyone would be glad to accommodate. Keep the question to one sentence if you can—the more you elaborate and explain, the more resistance you'll tend to run into.

4. An *appreciation statement*. This reinforces the behavior of the other person saying yes to you. It makes them feel that you value what they're doing. Here are some examples:

    *   "This will really help me out."

    *   "Thanks for your effort with this."

    *   "This will make a real difference."

    *   "This is much appreciated."

When the components are strung together, simple requests can look like these:

*   *In a restaurant:* "The sun's really bright. Would you mind lowering the shade a little? Thanks so much."

*   *In a subway car:* "It's a bit tight here. Could you please move your briefcase off the seat to make some room? I really appreciate it."

*   *Driving with a friend:* "I'm nervous to drive this close, especially at this speed. Would it be okay with you to leave a little more room between us and the car in front? Thanks for indulging me on this one."

Exercise: Making a Simple Request ⊠

If you sometimes find making requests challenging, you can practice in lots of everyday situations. Try some of these suggestions:

- *On the street:* Asking for the time, for directions, where someone bought a particular article of clothing, for change.

- *In stores:* Asking to examine merchandise, for information (for example, a return policy), to see something less expensive or in a different color, for advice regarding a purchase (for example, "Do these colors go together?"), for change.

- *At work:* Asking for information, for a little bit of help, for an extended deadline, for a moment of someone's time, for an opinion.

- *At home:* Asking for a change in schedule, for assistance, for time together, for help changing the environment ("Would you mind if we moved this chair to the kitchen?").

- *With friends and family:* Asking for a favor, for time, for a ride, for someone to stop something that's annoying.

- *With a teacher or therapist:* Asking for information, for help with a problem, for advice.

If you plan to work on this skill, choose *one* of the above options (or develop ones of your own) to work on *each day*. Either at breakfast or just before going to bed, identify the next day's challenge. Decide on the time and situation in which you plan to practice. Write it in your calendar to help you remember. Then do it.

ASSERTIVENESS SCRIPTS ⊠

As you read in the last chapter, assertiveness is a critical skill to maintaining healthy relationships. Without it, you'll be forced into passive or aggressive patterns that destroy the fabric of trust and intimacy.

Assertiveness is most easily learned by using a simple script. It will help you give structure to what you want to say and keep you focused. A script also has the advantage of permitting you to develop a statement in advance, practicing it by yourself or with someone you trust, and finally (at a time you choose) delivering it with greater confidence.

There are two basic components to an assertiveness statement and two optional components.

1. *"I think."* This part focuses on the facts and your understanding of what's going on. It should *not* include judgments or assumptions about the other person's motives. It should *not* in any way attack. "I think" is a clear description of events and experiences that you need to talk about—and perhaps change. Here are some examples:

   - "I think we haven't spent much time together lately—two nights last week, one the week before."

   - "You've billed me for a repair I didn't authorize."

- "Looking back at the recent past, I think you've been late for the majority of our meetings."

- "I'm getting back from the airport late—around 11:00 o'clock—and…"

Notice that there isn't much hint of emotion in these statements, and there's no disapproval in the statement of facts.

2. *"I feel." (optional):* This is a component that you'd likely use with a friend or family member but not with your garage mechanic. The purpose is to give a brief, nonjudgmental description of any emotion triggered by the situation. Communication specialists call this component of assertiveness the "I" statement. That's because it's about you and your particular feelings. Appropriately, any sentence about your emotions should start with "I."

- "I feel scared."

- "I feel lonely."

- "Lately, I feel sad about us."

- "I feel hurt, with a twinge of giving up."

- "I feel kind of lost and invisible and more and more disconnected."

- "I feel rejected."

- "I feel hopeful but nervous."

Each example, while naming feelings of varied complexity, never makes the other person sound bad or wrong. That doesn't work—when you blame someone for how you feel, it just makes them defensive and less willing to give you anything. Accusations and blame statements often start with the word "you"—so they're called "you" statements. Do your best *not* to use "you" statements when making an assertive statement. Examples of "you" statements include:

- "You're hurting me."

- "You don't care about us."

- "You're always late."

- "You're ruining our business."

Some people dress up "you" statements to *look* like "I" statements. However, this charade is usually obvious because the sentence starts with "I feel that you…"

- "I feel that you're selfish."

- "I feel that you're never home."

- "I feel that you manipulate me."

Notice that a judgment, not a true feeling, forms the core of these types of "you" statements. And while it might sound safer than using an "I" statement—because the speaker is less vulnerable— it communicates nothing about your own emotional experience. These types of statements only assess blame and make the listener less likely to hear what you want.

3. *"I want."* This component is the whole point of assertiveness, and you need to think it through carefully. Here are some guidelines to follow:

    - *Ask for behavioral, not attitudinal, change.* You can't reasonably expect someone to change what they believe or feel just because you don't like it. Beliefs and feelings aren't usually in voluntary control. But you *can* ask someone to change how they act and what they do.

    - *Ask for one change at a time.* Don't give a laundry list. That overwhelms people and makes them feel pressured.

    - *Ask for something that can be changed now.* "The next time we go on vacation, I want you to…" is a poor "I want" statement because it'll be long forgotten when the next vacation finally arrives.

    - *Be specific and concrete.* Vague requests like "Be nicer" don't get you anywhere because nobody has a very clear picture of what they mean. Describe what new behavior you expect, and say when and where you'd want it to occur. Asking someone for twenty minutes of help doing research on the Internet is more effective than requesting "technological assistance."

4. *Self-care solution (optional):* Just asking for things isn't always enough. Sometimes you need to give people encouragement (reinforcement) before they're motivated to do something for you. The encouragement that works best is a fourth (optional) component of your assertive script called the *self-care solution.* This amounts to nothing more than telling the other person what you'll do to take care of yourself if they don't comply with your request. The self-care solution isn't the same thing as threatening someone or punishing them. Its purpose is to give information and show that you're not helpless, that you have a plan to solve the problem. Here are some examples.

    - "If you can't leave for the party on time, I'll take my own car."

    - "If you can't help with the cleaning, I'll hire a maid and we'll divide that expense."

    - "If you can't find a way to keep the party noise down, I'll ask the police to help you."

    - "If you want to drive without insurance, I'll transfer the title to your name and you can take over the payments as well."

None of these self-care solutions is designed to hurt the other person; they're about protecting your rights and taking care of your own needs.

Integrating the Components of Being Assertive

Now, let's integrate the components of an assertive statement so you can see how they fit together. Here are some examples:

Example #1

I think: *It's been three years since we've had a cost-of-living raise, and prices have increased more than 10 percent in that time.*

I feel: *I feel left out, because the company's doing well and I'm not participating in that.*

I want: *I'd like a 10 percent cost-of-living adjustment soon so my income can keep pace with inflation.*

Self-care: *If we can't work this out, I'm going to have to look for something else so I can better support my family.*

Example #2

I think: *I've been working against a deadline tonight and haven't had time to cook dinner.*

I feel: *I'm pretty anxious and overwhelmed that I might not get this done.*

I want: *Could you whip something together from leftovers so I can keep going?*

Self-care: *If that doesn't work for you, I can order a pizza.*

One way to use your self-care solution is to hold it in reserve—only using it if the other person refuses your preferred solution. Saving the "big guns" for later is often an effective strategy.

Exercise: Developing Your Own Assertiveness Scripts

Now it's time to practice developing your own scripts. Start with identifying three situations in which something feels wrong and you want things to change. Write the information down in the space provided.

Problem #1

1.   The problem: _____

_____

_____

2. What I want changed: _____

_____

_____

Problem #2

1. The problem: _____

_____

_____

2. What I want changed: _____

_____

_____

Problem #3

1. The problem: _____

_____

_____

2. What I want changed: _____

_____

_____

Now let's turn this knowledge into actual scripts:

Problem #1

I think: _____

_____

I feel: _____

_____

I want: _____

_____

How I'll take care of myself: _____

_____

Problem #2

I think: _____

_____

I feel: _____

_____

I want: _____

_____

How I'll take care of myself: _____

_____

Problem #3

I think: _____

_____

I feel: _____

_____

I want: _____

_____

How I'll take care of myself: _____

_____

ASSERTIVE LISTENING ⌫

Everyone knows that good communication is a two-way street. But what a lot of people don't know is that listening is an active rather than passive process. It requires a full commitment to really understand what the other person thinks and feels about the problem, and wants to do to change it. In other words, the same three things you're learning to express assertively, you'll also need to listen for and elicit with questions.

If, while listening, you have any uncertainty about the other person's feelings or wishes, ask a direct question. "I'm not really sure how you feel about that—could you tell me more?" "What do you think we should try to change in this situation?"

The more active your questions, the more you learn and the better equipped you'll be to find solutions and compromises that serve both people's needs. Key questions to ask others are as follows:

- "What's the central problem, as you understand it?"

- "How do you make sense of the situation? What do you think is happening?"

- "When you're struggling with (*name the problem*) _____ , how does it make you feel?"

- "When you're dealing with (*name the problem*) _____ , what does it make you want to do?"

- "What do you think needs to change?"

- "What would you like me to do to help with this?"

For example, Ron noticed that a coworker seemed irritated with a new order-processing system Ron had just initiated. When Ron asked, "What do you think needs to change?" he got a wealth of helpful feedback, and the whole emotional climate changed.

Assertive listening is extremely valuable, but remember—just because you found out what someone needs, it doesn't mean you have to give it to them. Your needs and opinions matter too. So before you give in to the requests and suggestions of other people, make sure that you also consider what is important to you.

Blocks to Listening

Here are ten ways that people sabotage their effective listening abilities (adapted from McKay et al., 1983). Right now, put a check (✔) by the listening blocks you're aware of using. But don't judge yourself—everybody does some of this.

☐ *Mind reading:* Assuming you know what the other person feels and thinks—without asking.

☐ *Rehearsing:* Planning what you want to say next and missing what's being said now.

☐ *Filtering:* Listening only to things that are important or relevant to you and ignoring the rest (even if it's important to the other person).

☐ *Judging:* Evaluating the other person and what they say rather than really trying to understand how they see the world.

- ☐ *Daydreaming:* Getting caught in memories or fantasies while someone is talking to you.

- ☐ *Advising:* Looking for suggestions and solutions instead of listening and understanding.

- ☐ *Sparring:* Invalidating the other person by arguing and debating.

- ☐ *Being right:* Resisting or ignoring any communication that suggests you are wrong or should change.

- ☐ *Derailing:* Flat out changing the subject as soon as you hear anything that bothers or threatens you.

- ☐ *Placating:* Agreeing too quickly ("I know…You're right…I'm sorry") without really listening to the other person's feelings or concerns.

Exercise: Listening Blocks

In the left-hand column of the following table, describe three situations where communications broke down between you and someone else. In the right-hand column, see if you can identify at least one of the listening blocks that kept you from hearing or understanding everything that was said.

Listening Blocks

Situation	Blocks to Listening

During the next week, notice how often you use your favorite listening blocks. Commit to replacing them with assertive listening (see key questions under "Assertive Listening").

SAYING NO ⌫

The ability to say no is a vital part of healthy communication. Without it, any relationship is dangerous—it's like getting in a car with a gas pedal and no brakes. You have no control over what people do to you.

Saying no is simple and hard at the same time. The words are simple, but often it takes courage to say them. Let's start with the "how" of saying no. There are only two steps:

1. Validate the other person's needs or desires.

2. State a clear *preference* not to do it.

   Here are some examples:

   • "Action movies with a high body count are a lot of fun, but *I'd prefer* something calmer tonight."

   • "I've seen purple used to good advantage—it's a dynamic color—but *I'd prefer* something softer and pastel in the bedroom."

   • "I can see why you want to confront Ian (our son), but *I don't feel comfortable* with an approach that risks him turning his back on us."

   • "I can see why you want to go late, out of the hot sun, but *I'm not comfortable* trying to stay up so long after my bedtime."

Notice that the key phrases are "I'd prefer" and "I'm not comfortable." You don't offer a lot of justification for your position; you don't argue. You just validate and decline. The important thing is *not* giving the other person anything to use against you. No one can really argue with preferences or feelings.

Exercise: Building an Assertive Hierarchy

Learning assertiveness (including saying no) requires practice and willingness to take some risks. But you need to get your feet wet in low-risk situations, then work toward more anxiety-provoking encounters.

Make a list of situations where you want to make a change, say no, or set limits. Include problems with family, friends, people who work for or with you, authorities, and so on. Now rank the list from 1 to 10 in terms of risk and difficulty, with 1 being the least challenging and 10 being the most challenging situation. Do your best to list a variety of situations that span the hierarchy in terms of difficulty, with some easier ones and some more difficult ones. (Visit http://www.newharbinger.com/44581 to download the Assertive Situation Hierarchy form.)

Assertive Situation Hierarchy

Rank	Situation
10.	
9.	
8.	
7.	
6.	
5.	
4.	
3.	
2.	
1.	

Now start with the lowest-ranked situations and do four things:

1. Write your script ("I think...I feel...I want").

2. Rehearse your script.

3. Identify the time and place you want to use it.

4. Commit yourself to making your assertive statement on a specific date.

When you've completed your first assertive goal, evaluate what worked and what needs improvement. For example, do you need to be firmer, with less arguing or excuse making? Whatever you learned from your first step, incorporate it into the preparations for the second-ranked situation. Keep moving up the hierarchy. As you do, you'll find your confidence and skill growing. And your relationships will gradually become more rewarding.

COPING WITH RESISTANCE AND CONFLICT

We looked earlier at how to improve your ability to hear others. But what happens if someone isn't listening to *you*? The answer is in the following five conflict management skills:

1. Mutual validation

2. Broken record

3. Probing

4. Clouding (assertive agreement)

5. Assertive delay

Mutual Validation

When people aren't listening to you, one of the most common reasons is that they feel invalidated. They don't experience that they're being heard, so they keep pouring on their arguments and assertions. You can short-circuit the problem with mutual validation. Validating someone doesn't mean agreeing with them. It means, instead, that you understand their *needs*, *feelings*, and *motivations*. You get it—you see how the other person could think and feel that way.

Thus, mutual validation means you acknowledge and appreciate their experience, you understand where they're coming from, and then you validate your own experience as well. Here are some examples:

*   "*I understand* that it's scary to take a financial risk like this; you have every right to be cautious. *On my end*, I feel a pressure to make some higher-yield investments so we'll have a bit more when we retire. We're both coming from a reasonable place, just different."

*   "*I understand* that my saying you're not pulling your weight hurt you. That would be hard for anyone—me included—to hear. *On my end*, I'm scared this project is in danger of going over budget and I'll have to answer for that. I need everyone to pull together."

*   "*I understand* you're concerned about my safety, and that's why you replaced the part. I appreciate that very much. *On my end*, I've got a budget so tight I can't afford repair work that isn't literally keeping the car running. Safety isn't my highest concern right now."

Notice that each example of mutual validation includes a sentence that starts "I understand," and another one that begins "On my end." These two sentences establish that you appreciate both points of view.

Broken Record ⊠

You use this technique when someone isn't getting the message. Formulate a short, specific, easy-to-understand statement about what you want. Ideally, keep it to one sentence. Offer no excuses or explanations. Stand or sit straight, and talk in a strong, firm voice. Then just keep repeating the statement as many times as necessary, varying a word here or there—but not much else.

Don't argue, don't get angry, and don't try to debate or refute anything the other person says. Don't answer any "why" questions ("Why do you want to…") because that just gives the other person ammunition for their arguments. Respond by saying "I just prefer it" or "That's just how I feel." Under no circumstances should you offer additional information or evidence for your point of view. Just repeat, politely and clearly, like a broken record. Here's an example:

Sam: Your tree has a large branch suspended over my roof. I'm concerned that the next big storm could bring it down on my house. I'd like you to get an arborist to cut off the limb.

Bill: It's been like that for years; I wouldn't worry about it.

Sam: I think that branch is a danger to my house, and I'd like you to have it removed.

Bill: Relax; that branch will still be up there long after we're pushing up daisies.

Sam: It's hanging over my roof, and I'm concerned about it. I'm asking you to remove it, Bill, before it falls.

Bill: Why have you gotten so nervous about it all of a sudden?

Sam: The branch is over my roof, Bill, and it needs to come down.

Probing

The key phrase here is this:

- "What is it about (*name the situation*) _____ that bothers you?"

Just keep asking it until you get something useful.

Let's return to a previous example of a person who was accused of not pulling his weight. Imagine that you were criticized in that way. Here's how probing could help you.

Critic: You're not pulling your weight around here.

You: What is it about my work that bothers you?

Critic: Everybody else is working overtime. You waltz out every night at 5:00.

You: What is it that bothers you about me leaving the office on time?

Critic: The work has to be done. I'm responsible to see that it is. And you just work by the clock.

You: What is it that bothers you when I work by the clock?

Critic: Somebody else has to finish your work—often me. I want you to stay until it's done.

You: I appreciate your explaining to me.

If you wish to probe with more varied questions, review the sample queries in the "Assertive Listening" section.

Clouding

This technique allows you to "agree in part" with someone without accepting that everything they say is true. This often calms people down and stops the win/lose arguing game.

The key is to find some part of what's being said that you can accept and then to acknowledge that the other person is right about that. Ignore the rest of their argument. One way to agree is to modify words of sheer exaggeration, such as "always" and "never."

Example #1

Critic: You always get pissed off over little things.

You: It's true, there are times I find myself getting irritated.

Example #2

Critic: You never support me when I need something.

You: It's true, there have been several times when I couldn't completely support what you were asking.

Notice how clouding steals your critic's thunder and neutralizes his or her argument. Now the door is open to real negotiation of legitimate, yet very different needs.

Assertive Delay

This technique gives you room to wait, particularly when things threaten to get hot and angry. People will often pressure you to make a decision or agree with a plan right away. Assertive delay allows you to take a break—whether for a few minutes or several hours. During the interval, you can calm down, think carefully about what's being said, and prepare a good response. For example, "You've told me a lot, and I need time to sift through and see what I think." Or, "Give me an hour. This is important, and I want to think carefully before I say anything."

HOW TO NEGOTIATE ⊠

When a conflict arises that requires negotiation between you and someone else, you need to start from the position that *each of you has valid needs*. The RAVEN guidelines will keep you on track.

RAVEN stands for the following:

Relax. Accept conflict calmly. Take a deep breath before you say the next thing. Release tension as you exhale.

Avoid the aversive. Keep in mind the aversive strategies you might be tempted to use, and monitor what you say in order to avoid them.

Validate the other person's need or concern. Focus on a fair, mutually agreeable outcome where *both* people can get *some* of their needs met.

Examine your values. How do you want to be treated in a relationship, and how do you want to treat others? What do you want to achieve, not only regarding the conflict, but in this relationship?

Neutral voice. Keep anger and contempt out of your voice.

Once you're committed to staying within the RAVEN guidelines, it's time to start the actual negotiation process. It begins by each person taking turns and offering solutions. Make sure that a solution you offer addresses at least some of the needs of the other person. If you aren't sure what those needs are, ask them.

Once you've each offered several alternative solutions—without agreement—it's time to look for a compromise. Here are some classic compromise solutions:

- *I'll cut the pie; you choose the first piece.* After the divorce, Sharon divided the artwork into two groups—but Lawrence got to choose which group he'd take.

- *Take turns.* Linda and Moe alternated between going to the mountains and the beach on their vacations.

- *Do both; have it all.* Take care of both people's needs simultaneously.

- *Trial period.* Agree to a solution only for a specific length of time, after which you'll reevaluate. If one party feels the solution isn't working, negotiations are reopened.

- *My way when I'm doing it; your way when you're doing it.* Each person, as he or she deals with a problem, gets to use their own method. Sam and Katrina were partners in a small boutique. Sam thought the big "come on in" sign that Katrina made was garish. They agreed he wouldn't use it on his days watching the store.

- *This for that.* Roommates Jill and Denise agreed that if Jill cleaned the bathroom once a week, Denise would dust and vacuum once a week.

- *Part of what I want with part of what you want.* Two friends and coworkers planned to travel together to a convention. One wanted to relax on the train; one wanted to get there in a hurry by air. They agreed to fly one way and take the train the other.

- *Split the difference.* This often works with haggling over a price or how much time to spend doing something.

Exercise: How to Negotiate

Recall three recent conflicts where you had very different needs from someone else. For each conflict, work out two possible compromises from the above list. Describe specifically how you would implement them.

Conflict	Compromises
1.	a. b.
2.	a. b.
3.	a. b.

When working toward compromise, it's crucial to maintain flexibility. Holding a fixed, entrenched position makes negotiation difficult. Be open to creative, unexpected solutions. Be prepared to give something up to get something you want.

HOW TO ANALYZE PROBLEM INTERACTIONS

You need a way to figure out what happened when communications go wrong. Inevitably, problems and conflicts will show up in your relationships. Sometimes you will blow up or shut down. But the key is to learn from what happened and use that to polish your skills. No setback is completely negative if it helps you be more effective next time.

The following checklist will help you review interpersonal problems and become clearer about their causes. (Visit http://www.newharbinger.com/44581 to download the Communication Effectiveness Checklist.)

COMMUNICATION EFFECTIVENESS CHECKLIST

1. Were you clear about your goals?

    ☐   Did you know what you wanted?

    ☐   Did you know what you *didn't* want—so you could say no?

    ☐   Were you aware of your values, how you wanted to treat others, and how you'd like to be treated in return?

2. Did you use aversive strategies?

    ☐   Discounting

    ☐   Withdrawing/abandonment

    ☐   Threats

    ☐   Blaming

    ☐   Belittling/denigrating

    ☐   Guilt-tripping

    ☐   Derailing

    ☐   Taking away

3. Did you use passive strategies?

    ☐   Avoiding/withholding

    ☐   Shutting down/stonewalling

4. What were the blocking factors?

    ☐   High emotion (see page 223)

    ☐   Fear and "what ifs" (see page 224)

    ☐   Toxic relationships (see page 226)

    ☐   Myths (see page 226)

    •   If I need something, it means there is something wrong or bad about me.

    •   I won't be able to stand it if the other person gets mad or says no.

- It's selfish to say no or ask for things.
- I have no control over anything.

5. Intensity level

   ☐   Too high?

   ☐   Too low?

6. Assertiveness problems?

   ☐   Judgments instead of facts (see page 234)

   ☐   "You" statements instead of "I" statements (see page 235)

   ☐   No specific behavioral description of what you want (see page 236)

7. Blocks to listening? (see page 240)

   ☐   Mind reading

   ☐   Rehearsing

   ☐   Filtering

   ☐   Judging

   ☐   Daydreaming

   ☐   Advising

   ☐   Sparring

   ☐   Being right

   ☐   Derailing

   ☐   Placating

8. Forgot the conflict management strategies?

   ☐   Mutual validation (see page 244)

   ☐   Broken record (see page 244)

   ☐   Probing (see page 245)

   ☐   Clouding (see page 246)

   ☐   Assertive delay (see page 246)

9. Negotiation breakdown?

☐ Did you forget to use RAVEN?

- **R**elax

- **A**void the aversive

- **V**alidate the other person's need or concern

- **E**xamine your values

- **N**eutral voice

10. Didn't use compromise solutions?

The Communication Effectiveness Checklist is a starting point to evaluate interactions that you wish could have gone better. Identify the problems first, then decide which ones you want to work on. Review the sections in this and the previous chapter regarding skills you want to improve. Finally, make a specific plan for how you are going to change your behavior *next time*. Don't try to fix too many things at once because you'll never remember it all. Just focus on a few changes that might lead to big improvements. Write down specifically what you're going to do differently and in which situations.

Here's an example. Laura used the Communication Effectiveness Checklist to evaluate an angry interaction with her boss. She had asked for lighter duties because of a sprained wrist. These are the items she checked as problems.

- Denigrating (*I told him the company didn't take very good care of its employees.*)

- High emotion (*I got quickly upset and forgot some of my skills.*)

- Myths (*I feel like there's something wrong with me if I ask for anything special.*)

- "You" statements (*I said, "I feel like you don't really care what happens to people."*)

- No behavioral description of need (*I didn't specify exactly what "light duty" I was asking for.*)

- Blocks to listening (*I used judging and sparring.*)

- Mutual validation (*I didn't validate his concerns.*)

- Probing (*I never found out his concerns.*)

Laura realized she couldn't deal with everything on her list, so she decided to focus on just a few things:

- Denigrating and "you" statements

- High emotion

- Behavioral description of need

- Probing

Here's Laura's written plan:

When I discuss this with Bob again, I'm going to do the following:

1. Be extremely careful to make no critical statements about Bob or the company—no matter how upset I get.

2. Do a few minutes of mindful breathing to calm down before I talk to him.

3. Watch out for when I feel hot or I'm raising my voice—take a couple of deep breaths to calm down then.

4. Tell him I can do anything but collating, copying, and working with a mouse. I need to stop doing those things until my wrist is better.

5. If he objects, I'll ask what his concern is about temporarily changing my duties. Then I'll try to negotiate.

The most important thing to remember about your new interpersonal skills is to keep working at them. Your persistence will benefit you. Shrug it off when things go wrong, figure out what happened, and then make a new plan. You have the ability to change your relationships and your life. All you have to do is keep trying.

CHAPTER 11

Exposure-Based Cognitive Rehearsal

So far you have learned multiple techniques to increase distress tolerance, improve mindfulness skills, regulate overwhelming emotions, and improve your interpersonal relationships. Some of those skills have effectively helped you, some have not, and perhaps there are others that you still haven't tried. Inevitably, there will be some techniques and skills that seem to work when you're calmly sitting at home or in your dialectical behavior therapy group, but then don't work as well when you're in the middle of an upsetting situation. Maybe you either don't remember what that effective skill was that you learned or you feel too emotionally triggered to pull it off. This chapter will show you how to rehearse these skills—in an emotionally activated state—so you can use them effectively anytime and anywhere, even if you're very upset.

THE PROBLEM OF STATE-DEPENDENT LEARNING

State-dependent learning is a phenomenon that occurs when you can more easily recall information when you are in the same emotional or physical state as you were when you initially learned that information (Weingartner, Miller, & Murphy, 1977; Bower, 1981; Szymanski & O'Donohue, 1995; Nutt & Lam, 2011). For example, if you study for a test while in a relaxed, quiet environment, you are more likely to recall that same information while you are also in a relaxed, quiet environment. However, unfortunately, the opposite can also be true. Things we learn in a calm, relaxed state are sometimes unavailable to us when we feel angry and emotionally overwhelmed. In this way, state-dependent learning can sometimes affect your coping skills. If you only learn the skills and practice them while you are very relaxed, it might be harder to recall them when you need them in a very different emotional condition—such as feeling angry, fearful, or ashamed. Then you may be unable to recall how you planned to cope.

To help overcome this problem and prepare you to cope in an emotional state, you need to learn *exposure-based cognitive rehearsal*. This will give you a chance to practice your new skills *while feeling the very emotions for which you'll need the coping techniques*. But don't worry—this will be done in a safe, systematic way.

EXPOSURE-BASED COGNITIVE REHEARSAL: PRACTICING YOUR COPING SKILLS

In chapter 2, you read about cognitive rehearsal as a way to practice values-based behavior. Now we'll apply this same technique to any emotion coping skill you want to learn or have had trouble using (McKay & West, 2016). Here are the steps:

1. Select the emotion coping skill you want to learn or practice. Make sure you are familiar with the steps to implement the skill. The emotion coping skills you've learned include these:

    -   Radical acceptance

    -   Distraction

    -   Self-soothing

    -   Safe-place visualization

    -   Cue-controlled relaxation

    -   Time-out

    -   Living in the present moment

    -   Physiological coping skills

    -   Mindful breathing

    -   Defusion (thoughts, feelings, and judgments)

    -   Focus shifting

    -   Watching and accepting emotions

    -   Balancing thoughts and feelings

    -   Opposite action

    -   Problem solving

    -   Wise mind

    -   Coping thoughts

    -   Assertive communication

2. Identify a recent emotionally upsetting experience where that coping skill might have helped. This event should be something that you can easily visualize and something that can evoke a moderate emotional reaction when you do.

3. Visualize the emotionally triggering experience. Really try to get into it. Imagine details about the setting and situation. Visualize who's there and what they're doing. Try to "hear" any sounds

associated with the scene, including voices and conversation. Notice any sensations in your body—such as feelings of heat or tension. Stay with the scene until you can feel a moderate level of emotion.

4. Rate your emotion for level of intensity on a ten-point scale, from 0 (no emotion) to 10 (your most intense experience of that emotion). Shut the scene off as soon as emotional intensity is somewhere between 4 and 6.

5. Now begin to use one or more coping skills. Focus on practicing the skill(s), not on the upsetting scene. Stay active with the coping process until your emotional intensity has dropped noticeably (two or three points).

6. Then return to visualizing the upsetting scene again and repeat steps 3, 4, and 5.

Example: Ricardo Using Mindful Breathing

Ricardo wanted to use mindful breathing more effectively when he was upset. He had tried it every day for about a week after reading the mindfulness chapter, but it never seemed to be much use when he was anxiously obsessing about something.

The combination of a tight deadline and a critical comment from his boss had recently triggered waves of anxiety—particularly at home when he had time to think about it. Ricardo started by remembering his boss's criticism and visualizing the room where his team had planning meetings. The anxiety shot up immediately and was heading past 6 when Ricardo cut off the scene.

Now he started mindful breathing, observing and counting his breaths. As he reached the count of 4 he started over. Thoughts kept intruding—about his boss, the possibility of losing his job, the deadline, his performance—and each time he returned attention to his breath. His mind wanted to worry, but he kept gently guiding his attention back to each breath.

It took five minutes for the intensity of his anxiety to get down to 3. But he could feel the difference in his body, and he began to realize that mindful breathing can reduce stress. Ricardo repeated the cognitive rehearsal exercise by once again visualizing his boss and work team. When anxiety reached 5, he shifted to mindful breathing.

Cognitive rehearsal gave Ricardo practice while anxiously distressed, but it also provided confidence that he had a tool to cope. Several times a day, until the deadline was over, Ricardo used mindful breathing to shift away from anxious thoughts and feelings.

Example: Wendy Using Distraction plus Self-Soothing

Wendy had health problems related to her lifestyle and eating habits. She was ashamed of her symptoms and her weight—to the point of feeling waves of depression.

The image Wendy chose was a recent event where she had trouble walking up the stairs and she thought her neighbors were looking at her and disapproving. She imagined their silent stares, and within a few moments the sense of shame and sadness rose to a 6.

Now she shut off the image and began several coping skills in combination. Wendy distracted herself by thinking about her granddaughter and a plan she was forming to do something nice for the child. Then she self-soothed with (1) slow, deep breaths, (2) the sound of the sea (which she loved) on a smartphone app, and (3) touching the smooth lapis ring given to her by her mother. Wendy kept the process up—sweet plans for her granddaughter, the slow breaths, and self-soothing until the emotional pain diminished to between 3 and 4.

When she felt noticeably better, Wendy repeated the cognitive rehearsal. It worked again, and she began using this combo (plus other distraction and self-soothing skills) whenever shame or depression began surging up.

Example: Arden Using Coping Thoughts plus Watching and Accepting Emotions

Arden was sensitive to rejection. Any remark that seemed critical could send her into a tailspin of hurt and self-attack. She decided to use coping thoughts, such as these:

- "I have flaws, but I'm a decent person."

- "My feelings are like a wave that comes and goes."

- "I can get through this feeling—I have before—and I'll be okay in a little while."

In addition, she would watch and accept the emotion—letting it pass without attempting to resist or control it.

Arden chose a recent moment of hurt to visualize. She had just visited a friend who appeared cold and strangely uninterested in her. The whole thing seemed awkward, and it didn't take more than a minute visualizing the scene before Arden felt a flood of inadequacy—up to 7.

Now she turned off the image and started to observe—without judgment—the feeling of hurt. As she watched, she noticed the hurt was tinged with shame—and a sense of loss., as if her friend's cold demeanor had taken something precious from her.

Arden reminded herself that "this feeling is just a wave that comes and goes." And, "You'll be okay again in a little while." And, "Just wait and you'll get through it." Then she watched the feeling again, noticing that the hurt wasn't quite as strong as before. It took a little more than five minutes, but Arden watched the feeling of hurt get down to a 4 and she was amazed to feel somewhat better.

When Arden returned to the scene for another rehearsal, she learned something important: the more she thought about her friend and their relationship, the worse she felt. But if she just observed and accepted the hurt feeling while reminding herself it would pass, then the pain began to diminish.

THE PRACTICE EFFECT

Exposure-based cognitive rehearsal works because you learn to cope with your emotions *while they are happening*. The more you practice—particularly for coping skills you find difficult to remember or use—the more accessible the skill will become, and the more likely you are to remember to use it.

Twice through a cognitive rehearsal may be enough in some cases to add a skill to your coping repertoire. But often more practice will be needed. Try rehearsing the skill with different emotionally triggering scenes. The more you vary the imagery exposure, the more your confidence will grow in each coping skill.

Plan Ahead

Cognitive rehearsal can also be used for another very important function: planning ahead for how you'll cope with emotionally triggering events in the future. Depending on the type of anticipated stress or triggers you'll encounter, you should select one or more emotion coping strategies you think might protect you from being overwhelmed.

Now follow the same procedure as before—except that you'll visualize an upsetting scene or situation that hasn't yet happened. Imagine who will be there, what will be said, and the likely events that will unfold. Stay with the visualization until the emotion reaches a moderate intensity (4 to 6 on the ten-point scale).

Now shut off the scene and turn your attention to the coping skills you've selected to rehearse. Keep working at them until the intensity level has dropped two to three points. Some of your coping skills may work better than others; some may not work at all. Drop any coping skills that didn't work during your next rehearsal. You may also wish to test different skills during subsequent rehearsals.

Remember the practice effect. Continue cognitive rehearsal until you feel confident in the coping skills you've selected. Rehearsal doesn't guarantee success, but it will greatly improve your chances of facing stress or provocation without getting overwhelmed.

Example: Marty Using Radical Acceptance and Cue-Controlled Relaxation

Marty was flying to Omaha to visit his parents—it was the first time in three years. He loved them, but they were emotionally cold and critical, radiating quiet disapproval for his sexual orientation and generally how he lived his life. Marty chose radical acceptance as a coping skill because, in truth, the situation with his parents wasn't going to change. Here's what he wrote to remind himself:

- "I am not the son they wanted, nor do I live by some of the rules they hold dear. I can't change that."

- "It is also true that we love each other…"

- "…and that I live by and believe in my values, even if so very different from theirs."

The second coping strategy Marty chose was cue-controlled relaxation. He selected the cue word "meadow" because it was a place where he felt the most peace. Marty practiced saying to himself, "Breathe in," and as he was about to exhale, he thought "Meadow." During each exhale, he focused on relaxing all his muscles, head to toe. He was getting good at it.

The imagery exposure was easy. He imagined his mother sitting stiffly with folded hands, and his father, with a pained expression asking, "What are you doing with your life now, son?" He reached level 6 in just thirty seconds, feeling some combination of anger, sadness, and anxiety.

Now Marty interlaced cue-controlled breaths with his radical acceptance coping thoughts, over and over until the emotional intensity reached a 3. He repeated this process twice a day until arriving in Omaha. The outcome was better than Marty had originally expected. He and his parents managed a few stiff declarations of love for each other, and he was sad at times but not overwhelmed.

CHAPTER 12

Putting It All Together

The skills you have learned in this book will grow stronger each day that you practice them. Conversely, if your skills aren't used, they'll slip further from your grasp. They'll cease to be real choices and real ways to change. Instead, they'll just become mere ideas, vaguely recalled, with no power to help you. Equally important is to practice your coping skills using exposure-based cognitive rehearsal so that you gain confidence using them even when you feel emotionally upset, scared, nervous, or angry.

Keeping and strengthening your skills will take sustained effort. There's an old saying that victory belongs to the most persevering, which is exactly what's needed now: a commitment to practice your skills daily—over time.

You may wonder—legitimately—where you'll find the motivation to keep doing something so challenging. And all this talk of perseverance may sound very old-fashioned, but there is a way to practice daily what you've learned, and it doesn't take a huge amount of willpower. What it requires is getting in the *habit* of spending about fifteen minutes a day practicing your skills.

DAILY PRACTICES FOR EMOTIONAL HEALTH

The *daily practices* are, in essence, an exercise regimen to maintain your emotional and psychological health. The practices have five parts:

1. Mindfulness

2. Deep relaxation

3. Self-observation

4. Affirmation

5. Committed action

The daily practices take a total of about fifteen minutes. They should be done, ideally, at the same time each day—so they can become a healthy habit. Choose a period in your day when you can be alone and have some quiet time to yourself. It could be just after your morning coffee or in your workspace just before going to lunch. It could be how you destress when you come home at night or part of your bedtime routine. Whatever time you choose, stick to it. Don't let other events or commitments interfere. Consider the time spent in daily practices as an appointment with yourself—no less important than all the other commitments that you keep.

Your daily practices will be assembled from a menu of choices. Here's how that works:

1. Mindfulness. *Three to five minutes.* Choose to do one of the following:

   • Mindful breathing (see chapter 4)

   • Wise-mind meditation (see chapter 5)

2. Deep relaxation. *Three minutes.* Choose to do one of the following:

   • Cue-controlled relaxation (see chapter 2)

   • Band of light (see chapter 4)

   • Safe-place visualization (see chapter 2)

3. Self-observation. *Three minutes.* Choose to do one of the following:

   • Thought defusion (see chapter 4)

   • Be mindful of your emotions without judgment (see chapter 8)

4. Affirmation. See chapter 2 for a list of self-affirmations or create a self-affirmation yourself. Repeat the affirmation five times while taking slow, long breaths. You can choose a different affirmation each day—or keep working on the same one.

5. Committed action. *Three minutes.* Choose to do one of the following:

   • Plan to implement today's (or tomorrow's) committed action (see chapter 2).

   • Plan for what you can do today (or tomorrow) to connect to your higher power (see chapter 2).

Each component of your daily practices is designed to strengthen one or more core skills. First and foremost are mindfulness skills, because all of the others depend, to some degree, on mindful awareness. Deep relaxation is a key to distress tolerance, while self-observation and affirmation will help with emotion regulation. Finally, a plan for committed action will strengthen emotion regulation and interpersonal effectiveness skills.

The concept of committed action deserves special note. Your daily practices should include a plan for something you'll do—that day or the next—to solve a problem, deal effectively with a difficult situation or person, or strengthen awareness of your higher power. You can connect to your higher power through prayer, an act of kindness, or some giving of yourself to others. What you choose is up to you, but committed action—in some form—is necessary to make any real change in your life.

Right now, choose the five daily practices you will use tomorrow. Then, write them here as part of your commitment to really *do* them. (Visit http://www.newharbinger.com/44581 to download the My Daily Practices form.)

MY DAILY PRACTICES

Mindfulness: _____

Deep relaxation: _____

Self-observation: _____

Affirmation: _____

_____

Committed action plan: _____

_____

_____

What time each day will you do your practices? Please write that here:_____

_____

So far, so good—you know what you'll do for your daily practices and when you'll do them. But now comes the most important part: persevering—spending those fifteen minutes every day strengthening your skills.

How do you persevere? The answer is one day at a time—making sure that on *this* day, at the appointed time, you do your practices. And the next day you do the same thing...and the next. A commitment isn't something you make once, and you're set for life. It's something you keep making, every day.

The daily practices will change your life because they will help you shape new responses to old struggles. Life isn't about hopes or intentions. It's about *doing*. It's about *being* effective. Now, as we close the book, we're asking you to live what you've learned. You can do this, maybe not perfectly, but enough to make real changes.

The poet and author Samuel Johnson once said, "The future is purchased by the present." Similarly, by investing in your dialectical behavior therapy skills and practices today, you can create a happier and healthier tomorrow.

The DBT Diary

Note how many times each day you use these key skills. For items marked with *, briefly describe what you did in the "Specifics" column. Make copies of the blank diary before using it and do your best to complete one every week.

(Visit http://www.newharbinger.com/44581 to download The DBT Diary.)

Core Skills	Coping Strategies	Mon.	Tues.	Wed.
Distress Tolerance	Stopped Self-Destructive Action			
	Used REST Strategy			
	Used Radical Acceptance			
	Distracted from Pain			
	Engaged in Pleasurable Activities*			
	Soothed Myself*			
	Practiced Relaxation			
	Committed to Valued Action*			
	Connected with My Higher Power			
	Used Coping Thoughts & Strategies*			
	Analyzed Feelings-Threat Balance			
	Used Physiological Coping Skills*			
Mindfulness	Practiced Thought Defusion			
	Practiced Mindful Breathing			
	Used Wise Mind			
	Practiced Beginner's Mind			
	Practiced Self-Compassion			
	Practiced Doing What's Effective			
	Completed a Task Mindfully			
	Practiced Loving-kindness Meditation			

Thurs.	Fri.	Sat.	Sun.	Specifics

Core Skills	Coping Strategies	Mon.	Tues.	Wed.
Emotion Regulation	Was Able to Recognize My Emotions			
	Dealt with Physical Pain Appropriately*			
	Ate in a Balanced Way			
	Didn't Use Drugs or Alcohol			
	Got Sufficient Sleep			
	Exercised			
	Experienced Positive Events/Emotions*			
	Let Go of Thoughts or Judgments			
	Watched and Named Emotions			
	Didn't Act on Emotions			
	Used Opposite Action			
	Used Problem Solving			
Interpersonal Effectiveness	Practiced Compassion for Others			
	Practiced Fear Mgmt.—Risk Assessment			
	Made an Assertive Request			
	Said No Assertively			
	Negotiated Agreements			
	Listened to and Understood Others			
	Validated Others			
Rate Your Overall Mood for the Day (1 to 10) 1=Very Poor, 5=Mediocre, 10=Excellent				

Thurs.	Fri.	Sat.	Sun.	Specifics

References

Alberti, R. E., & Emmons, M. (1990). *Your perfect right* (6th ed.). San Luis Obispo, CA: Impact Press.

Anderson, W. P., Reid, C. M., & Jennings, G. L. (1992). Pet ownership and risk factors for cardiovascular disease. *Medical Journal of Australia, 157*(5), 298–301.

Babyak, M., Blumenthal, J. A., Herman, S., Khatri, P., Doraiswamy, M., Moore, K., et al. (2000). Exercise treatment for major depression: Maintenance of therapeutic benefit at 10 months. *Psychosomatic Medicine, 62*(5), 633–638.

Baer, R. A. (2003). Mindfulness training as a clinical intervention: A conceptual and empirical review. *Clinical Psychology: Science and Practice, 10,* 125–143.

Barker, L. L. (1990). *Listening behavior.* New Orleans, LA: SPECTRA.

Barrowcliff, A. L., Gray, N. S., MacCulloch, S., Freeman, T. C. A., & MacCulloch, M. J. (2003). Horizontal rhythmical eye movements consistently diminish the arousal provoked by auditory stimuli. *British Journal of Clinical Psychology, 42,* 289–302.

Barrowcliff, A. L., Gray, N. S., Freeman, T. C. A., & MacCulloch, M. J. (2004). Eye movements reduce the vividness, emotional valence, and electrodermal arousal associated with negative autobiographical memories. *Journal of Forensic Psychiatry and Psychology, 15,* 325–345.

Beck, A. T., Rush, A. J., Shaw, B. F., & Emery, G. (1979). *Cognitive therapy of depression.* New York: Guilford Press.

Bower, G. H. (1981). Mood and memory. *American Psychologist, 36*(2), 129–148.

Bower, S. A., & Bower, G. H. (1991). *Asserting yourself: A practical guide for positive change* (2nd ed.). Reading, MA: Addison-Wesley Publishing.

Cappo, B. M., & Holmes, D. S. (1984). The utility of prolonged respiratory exhalation for reducing physiological and psychological arousal in nonthreatening and threatening situations. *Journal of Psychosomatic Research, 28*(4), 265–273.

Cautela, J. (1971, September). *Covert modeling.* Paper presented at the fifth annual meeting of the Association for Advancement of Behavior Therapy, Washington, DC.

Chodron, P. (2003, March). How we get hooked, how we get unhooked. *Shambala Sun,* 30–35.

Chodron, T. (1991, May) How teachings should be studied and taught. A series of teachings based on *The Gradual Path to Enlightenment (Lamrim)*. Dharma Friendship Foundation, Seattle. Lecture. Retrieved from https://thubtenchodron.org/1991/05/qualities-teacher-student.

Clark, M. E., & Hirschman, R. (1990). Effects of paced respiration on anxiety reduction in a clinical population. *Biofeedback and Self-Regulation, 15*(3), 273–284.

Davis, M., Eshelman, E. R., and McKay, M. (1980). *The relaxation & stress reduction workbook*. Oakland, CA: New Harbinger Publications.

Denning, P. (2000). *Practicing harm reduction psychotherapy: An alternative approach to addictions*. New York: Guilford Press.

Dishman, R. K. (1997). Brain monoamines, exercise, and behavioral stress: Animal models. *Medicine and Science in Sports and Exercise, 29*(1), 63–74.

Dodge, K. A. (1989). Coordinating responses to aversive stimuli: Introduction to a special section on the development of emotion regulation. *Developmental Psychology, 25*(3), 339–342.

Downing, S. (2016). Low, moderate, and high intensity exercise: How to tell the difference. https://coach.nine.com.au/2017/02/01/07/25/exercise-intensity.

Feldman, C. (1998). *Thorsons principles of meditation*. London: Thorsons.

Fisher, R., & Ury, W. (1991). *Getting to yes: Negotiating agreement without giving in* (2nd ed.). New York: Viking Penguin.

Franklin, J. C., Hessel, E. T., Aaron, R. V., Arthur, M. S., Heilbron, N., & Prinstein, M. J. (2010, October 11). The functions of nonsuicidal self-injury: Support for cognitive-affective regulation and opponent processes from a novel psychophysiological paradigm. *Journal of Abnormal Psychology*. Advance online publication. doi: 10.1037/a0020896.

Gibala, M. J., & McGee, S. L. (2008). Metabolic adaptations to short-term high-intensity interval training: A little pain for a lot of gain? *Exercise and Sport Sciences Review 36*(2), 58–63.

Gibala, M. J., Little, J. P., MacDonald, M. J., & Hawley, J. A. (2012). Physiological adaptations to low-volume, high-intensity interval training in health and disease. *Journal of Physiology, 590*(Pt. 5), 1077–1084.

Gooden, B. A. (1994). Mechanism of the human diving response. *Integrative Physiological and Behavioral Science, 29*(1), 6–16.

Greenwood, K. A., Thurston, R., Rumble, M., Waters, S. J., & Keefe, F. J. (2003). Anger and persistent pain: Current status and future directions. *Pain, 103*(1–2), 1–5.

Hayes, S. C., Strosahl, K. D., & Wilson, K. G. (1999). *Acceptance and commitment therapy: An experiential approach to behavior change*. New York: Guilford Press.

Hirsch, J. A., & Bishop, B. (1981). Respiratory sinus arrhythmia in humans: How breathing pattern modulates heart rate. *American Journal of Physiology, 241*(4), H620–629.

Inayat Khan, P. V. (2000). *Awakening: A Sufi experience*. New York: Tarcher/Putnam.

Jacobson, E. (1938). *Progressive relaxation*. (rev. 2nd ed.). Chicago: University of Chicago Press.

Johnson, S. M. (1985). *Characterological transformation: The hard work miracle*. New York: W. W. Norton & Company.

Jung, M. E., Bourne, J. E., & Little, J. P. (2014). Where does HIT fit? An examination of the affective response to high-intensity intervals in comparison to continuous moderate- and continuous vigorous-intensity exercise in the exercise intensity-affect continuum. *PLOS ONE*, 9(12): e114541. doi.org/10.1371/journal.pone.0114541.

Kabat-Zinn, J. (1982). An out-patient program in behavioral medicine for chronic pain patients based on the practice of mindfulness meditation: Theoretical considerations and preliminary results. *General Hospital Psychiatry*, 4, 33–47.

Kabat-Zinn, J. (1990). *Full catastrophe living: Using the wisdom of your body and mind to face stress, pain, and illness.* New York: Delacorte.

Kabat-Zinn, J. (2003). Mindfulness-based interventions in context: Past, present, and future. *Clinical Psychology: Science and Practice*, 10(2), 144–156.

Kabat-Zinn, J., Lipworth, L., & Burney, R. (1985). The clinical use of mindfulness meditation for the self-regulation of chronic pain. *Journal of Behavioral Medicine*, 8, 163–190.

Kabat-Zinn, J., Lipworth, L., Burney, R., & Sellers, W. (1987). Four-year follow-up of a meditation-based program for the self-regulation of chronic pain: Treatment outcomes and compliance. *Clinical Journal of Pain, 2*, 159–173.

Kabat-Zinn, J., Massion, M. D., Kristeller, J. L., Peterson, L. G., Fletcher, K. E., Pbert, L., et al. (1992). Effectiveness of a meditation-based stress reduction program in the treatment of anxiety disorders. *American Journal of Psychiatry*, 149, 936–943.

Kerns, R. D., Rosenberg, R., & Jacob, M. C. (1994). Anger expression and chronic pain. *Journal of Behavioral Medicine*, 17(1), 57–67.

Kinoshita, T., Nagata, S., Baba, R., Kohmoto, T., & Iwagaki, S. (2006). Cold-water face immersion per se elicits cardiac parasympathetic activity. *Circulation Journal*, 70(6), 773–776.

Klonsky, E. D. (2007). The functions of deliberate self-injury: A review of the evidence. *Clinical Psychology Review*, 27, 226–239.

Kristeller, J. L., & Hallett, C. B. (1999). An exploratory study of a meditation-based intervention for binge eating disorder. *Journal of Health Psychology*, 4, 357–363.

Lee, C. W., & Cuijpers P. (2013). "A meta-analysis of the contribution of eye movements in processing emotional memories." *Journal of Behavior Therapy and Experimental Psychiatry*, 44(2), 231–239.

Lehrer, P. M. & Gevirtz, R. (2014, July 21). Heart rate variability biofeedback: How and why does it work? *Frontiers in Psychology*, 5(Article 756). doi.org/10.3389/fpsyg.2014.00756.

Linehan, M. M. (1993a). *Cognitive-behavioral treatment of borderline personality disorder.* New York: Guilford Press.

Linehan, M. M. (1993b). *Skills training manual for treating borderline personality disorder.* New York: Guilford Press.

Linehan, M. M. (2015). *DBT skills training manual* (2nd ed.). New York: Guilford Press.

Little, J. P., Safdar, A., Wilkin, G. P., Tarnopolsky, M. A., & Gibala, M. J. (2010). A practical model of low-volume high-intensity interval training induces mitochondrial biogenesis in human skeletal muscle: Potential mechanisms. *Journal of Physiology*, 588(6), 1011–1022.

Little, J. P., Gillen, J. B., Percival, M. E., Safdar, A., Tarnopolsky, M. A., Punthakee, Z., Jung, M. E., & Gibala, M. J. (2011). Low-volume high-intensity interval training reduces hyperglycemia and increases muscle mitochondrial capacity in patients with type 2 diabetes. *Journal of Applied Physiology, 111*(6), 1554–1560.

Marra, T. (2005). *Dialectical behavior therapy in private practice: A practical and comprehensive guide.* Oakland, CA: New Harbinger Publications.

McCaul, K. D., Solomon, S., & Holmes, D. S. (1979). Effects of paced respiration and expectations on physiological and psychological responses to threat. *Journal of Personality and Social Psychology, 37*(4), 564–571.

McKay, M., Davis, M., & Fanning, P. (1983). *Messages: The communication skills book.* Oakland, CA: New Harbinger Publications.

McKay, M., Davis, M., & Fanning, P. (1997). *Thoughts and feelings: Taking control of your moods and your life.* Oakland, CA: New Harbinger Publications.

McKay, M., Fanning, P., & Paleg, K. (1994). *Couple skills: Making your relationship work.* Oakland, CA: New Harbinger Publications.

McKay, M., Rogers, P. D., & McKay, J. (2003). *When anger hurts: Quieting the storm within* (2nd ed.). Oakland, CA: New Harbinger Publications.

McKay, M., & West, A. (2016). *Emotion efficacy therapy: A brief, exposure-based treatment for emotion regulation integrating ACT and DBT.* Oakland, CA: Context Press.

McKay, M., & Wood, J. (2019). *The new happiness: Practices for spiritual growth and living with intention.* Oakland, CA: Reveal Press.

Merton, T. (1960). *Spiritual direction and meditation.* Collegeville, MN: Order of St. Benedict.

Migala, J. (2017, August 7). 7 HIIT mistakes you're probably making. https://dailyburn.com/life/fitness/hiit-workout-mistakes.

Nes, B. M., Janszky, I., Wisløff, U., Stølen, A., & Karlsen, T. (2013). Age-predicted maximal heart rate in healthy subjects: The HUNT Fitness Study. *Scandinavian Journal of Medicine & Science in Sports, 23*(6), 697–704.

Nutt, R. M., & Lam, D. (2011). Comparison of mood-dependent memory in bipolar disorder and normal controls. *Clinical Psychology and Psychotherapy, 18,* 379–386.

Olerud, J. C., & Wilson, K. G. (2002, May). *Evaluation of an ACT intervention in a preventive program for chronic pain at the worksite.* Paper presented at the meeting of the Association for Behavior Analysis, Toronto, Canada.

Physical Activity Guidelines Advisory Committee. (2008). *Physical Activity Guidelines Advisory Committee Report.* Washington, DC: US Department of Health and Human Services.

Pinson, D. (2004). *Meditation and Judaism: Exploring the Jewish meditative paths.* Northvale, NJ: Jason Aronson.

Rahula, W. (1974). *What the Buddha taught* (2nd ed.). New York: Grove Press.

Robinson, M. M., Dasari, S., Konopka, A. R., Johnson, M. L., Manjunatha, S., Esponda, R. R., et al. (2017). Enhanced protein translation underlies improved metabolic and physical adaptations to different exercise training modes in young and old humans. *Cell Metabolism, 25,* 581–592.

Rogers, C. R. (1951). *Client-centered therapy.* New York: Houghton Mifflin Company.

Russ, M. J., Roth, S. D., Lerman, A., Kakuma, T., Harrison, K., Shindledecker, R. D., et al. (1992). Pain perception in self-injurious patients with borderline personality disorder. *Biological Psychiatry, 32,* 501–511.

Salzberg, S. (1995). *Lovingkindness: The revolutionary art of happiness.* Boston: Shambhala.

Salzberg, S. (1997). *A heart as wide as the world: Living with mindfulness, wisdom, and compassion.* Boston: Shambhala.

Salzberg, S. (2005). *The force of kindness: Change your life with love & compassion.* Boulder, CO: Sounds True.

Segal, Z. V., Williams, J. M. G., & Teasdale, J. D. (2002). *Mindfulness-based cognitive therapy for depression: A new approach to preventing relapse.* New York: Guilford Press.

Serpell, J. (1991). Beneficial effects of pet ownership on some aspects of human health and behaviour. *Journal of the Royal Society of Medicine, 84*(12), 717–720.

Shapiro, F. (2001). *Eye movement desensitization and reprocessing (EMDR): Basic principles, protocols, and procedures.* New York: Guilford Press.

Shapiro, S. L., & Schwartz, G. E. (2000). The role of intention in self-regulation: Toward intentional systemic mindfulness. In M. Boekaerts, P. R. Pintrich, & M. Zeidner (Eds.), *Handbook of self-regulation* (pp. 253–273). New York: Academic Press.

Sherman, A. (1975). The realm of possibility. In T. Tulku (Ed.), *Reflections of mind: Western psychology meets Tibetan Buddhism* (pp. 69–83). Berkeley, CA: Dharma Publishing.

Ströhle, A. (2009). Physical activity, exercise, depression, and anxiety disorders. *Journal of Neural Transmission, 116,* 777–784.

Suzuki, S. (1970). *Zen mind, beginner's mind: Informal talks on Zen meditation and practice.* New York: Weatherhill.

Szymanski, J., & O'Donohue, W. (1995). The potential role of state-dependent learning in cognitive therapy with spider phobia. *Journal of Rational-Emotive & Cognitive-Behavior Therapy, 13*(2), 131–150.

Tart, C. T. (1994). *Living the mindful life: A handbook for living in the present moment.* Boston: Shambhala.

Teasdale, J. D., Segal, Z. V., Williams, J. M. G., Ridgeway, V. A., Soulsby, J. M., & Lau, M. A. (2000). Prevention of relapse/recurrence in major depression by mindfulness-based cognitive therapy. *Journal of Consulting and Clinical Psychology, 68,* 615–623.

Trost, S. G., Owen, N., Bauman, A. E., Sallis, J. F., & Brown W. (2002). Correlates of adults' participation in physical activity: Review and update. *Medicine & Science in Sports & Exercise, 34,* 1996–2001.

Warburton, D. E., Nicol, C. W., & Bredin, S. (2006). Health benefits of physical activity: The evidence. *Canadian Medical Association Journal, 174,* 801–809.

Weingartner, H., Miller, H., & Murphy, D. L. (1977). Mood-state-dependent retrieval of verbal associations. *Journal of Abnormal Psychology, 86*(3), 276–284.

Wilson, K. G. (2002). The Valued Living Questionnaire. Available from the author at Department of Psychology, University of Mississippi, University, MS.

Wilson, K. G., & Murrell, A. R. (2004). Values work in acceptance and commitment therapy: Setting a course for behavioral treatment. In S. C. Hayes, V. M. Follette, & M. M. Linehan (Eds.), *Mindfulness and acceptance: Expanding the cognitive-behavioral tradition* (pp. 120–151). New York: Guilford Press.

Wolpe, J. (1958). *Psychotherapy by reciprocal inhibition.* Stanford, CA: Stanford University Press.

An excerpt from

The New Happiness:
Practices for Spiritual Growth
and Living with Intention

by Matthew McKay, PhD & Jeffrey C. Wood, PsyD
Foreword by Steven C. Hayes, PhD

Available from Reveal Press
An Imprint of New Harbinger Publications

Introduction

Every moment of your life is a spiritual opportunity—an occasion to strengthen your connection with your own inner wisdom, other people, and the universal truth that transcends time and space. For some people, "spirituality" implies a belief in God, gods, or an afterlife, but it doesn't have to. In its simplest form, spirituality can mean living a life based on choices and actions that make you feel more connected with your deepest values.

The *old* definition of happiness says that your satisfaction and contentment in life are based on what you *have*—things like wealth, achievements, possessions, and recognition by others. But unfortunately, when those things fade and disappear, so too will your happiness. The promise of *The New Happiness* is that there is a better way to experience satisfaction and contentment in life based on your spiritual values and actions; this is a happiness that lasts even when you come up against unavoidable obstacles and losses in life.

Spirituality Based on Psychological Principles

Built upon the research and principles of acceptance and commitment therapy (ACT)[vi]—namely, establishing values, developing mindfulness,[vii] and committing to acceptance—*The New Happiness* will lead you through a course of self-introspection and skills-building to help you develop your own set of spiritual principles. ACT is a successful, modern form of psychotherapy designed to help people in emotional and psychological pain. While this book draws

---

vi   The processes of ACT have been shown to strengthen and support spiritual growth (Hawkes et al., 2014; Dworsky et al., 2016; Santiago and Gall, 2016; Nieuwsma et al., 2015; Nieuwsma, Walser, and Hayes, 2016; Amin, Maroufi, and Sadeghi, 2017).

vii   Mindfulness and meditation have been shown across hundreds of empirical studies to significantly improve physical, psychological, and spiritual well-being (Murphy and Donovan, 1997; Baer, 2003; Walsh and Shapiro, 2006).

on those principles—as well as on key practices from a multitude of religions, faiths, and philosophies—it goes *beyond* what is usually discussed in the therapy room.

The focus here is not on treating depression, anxiety, and other forms of psychological problems (although that might happen naturally while working with this book). Instead, the focus is on improving the overall quality of your life and your sense of well-being. *The New Happiness* will help you shape your spirituality through your values-based actions, rather than helping you define your religious and philosophical beliefs. In short, *The New Happiness* defines spirituality as a process of "doing" rather than a process of "believing."

Doing Versus Believing

For some people, beliefs related to faith, religion, and spirituality can be confusing or even harmful. Maybe you were raised without spiritual beliefs of any kind and now you feel like something is lacking in your life. Or maybe you once held certain religious beliefs but now you question their validity. Or worse, maybe you were once the target of abuse in the name of religious beliefs, and as a result, you gave up believing in anything spiritual. If you fall into any of these categories, you're not alone. For thousands of years, scholars, theologians, and believers have argued and fought in favor of their own beliefs about God, spirituality, and religion. But rather than get bogged down in these debates, *The New Happiness* encourages you to engage in spiritual actions without arguing about who's right or telling you what you should believe. We're proposing that you can still feel spiritually fulfilled without knowing the answers to all of the spiritual questions. If you believe in God, that's okay, but if you don't believe in God, that's okay too.

The New Happiness is an action-based spiritual system—*not* a belief-centered spiritual system. It is designed to help you identify your spiritual values and live according to those values, in order to give your life a deeper sense of meaning. (Throughout this book we'll use "spiritual values" and "values" interchangeably to mean the same thing: the principles and standards that guide you toward a more rewarding and spiritual life.) In many ways, this book is a secular guide to spirituality and no previous belief system is required! We, the authors, are encouraging you to embody your spirituality and to allow it to inform everything you do, to affect all of your choices; to live your life according to your spiritual values and allow your behaviors to be an expression of your spirituality. This is the true "secret" to lasting happiness.

Why Choose The New Happiness?

If you're reading this book, it is likely that you fall into one or more of the following categories:

1. You want to be happy in your life and the thought of finding a "new" kind of happiness sounds hopeful.

2. You feel like something is missing in your life, and you suspect that seeking spirituality will fill the gap.

3. You're familiar with the principles of ACT—or you've been in ACT treatment—and you want to try something new and related.

4. You've been in other forms of psychological treatment, such as dialectical behavior therapy (DBT), and after finding success stabilizing your emotions, you aren't sure what to do next. You may be thinking, *Now what? Where do I go from here?*

In each of these cases, connecting with spirituality is your next step—identifying your values, your life purpose, and your actions during moments of choice, and finding out where true happiness comes from.

What to Expect

Throughout this workbook, you'll be led through various exercises. It's important that you follow the chapters in the order in which they appear, because each of the new skills builds on the skills learned in previous chapters. In total, the book is a gradual learning process, taking you from simple spiritual exercises in the beginning to more advanced skills in the latter chapters.

*   First, we'll help you redefine what spirituality means, focusing on "what you do" rather than "what you believe."

*   You'll learn a simple form of mindful meditation.

*   You'll work on discovering your values and acting on those values during the moments of choice in your life, when you have to decide: "What should I do?"

- You'll learn another wisdom meditation to help you connect both with your own inner wisdom—to help you make wiser choices—and with something spiritual outside of yourself—whether that's your own sense of God, a higher power, or the universe—to feel connected and gain guidance.

- You'll learn about barriers to spirituality and how to overcome them.

- Finally, four of the last chapters of the book deal with advanced concepts of spirituality to help you develop even deeper connections with people and the things you value. You'll learn about compassion, making amends to others, the importance of accepting impermanence, and finding a personal state of grace—a lasting sense of happiness that is created through living a spiritual life.

As you begin learning the various skills in this book, you'll notice that many of them require you to find a few minutes of your day when you can sit still, in a quiet place, and breathe. We are not going to ask you to isolate yourself for several hours each day, but we do hope that in the beginning you can find at least three to five minutes. (Later in your practice you can spend more time as needed.) In addition, you might want to think about creating a special "spiritual" environment for your skills exercises. Maybe find a quiet room or a corner of your garden where you can put a comfortable chair or cushion to sit on, place some inspirational spiritual pictures or decorations in the space, and begin looking for a spiritual "talisman" to use in your exercises—an object that holds special spiritual significance for you.

In addition, it's important to understand that changing anything in your life requires a combination of work, motivation, and determination. Creating a spiritually fulfilling life for yourself is no different, but it's well worth your efforts. This book requires you to make changes in what you *do*, rather than just making changes in what you *think*. You're going to learn new actions to help you change old habits and learn how to make more fulfilling choices in your life. But don't be intimidated—the process is gradual, and you'll be rewarded along the way with a feeling of connection to other people, your own inner wisdom, and a greater sense of knowledge bigger than yourself.

Remember, your life is a creative process. Each day you get to choose how you will act, *regardless of your circumstances*. Each day you get to choose between doing "business as usual" and maybe finding happiness, *or* living according to your spiritual principles and being happy no matter what happens. We hope you'll choose to make your life a creative *spiritual* process and find new happiness for the rest of your life.

Matthew McKay, PhD, is a professor at the Wright Institute in Berkeley, CA. He has authored and coauthored numerous books, including *The Dialectical Behavior Therapy Skills Workbook, The Relaxation and Stress Reduction Workbook, Self-Esteem, Thoughts and Feelings, When Anger Hurts,* and *ACT on Life Not on Anger.* McKay received his PhD in clinical psychology from the California School of Professional Psychology, and specializes in the cognitive behavioral treatment of anxiety and depression.

Jeffrey C. Wood, PsyD, lives and works in Las Vegas, NV. He specializes in brief therapy treatments for depression, anxiety, and trauma. He also provides coaching for spiritual development, communication skills development, and life-skills coaching. He is coauthor of *The New Happiness, The Dialectical Behavior Therapy Skills Workbook, The Dialectical Behavior Therapy Diary, The Cognitive Behavioral Therapy Workbook for Personality Disorders,* and *Getting Help.*

Jeffrey Brantley, MD, is a consulting associate in the Duke department of psychiatry, and founder and director of the Mindfulness Based Stress Reduction (MBSR) Program at Duke University's Center for Integrative Medicine. He has represented the Duke MBSR program in numerous radio, television, and print interviews. He is author of *Calming Your Anxious Mind,* and coauthor of *Five Good Minutes.*

Real change *is* possible

For more than forty-five years, New Harbinger has published proven-effective self-help books and pioneering workbooks to help readers of all ages and backgrounds improve mental health and well-being, and achieve lasting personal growth. In addition, our spirituality books offer profound guidance for deepening awareness and cultivating healing, self-discovery, and fulfillment.

Founded by psychologist Matthew McKay and Patrick Fanning, New Harbinger is proud to be an independent, employee-owned company. Our books reflect our core values of integrity, innovation, commitment, sustainability, compassion, and trust. Written by leaders in the field and recommended by therapists worldwide, New Harbinger books are practical, accessible, and provide real tools for real change.

 newharbingerpublications

MORE *from* NEW HARBINGER PUBLICATIONS

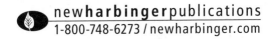

THE NEXT STEP *for* POSITIVE CHANGE

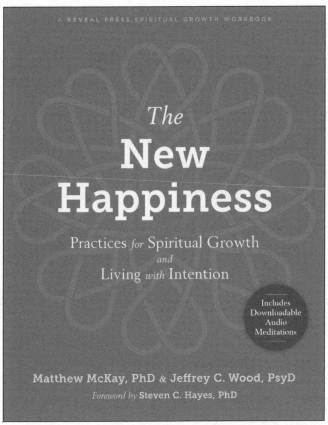

ISBN: 978-1684034581 / US $21.95

Now that you've completed the exercises in *The Dialectical Behavior Therapy Skills Workbook,* are you ready to move to the next level?

Check out *The New Happiness* by Matthew McKay and Jeffrey C. Wood.

The New Happiness blends timeless spiritual practices with contemporary psychology to help you develop your own "action plan" for real, lasting happiness. Using the practical exercises in this guide, you'll learn to set daily intentions that align with what *really* matters to you, make important decisions with confidence and clarity, and uncover your inner wisdom.

REVEAL PRESS
An Imprint of New Harbinger Publications

Register your **new harbinger** titles for additional benefits!

When you register your **new harbinger** title—purchased in any format, from any source—you get access to benefits like the following:

- Downloadable accessories like printable worksheets and extra content
- Instructional videos and audio files
- Information about updates, corrections, and new editions

Not every title has accessories, but we're adding new material all the time.

Access free accessories in 3 easy steps:

1. Sign in at NewHarbinger.com (or **register** to create an account).

2. Click on **register a book**. Search for your title and click the **register** button when it appears.

3. Click on the **book cover or title** to go to its details page. Click on **accessories** to view and access files.

That's all there is to it!

If you need help, visit:

NewHarbinger.com/accessories

new harbinger
CELEBRATING
40 YEARS